THE TH

Understanding Narrative

EDITED BY

James Phelan
and Peter J. Rabinowitz

OHIO STATE UNIVERSITY PRESS

COLUMBUS

Chapter 5 is drawn from a chapter in Judith Mayne's *Cinema and Spectatorship* (Routledge, 1993).

Library of Congress Cataloging-in-Publication Data

Understanding narrative / edited by James Phelan and Peter J. Rabinowitz.
     p.   cm. — (The theory and interpretation of narrative series)
    Includes bibliographical references and index.
    ISBN 0-8142-0633-6. — ISBN 0-8142-0634-4 (pbk.)
    1. Narration (Rhetoric) I. Phelan, James, 1951– . II. Rabinowitz, Peter J.,
1944– . III. Series.
    PN212.U64 1994
    809.3'923—dc20   94-5731
                                                  CIP

Text and jacket design by Nighthawk Design.
Type set in Palatino by Focus Graphics, St. Louis, MO.
Printed by Patterson Printing, Benton Harbor, MI.

9 8 7 6 5 4 3 2 1

CONTENTS

· v ·

Contents

Introduction

Understanding Narrative

JAMES PHELAN

PETER J. RABINOWITZ

*From Understanding to Self-Consciousness, from Fiction
to Narrative*

By design, our title refers to Brooks and Warren's influential
textbooks, especially *Understanding Fiction*. In establishing this
intertextuality, we are neither claiming kinship with Brooks and
Warren's 1943 volume nor launching yet another assault on New
Criticism. Instead, we are invoking their familiar title in order to fix
a point of orientation in an increasingly complicated critical landscape, a point that will help us define the ways that the terms
understanding, *fiction*, and *narrative*—as well as the institutional
practices to which they are tied—have altered in the past fifty years.

In the most general sense, *understanding fiction* and its signifieds
have weathered this period the way that any social construct (a
string quartet, a baseball franchise, a family, an English depart-
ment) survives a half-century: the signifiers have remained intact
while the signifieds have been continuously transformed. But the
trajectory of the relations between signifier and signified in the
phrase *understanding fiction* is especially complex, partly because
the signifier-signified relation of each separate term has evolved
differently, partly because these divergent changes have led to a

change in their relation to each other. Adapting Umberto Eco's metaphor of semiotic space, we can say that, while the two terms have remained in each other's gravitational field, each has, in its own way, been realigning its relationships to numerous other signifiers and signifieds in nearby orbits.

On the one hand, *understanding* has been adding signifieds as theorists have developed new ways of reading, new ideas about the interconnectedness of reading and writing, new theories about the difficulty, even impossibility, of reading, and, indeed, new understandings of understanding itself. That is, not only are there now multiple, noncompatible theories claiming to offer the best account of the way the particulars of a text form—or resist forming—a larger gestalt; but theorizing about understanding by everyone from Hirsch to Irigaray has also profoundly altered our relation to the activity. In short, our understanding of understanding has been pluralized, and one increasingly important use of the term holds that understanding is a self-reflexive and self-questioning act, one in which the process and the subject matter are inextricably tangled. In this use of the term, understanding entails not only the interpreter's translation of the object into other terms but also the critic's self-conscious awareness of her relation to the "terministic screen" or "critical framework" or "metaphysical assumptions" or "situated subjectivity" or "horizon of expectations" that mediate between her and the object. Wayne Booth's essay exemplifies both dimensions of the shift in our understanding of understanding. Booth distinguishes several different kinds of reading, each entailing a different kind of understanding: "reading-with" (accepting the apparent demands made upon us by the text), "reading-against" (seeking what is unintended or even "banned" by the text), and "critical rereading," which searches a text anew, either for "deeper meaning" or for "an understanding of structure." Despite certain echoes in its terminology, Booth's third category is clearly distinct from Brooks and Warren's notion of understanding as an account of the "organic relation" existing among a text's elements, for it inevitably reflects back on the act of reading itself: it can lead us, for instance, to "deplore" what we have done before or, alternatively, to acquire a "heightened admiration" through a heightened questioning of the ethical quality of our reading experience. In particular, the assumptions about the values of structural understanding that serve as the *basis* for Brooks and Warren's analyses become the *subject* of Booth's inquiry into Henry James's *Wings of the Dove*. Susan McClary's analysis of Mozart's *Prague* Symphony similarly builds from one kind of understanding to another: her investigation of Mozart's structures leads into an interrogation of the reigning assumptions about their ideological neutrality.

While *understanding* has been adding signifieds, *fiction* has been expanding its borders, invading the space formerly controlled by other signifiers. Indeed, the borders have been changing in at least two ways at once. First, border-crossings have become bolder and more frequent, as theorists such as Hayden White and narrative artists such as Joan Didion, Tom Wolfe, Ishmael Reed, and Don DeLillo have called attention to the fictionalizing that they regard as inevitably a part of such nonfiction genres as history, biography, and autobiography. Second, the location of the borders has also changed: *fiction* has moved out from its home base in the province of *prose* to annex pieces of such surrounding territories as poetry, film, painting, music, and performance art. Indeed, as the signifier has stretched to cover all these different signifieds, its work of signification has increasingly been shouldered by another member of its family. Just as television sets, given their broadened functions, have been increasingly referred to as monitors, so the term *fiction* has increasingly been replaced by *narrative*.

Some theorists, of course, have called for resistance to what they see as a kind of imperialism in these expansionist tendencies, an imperialism that has led to a loss of attention to the special qualities of the individual domains that are being merged in the larger entity of *narrative*. The decreased differentiation between *history* and *fiction* has been particularly troubling. But for the moment we do not want to engage the question of whether these changes are for the better, for the worse, or—as is more likely—have mixed results. Our point is that these alterations in the landscape cannot be ignored. To take just one consequence, the realignment of relations among *fiction*, *nonfiction*, *history*, and *narrative* means that apparent similarities of terminology between old and new critical texts on these subjects frequently mask significant differences in their conceptual territories. Future theoretical discussions will no doubt further change the terrain in which we work, but it seems unlikely that the old map of the territory will ever be restored.

The superseding of *fiction* (with its silent partner *prose*) by *narrative* is reflected most clearly in this collection by the essays of Judith Mayne, Susan McClary, and Mary Louise Pratt. In her essay on the film version of *The Picture of Dorian Gray*, Mayne proposes a reconceptualization of the notion of spectatorship and then shows how attention to acts of spectatorship within the film raises previously submerged elements of its exploration of male/female and straight/gay relations. The essay is a self-sufficient contribution to film theory and practical criticism; but in the context of this collection it also invites questions about the similarities and differences between representations of spectatorship in film and representations of reading in the novel.

In her essay, McClary peels away "the polished surfaces and assuring reconciliations that characterize the public veneer" of Mozart's music. In particular, she demonstrates how what she calls "narrative inflections" intervene in the structure of Mozart's *Prague* Symphony, and how an examination of these inflections on two fronts (public and private) can reveal the ways in which he was "wrestling" with the historical tensions (including tensions over class, gender, and identity) of late eighteenth-century bourgeois culture. In so doing, McClary suggests how the music reveals "the contradictions bound up with subject formation" and provides "models for how bourgeois sensitivity might be constructed in the face of both oppressive authority and the temptation to regress into nostalgia."

Mary Louise Pratt's essay is, on the surface, more traditionally literary. But she too moves beyond the borders of a volume on "understanding fiction" as it was conceived by Brooks, Warren, and most of their contemporaries. Indeed, because the relatively straightforward travel narratives of eighteenth- and nineteenth-century

European explorers in the Americas and Africa appear not to "answer fully enough our basic interest about human action" in the way that such contemporaneous canonical fictions as *Clarissa* and *Wuthering Heights* do, they would seem perfect exemplars of the class of anecdotal texts that Brooks and Warren cast out in the opening pages of their book (1–4). Without denying this difference, Pratt establishes that these texts, too, have a great deal to offer to serious students of narrative, revealing through her careful analysis of the travel narratives' techniques of description and narration the ways they imply, reinforce, and promulgate their imperialist ideology. Just as Pratt's analyses of these narratives are partially informed by the work done on more canonical works and genres in the last fifteen years, so too does her analysis offer a fresh way to think about the subtle and not-so-subtle communication of ideologies in canonical fictional texts. More challenging still, her analysis invites us to question the very bases on which we sort out our literary categories.

Theorypractice: Rewriting the "New Reading"

The changes in the meanings of and relations between *understanding* and *fiction* are only a small part of much broader changes in narrative studies since the breakdown of the widespread New Critical orthodoxy established by such books as *Understanding Fiction*. To take one example, consider the issue of organic unity. Where Brooks and Warren could once proclaim with utter authority and confidence that "A piece of fiction is a unity, in so far as the piece of fiction is successful" (xx), contemporary critics of narrative share no such agreement about the relation between unity and success. This change is not simply the substitution of one dogma for another; that is, it is not simply the consequence of the rise of some monolithic "poststructuralism," or even of a clan of related poststructuralisms, that proclaims the impossibility of organic unity. Rather, even many individual critics who embrace few of the principles of poststructuralism find the search for organic unity a decreasingly rewarding critical pursuit. For example, Phelan's analysis of the relation between present tense narration and Coetzee's positioning of his implied audience in *Waiting for the Barbarians* has an unexpected side effect. In tracing the course of the audience's positionings, Phelan claims that Coetzee's narrative lacks one of the standard features of the coherent, unified text: the implied author's final judgment of the protagonist. In a traditional analysis, this lack would move to the center of the study: the critic would have to address the question of whether Coetzee had created a new kind of unity or frustrated the reader's desire for unity—or whether he had simply failed as an artist. For Phelan, however, this question is beside the point because he has shifted attention away from the form-in-itself and focused instead on the dynamics of the audience's response without worrying about the overall coherence of those dynamics. Thus Phelan's attention to the formal element of present tense narration implicitly throws into question what we mean by formal analysis. Similarly, Rabinowitz's essay is specifically focused on the way that the ending of *The Maltese Falcon* surreptitiously betrays the epistemological principles that had grounded the novel to that point. But here too the traditional questions about the narrative's unity drop out of the analysis as Rabinowitz seeks instead to interrogate the sources of this epistemological rupture in the intersection of narrative technique (specifically, the use of "second person narration") and ideology (specifically, that stemming from Hammett's anxieties about women). Rabinowitz first shows that Hammett's acceptance of his culture's dominant ideology of gender leads him to deny full subjectivity to Brigid O'Shaughnessey and, as a consequence, to choose a particular kind of second person narration at the climax. Rabinowitz then shows how this technical choice short-circuits the epistemological innovations Hammett was introducing into the evolving formula of the hard-boiled detective novel. In other words, rather than holding up unity as a goal to be achieved and a measure of aesthetic success, Rabinowitz focuses on how a rupture in organic unity allows us to read the novel as a site of conflict between ideologies.

Not surprisingly, this collection represents more than just the general critical shift away from a concern for unity. It also indicates how far we have traveled away from the larger program implied in Brooks and Warren's "Letter to the Teacher" and exemplified in the rest of *Understanding Fiction*. Although we all still live with the powerful legacy of the New Criticism, there is probably no single critical principle of *Understanding Fiction* that some prominent theorist has not repudiated in the last fifty years. Even more significant than the breakdown of the New Critical hegemony is the institution's refusal to replace it with any New Orthodoxy. We therefore doubt that we could propose any new set of principles for understanding narrative to which all our contributors, let alone all contemporary students of narrative, would subscribe. And yet this critical ferment does not, we believe, lead to theoretical anarchy. Indeed, although we can't be sure that any of the individual contributors would agree, we view this volume as a chance to stake out a program of critical activity—one quite different from that which followed in the wake of *Understanding Fiction*, not only in its particular critical principles, but also in its larger metatheoretical stance.

For the past fifty years, the journals have been full of essays offering new readings of Masterpieces Ancient and Modern, new keys to their meaning or, more recently, to their contradictory meanings or even their unreadability. We contend that the continued production of such essays is less and less profitable—in particular, that untheorized interpretation can make only a minor contribution to contemporary narrative studies. By untheorized, we mean interpretation that goes about proving its thesis without reflecting either on the principles informing its practice or on the relation of the essay's findings to more general issues in narrative theory. (By this definition, of course, many essays of the forties, fifties, and sixties were theorized; our aim is not to privilege a given theoretical content but rather to emphasize a kind of inquiry.)

An untheorized contribution is necessarily limited, in part, for a reason that others before us have articulated: as the number of new readings increases, the distinctiveness of any single reading fades away. What more is there to say about Joyce's attitudes toward

Stephen in *A Portrait of the Artist as a Young Man*? But we believe that such critical practice is limited for a more serious reason as well: it leaves out a vital dimension of critical inquiry at a time when the concept of understanding has been pluralized and when, as a consequence, many critics are engaged in an active and far-reaching conversation about the concepts underlying any proffered new understanding: author, audience, text, history, sign, structure, story, discourse, tense, character, style, ideology, politics, gender, ethics, and so forth. If we ignore this conversation, not only do we leave ourselves open to the possibility that the new reading has been undermined or recontextualized even before it is published. We also remain shut off from a significant dimension of our own practice—as if we were to announce from the outset that we are not interested in inquiring too closely into the underpinnings of our work. To put the point less negatively: if we ignore this conversation, we pass up, at the very least, opportunities to contribute to our own self-understanding and to an understanding of how our positions and practices relate to those of others in our critical community. In so doing, we miss the opportunity to transform the grounds of self-understanding, both for ourselves and others.

Again, the essays in this collection exemplify our point. While all of them could be discussed according to their double attention, to interpretation and to the grounds of interpretation, we will single out just two. Elizabeth Langland's analysis of the intertextual relations between Charlotte Brontë's *Shirley* and Thackeray's *Vanity Fair* also proposes a revisionary view of the concept of intertextuality, one that moves it away from traditional notions of influence and toward a postmodern conception of textuality informed by the theories of Barthes, Bakhtin, Foucault, and Irigaray. As Langland illustrates how Brontë's relation to Thackeray gets variously played out as "dialogue, discourse, theft, and mimicry," she also varies the tone and style of her own text, thus suggesting an intertextual relation between her essay and those of the theorists she is drawing upon. Barbara Foley's essay on the relation between the form of the bildungsroman and leftist politics in proletarian novels of the 1930s draws much of its strength from its rigorous interrogation of the theoretical assumption that a given form implies a particular politics—an interrogation that includes, among other things, a historical examination of the way the key terms *realism* and *bildungsroman* have shifted their meanings. Foley's self-conscious and self-reflexive readings of *Moscow Yankee* and *Yonnondio* demonstrate just how complicated the relation between form and politics can be; and this demonstration, as Foley points out, has considerable importance to our understanding of other writers "who are variously termed 'oppositional,' 'marginalized,' and 'subaltern.'"

At the same time that we are questioning the value of non-theoretical interpretation, we are also (and this may be a less popular position) skeptical about the value of noninterpretive narrative theory. Despite the initial enthusiasm surrounding narratologists' claims in the 1970s that they would describe the grammar of narrative and define (even quantify) the essence of narrativity, their efforts have not borne much fruit—especially when these efforts have been divorced from concrete problems of interpretation.[1] This result is no accident. In part, the program has failed because the attempt to fix the rules for proper functioning of narrative cannot stand up in the face of the multiple and incompatible principles of understanding that theorists have advanced. But more important, many critics have discovered that the task of interpretation may itself lead to revisions of the theoretical principles brought to the task. If the untheorized interpretation is not worth reading, the untested theoretical proclamation is not worth believing.

By "testing," we mean something more than application: our journals will not be significantly better if all those explications of Joyce's attitudes toward Stephen are replaced by Lacanian readings of Joyce's attitudes toward Stephen. Nor do we mean testing in the sense of simple confirmation. Indeed, as we have seen in thousands of literary essays, the easiest part of hypothesis testing is confirmation. To choose one particularly famous example: in *Is There a Text in This Class?* Stanley Fish tells the story of how his class in seventeenth-century English religious poetry was able to interpret a reading assignment left on the board from his previous class ("Jacobs-Rosenbaum / Levin / Thorne / Hayes / Ohman(?)") as a religious poem. Although Fish intends this example to persuade us that interpretive strategies wholly constitute texts, it functions much better as an example of the ease of hypothesis confirmation. Once one shifts the question from "Can the text be read as a poem?" to "Which hypothesis—that this 'text' is a poem or that it is a reading assignment—is more powerful?," Fish's argument begins to founder. To take just the most obvious piece of evidence, the word "Hayes" resists being incorporated into the poem interpretation, while "Hayes" is readily incorporated into the assignment interpretation.[2] Because hypothesis confirmation is typically easy, the critical essay whose theoretical principles are only being confirmed will be as unproductive as the untheorized new reading.

On the other hand, when the critic allows the text to resist the theoretical principles she is bringing to bear upon it—that is, when the text is treated as something other than inert matter on which a theoretical position can be stamped—she is able not only to come to a stronger understanding of the text, but to reconceptualize her theoretical ground as well. Again we single out just two essays that exemplify this point. In his essay "Naturalizing *Molloy*," Thomas Pavel certainly offers a new reading of Beckett's novel. But by highlighting the contrast between hermeneutics and poetics and the relation between tradition and innovation, he contextualizes that reading by asking us to rethink, on theoretical grounds, the consensus that has grown up around Beckett. As a consequence, when he proposes a shift in our orientation away from the traditional apocalyptic readings of *Molloy*, he revises our received notions not only of the novel but also, more generally and more provocatively, of the activity of naturalizing the strange. Ross Chambers similarly shows how theory and practice can be reciprocally illuminating by proposing that we think of the "loiterature of travel" as a new genre that is recognizable more for its counter-disciplinary functions than for any specific set of characters, events, or conventions. Chambers's conception of the new genre arises out of his adaptation of Foucault's concern with the relations among power, knowledge, and desire, along with his own ideas about how some narratives allow "room for maneuver" within the dominant ideology. At the same time, it is his analysis of the narratives of "strolling, touring, and cruising" that operationally defines the genre. In other words, the diverse texts that Chambers analyzes are able to shed light on each other once Chambers theorizes their generic similarity, even as his particular readings of those narratives flesh out his definition of the genre.

In calling for essays that combine theory and practice, then, we are calling for work that genuinely inquires into elements of both theory and text. The particular forms and purposes of such essays may be as plural as is understanding itself. As the essays in this collection show, some critics may give greater emphasis to theory, some to the text, some to historical context, some to formal structure, some to gender relations, some to technique. Foley and Chambers, for instance, have ends that are ultimately political. Others, such as Mayne, McClary, and Pavel, want to increase our cognitive knowlege of a text, both in its internal workings and in its relation to its sociohistorical situation. Phelan and Booth, for their part, focus on technique but emphasize the affective quality of the text, and thus attend to the way technique influences the emotional/ psychological/ethical experience of reading. Langland and Rabinowitz also attend to technique, but their purpose is to explore some of the differences gender makes in the construction of narrative. Because of the diversity of the field of narrative studies, we do not claim to have representatives of all the voices in the current conversation; indeed, our metatheoretical claim about the nature of literary criticism today would be undermined were we able to do so. But each of these essays does represent one rich kind of exploration of theory and interpretation.

Schools, Out!

To this point, we have emphasized the pluralizing of understanding and the diversity of current work on narrative, but we have not addressed the ways in which the essays in this collection might complicate or conflict with one another. Has our celebration of diversity either deflected our attention from potentially fruitful disagreement or led us to gloss over unresolvable conflict? Rather than answer this question directly, we would like to leave it for our readers and to discuss instead how the kind of theorypractice we have been calling for also entails a new understanding of the relation between one critic's work and another's.

As the theory revolution has developed, the "schools and movements" model (originally developed to distinguish among artistic productions) has become an increasingly dominant means of characterizing both individual critics and their relations to one another. This model charts out critical terrain by identifying a critic's allegiance to a school and then analyzing the convergences and divergences of these larger groups. For example, we might say that Brooks and Warren are New Critics, Booth a neo-Aristotelian, Foley a Marxist, Mayne a poststructuralist feminist. We might further fill in the details of this mosaic by saying that Booth shares the New Critical belief in the power of the autonomous text but departs from New Critical beliefs about literature being a special kind of language; that Foley insists not on the text's autonomy but on its relations to its sociohistorical context and its ideological import; that Mayne emphasizes the way the complexities of signifying in the film text reveal its gender ideologies. While this model helps sort out the diversity among critics—indeed, it may be a necessary step in any attempt to understand the larger critical landscape—it does so only by locking everyone into a predetermined grid of possibilities by emphasizing the static (critical positions) rather than the dynamic (critical questions). We therefore prefer to sidestep this model and to attend instead to the dynamic nature of the work of individual critics and of the larger field. By saying "School's out" (or "Schools, out!") we liberate our perceptions from the predetermined slots provided by the standard maps of the field, and we allow ourselves to recognize that critics increasingly draw upon the insights of different kinds of critical work as they formulate their questions, develop their methods, and reason to their answers. To take just one example, Foley's Marxist commitments are in dialogical relation to her neo-Aristotelian commitments to the power of genre; it is precisely this multiplicity that fuels her insightful analyses of *Moscow Yankee* and *Yonnondio* and her general reconfiguration of the relations between politics and form.

Shifting away from a "schools and movements" approach does not mean that we thereby either eliminate or ignore conflicts. But it does allow us to distinguish between divergence and disagreement: between the choice not to ask a question, for instance, and the belief that it shouldn't be asked—or between deciding not to make use of a particular theoretical insight and rejecting it entirely. Thus, for instance, neither of the two of us is committed, at the moment, to the search for unity; but neither of us would argue in principle against someone who is. That is, while unity may be a secondary, even tertiary concern in our respective projects, we do not thereby deem it a fallacy or a heresy to search for the principles of a given narrative's unity, as the more dogmatic New Critics were apt to cast out positions with which they did not agree.

This shift in perspective clarifies what is most striking about our critical climate. Although the "schools and movements" popularizers tend to obscure this fact, today's best practitioners do not stake out their arguments by opposition, but by interacting with different proportions of alternate methodologies in their eclectic mixes. That is, there inevitably are not only multiple sources of any critic's work, but also multiple dimensions to any critic's relation to another. Langland, for example, borrows heavily from Barthes, Bakhtin, Foucault, and Irigaray without fully endorsing their particular critical projects or, indeed, worrying about the possible compatibility or incompatibility of these theorists with each other. For her specific project of reconceptualizing intertextuality, she does not need to make any full endorsements or any totalizing synthesis of all their work. Instead, she needs to show that her eclectic conception of intertextuality has its own compelling logic and explanatory power—and here the practical criticism of her essay becomes crucial.

In summary, then, our call for theorypractice is a call to attend and contribute to the powerful dynamics of contemporary narrative studies. Unlike Theseus's famous boat, in which the planks, sails, masts, and other parts are replaced without changing the essential structure of the boat, narrative studies changes its shape as it changes its parts. Sometimes the new planks fashioned in response to a particular cargo of issues and questions don't quite fit the old construction, and so a new design is developed. But after a while, this design too becomes inadequate for accommodating another new cargo of issues and questions, and yet another renovation takes place. As the essays in this volume show, the signifieds of "understanding narrative" are plural—and always under construction.

Notes

We would like to thank Jane Greer for her editorial work, and especially for doing the index to this book.

1. It is worth distinguishing this work from the apparently similar program of moving beyond interpretation outlined by Jonathan Culler in *Structuralist Poetics* and *The Pursuit of Signs* (especially the essay "Beyond Interpretation"). Because Culler's work proceeds by examining specific interpretations by other critics, it offers worthwhile insights into conventions governing interpretive practice. Gerald Prince's *Narratology*, on the other hand, often proceeds by analyzing brief narratives that he devises specifically for analysis. Because these narratives are otherwise divorced from the social and historical contexts of both production and reception, the reach of Prince's conclusions remains limited to his own closed system.

2. For a fuller discussion of this example and Fish's general position, see Phelan, "Data, Danda, and Disagreement."

Bibliography

Brooks, Cleanth and Robert Penn Warren. *Understanding Fiction*. New York: Appleton-Century-Crofts, 1943.

Culler, Jonathan. *The Pursuit of Signs*. Ithaca: Cornell University Press, 1981.

———. *Structuralist Poetics: Structuralism, Linguistics, and the Study of Literature*. Ithaca: Cornell University Press, 1975.

Eco, Umberto. *A Theory of Semiotics*. Bloomington: Indiana University Press, 1978.

Fish, Stanley. *Is There a Text in This Class? The Authority of Interpretive Communities.* Cambridge: Harvard University Press, 1980.

Phelan, James. "Data, Danda, and Disagreement." *Diacritics* 13 (Summer 1983): 39–50.

Prince, Gerald. *Narratology: The Form and Functioning of Narrative.* Berlin: Mouton, 1982.

1

Strolling, Touring, Cruising: Counter-Disciplinary Narrative and the Loiterature of Travel

ROSS CHAMBERS

Avec le temps, la passion des grands voyages s'éteint.
> Nerval, *Les Nuits d'Octobre*

In a famous essay, Walter Benjamin tells a story of storytelling (*Erzählung*) as an agent of *Erfahrung*, the "experience" the traveler brings home from distant parts. According to Benjamin, *Erfahrung* has been degraded in modern times as a result of being split into "information" (the already interpreted), and "fiction" (by implication the interpretable).[1] But one can travel, of course, without leaving home; and Benjamin himself is clear that the value of *Erfahrung* is exclusively for a home audience and indeed that the category includes local experience. I want to look in what follows at a modern narrative genre—the genre of "loiterature"—that eludes definition as either "information" or "fiction" and has everything to do with forms of experience that are available without leaving home.[2]

Narrative is intimately connected with the production of knowledge, and so with effects of power and desire. Modern narratology, however, in defining itself very largely as a grammar and a rhetoric, has tended to elide these larger questions in favor of aspects of narrative that are amenable to more formal technical study, notably the analysis of narrative *structure* and of *narration* as a matter of relational positions, such as those of narrator and narratee or author and reader. Both as a grammar and as a rhetoric, narrative theory has had to deal with the vexed question of closure. As Ian Reid insists,[3] the closed structure of story is open to analysis, as a linear series of discursive substitutions or "exchanges"; the closed narrator-narratee relation coexists with an interpretive relation of reading that introduces all the effects of difference and deferral associated with textuality.[4] I propose that the questions of narrative structure and of the rhetorical production of relational subjectivity are themselves understandable as a function of narrative's status as a discourse of knowledge in which issues of power and desire are simultaneously at stake. For if narrative structure and narratorial relations each raise the problem of the relation of closure to discursive openness, there is also an epistemological issue of the same kind. This issue has to do with the ways disciplinary modes of knowledge can be seen as functioning in an exclusionary fashion and with the possibility of counterdisciplinary modes[5] as a less exclusionary, more open alternative. In the modern period (more specifically, since the latter part of the eighteenth century) narrative literature has been split, not only between Benjamin's genres of "information" and "fiction," but also between a disciplined exposition of knowledge and modes of narrative disclosure that enact "experience" as a counterdisciplinary event, with in each case correlative structural entailments and specific differences in the way narrative constructs subjectivity. The "loiterature" of travel will serve as my example of such counterdisciplinary narrative.

It is not my hypothesis that "disciplinary" and "counterdisciplinary" narrative constitute absolutely distinct genres: they are clearly locked in a relation of mutual entailment. Rather than showing that interrelationship, I will concentrate on exploring some features of loiterly narrative (on the assumption that narrative's "disciplined" mode is familiar enough to be recognizable without lengthy analysis). I will try to present it, in a rather artificial point-by-point way, as the structural, intersubjective, and epistemological "other" of the disciplinary mode. To do this, I will rely on Michel Foucault's analysis of discipline in *Surveiller et punir*, while pointing, by implication, to what is exclusionary in Foucault's own highly systematic and disciplined account of the emergence in the modern period of a society founded on discipline. That society was and is the site of counterdisciplinary impulses whose narrative manifestations are the subject of my own—also oversystematic— account.

Discipline, as Foucault describes it, emerges as a structuring in space and time of the activity of work: schoolchildren, hospital patients, factory workers, and soldiers, for instance, occupy a space that is rigorously delimited and divided, and their daily life is subject to no less rigorous scheduling, while their institutional career may be structured as a movement through a hierarchy— from student to teacher, say, or from worker to supervisor—that gives narrative shape to the disciplined development of the isolated individual subject. But discipline seeks also to mold "souls" in this way through training the body: the disciplined subject is one whose actions and reactions have been so trained to regularity and reliability that they do not need to be specifically commanded, thus realizing previously undreamt-of efficiencies, economies, and ef- fectiveness (for example, in the movement of troops or the produc- tion of goods). This subject is, finally, a subject of knowledge, both in the sense of being subjected to a system of surveillance and examination that becomes progressively internalized, and in the sense that such a system presupposes an examining subject and a systematic body of knowledge about the examinees. Foucault shows how, in the form of pedagogy, criminology, psychiatry, psycho- analysis, and so forth, the *sciences humaines* emerged historically as an epistemological offshoot of the disciplinary society, with, at its heart, the practice of the examination—and at the heart of the examination the construction of sets of *norms* against which indi- viduals may be measured and found to be either in conformity or wanting.

What this picture omits, however, is the degree to which, having become a norm in its own right, disciplinarity defines and pro- duces, beyond the criminals and the criminality that are Foucault's focus, various groups of marginalized and potentially oppositional misfits whose relation to delinquency is more ambiguous. What these groups have in common, I think, is an alienated relation to the world of work. Already in the famous opening pages of Balzac's *La Fille aux yeux d'or* [*The Girl with the Golden Eyes*], with its Dantean representation of Paris as a many-circled inferno of endless labor and relentless pleasure-seeking under the spur of ambition and gold, a few sentences are reserved for those—such as priests and those newly arrived from the provinces, the beautiful people of both sexes (society ladies and dandies) and "le peuple heureux des flâneurs"—who escape the frenzy. Balzac's major successor in the portrayal of urban modernity, Baudelaire, similarly distinguishes between an anonymous crowd given over to daily labor and the nightly burden of pleasure, and those isolated figures—denizens of the street such as beggars and rag-pickers, prostitutes and strolling entertainers, widows and "petites vieilles"—in whom he recognizes his own kin, his "congénères," as an artist. The subordinated subgroups of the bourgeoisie, such as artists (who are perceived as not working) and women (who are not permitted to work, their social function being purely ornamental), have in common with the street people (who are perceived as parasitic) a dubious, alienated status that derives from the sense that they are at once economically unproductive and, because not subject to disciplinary control, potentially rebellious. To these suspect groups can be added the sexual minorities whose identities emerged a little later, in part through their being identified as anomalous objects of the new disciplines of knowledge, and in part as an effect of the crisis in the system of gender identities that arose toward the end of the century.

To the extent that middle-class members of such groups inclined to oppositionality (something first seen in the phenomenon of "Bohemia"), the narrative genre I call "loiterature" was available to them, initially in the practices of what Daniel Sangsue has called "eccentric narrative,"[6] and of what is now generally called "flâneur realism," as a counterdisciplinary vehicle. Against disciplinary closure, loiterature proposes the values of the "writerly"—of difference, deferral, and limitless supplementation—and it offers the occasion for a witty and entertainingly seductive performance of failure that comments on the disciplinary values of productivity and mastery. In coining the word loiterature I am translating a pun of Maurice Blanchot's.[7] Blanchot uses the word *désoeuvrement* to describe the inability of writing, traversed as it is by a consciousness of linguistic lack, to achieve the monumental, completed status of *oeuvre*. In appropriating the term, I want to keep the primary sense of *désoeuvrement* (i.e. idleness), but at the same time to draw attention to the difference between a certain metaphysical pathos of failure, much exploited by Blanchot, and the political implications of a certain *failure to conform*, in the context of a social formation oriented toward disciplined efficiency and the power of norms, and in a literary system that values sublimity and promotes the concept of the *oeuvre* as masterpiece. In short, by opposing the monumental, the sublime, and the "ideal" in the aesthetic sphere, loiterature was simultaneously situating itself, in social terms, as a discourse of counterdisciplinarity. In doing so, it was led specifically to attempt a transvaluation of the *trivial*—something that foreshadows, I think, contemporary attempts such as those of Michel de Certeau[8] to deploy the concept of the "everyday" as a phenomenon of culture that can subvert from within—whether in art or in the domain of knowledge—the claims of *techne*.

If the body is the vehicle of disciplinary training, it is also a site of potential resistance (consider the soldier who farts on parade); and the trivial asserts, above all, the claims of the body. But the word has an interesting etymology: it derives from Latin *trivialis*, designating a place where three roads meet and where, by implication, prostitutes, pimps, confidence-tricksters, and other unsavory types were wont to loiter in expectation of opportunity (opportunism, as de Certeau has pointed out, is the defining characteristic of oppositional tactics, and it is the art of biding one's time).[9] The modern sense of "insignificant," however, seems to have attached to the word trivial as a result of the medieval division of the seven liberal arts into the quadrivium (which comprised the four number arts) and the trivium (which grouped the three language arts:

grammar, rhetoric, and logic). If suspicion of the trivial partakes of the Western tradition of privileging "mind" over "body," it also has to do with a no less complex social history of suspicion of loiterers, as tricky customers who can be assumed to be up to no good, and of discourse as a medium of knowledge less reliable and trickier than "sound" disciplines like mathematics and science.

But the modern genre of loiterature began to emerge in the latter part of the eighteenth century. It has specific characteristics that can be opposed point by point to the features of disciplinarity I've mentioned. A narrative art of digression and episodicity, modeled after Sterne's overwhelmingly influential *Tristram Shandy* and *A Sentimental Journey*, disrupts the sense of narrative as structural closure and mimes an experience of linear temporality. In lieu of the disciplined subject, the loiterly narrator has the persona of an engaging conversationalist, interesting by virtue of a seductive performance of personality, like the *parasitus* of classical times, or the pícaro of early modern times. Such a narrator produces knowledge, finally, that has little to do with system or examination, dispensing random observations and striking insights seriatim, according to the haphazard logic of the "collection." The loiterly subject is less interested in conceptual systems than in memory, as the site of re-collection where the random experience (the *Erfahrung*) of a life attuned to the dimension of time becomes unsystematically available. In addition to the founding texts of Sterne, let me randomly cite several others: *Jacques le fataliste* (for its identification of the discourse of fate with structural narrative closure, and for its counterpractice of interruption), early forms of flâneur realism such as Mercier's *Tableau de Paris* or Restif's *Les Nuits de Paris*, the *Rêveries d'un promeneur solitaire*, and finally X. de Maistre's *Voyage autour de ma chambre*, which brings me back to my specific subject through its witty exploitation of the theme of travel without leaving home, of idleness as a mode of *Erfahrung*.

I would myself like to linger over some of these texts, but I will restrict myself instead to some observations about the destructuring of narrative through an art of deferral, the situation of the loiterly narrative subject as a seductive performer, and the practice of collection/recollection as a counterdisciplinary epistemological and narrative mode. I will do so by reading, respectively, a characteristic work of flâneur realism written in the context of *feuilleton* culture (Nerval's *Les Nuits d'Octobre* [*October Nights*]), a novel of episodic construction, Colette's *La Vagabonde* [*The Vagabond*]), that is one of the few examples of loiterature by a woman writer, and a work in which the practice of gay history is figured as a form of cruising, Neil Bartlett's *Who Was That Man?* As the figure of cruising indicates, we will need to be sensitive to a subterranean thematic of desire that links these three texts: the subject of narrative knowledge is produced in Bartlett as a person of desire, as is Colette's narratee through a seductive act of narration, while in symptomatic fashion the dilatoriness of Nerval's belated narrator enacts the destructuring of narrative through digression as an art of deferral "founded" on lack. As an art of the trivial, loiterly writing deploys the tricky resources of desire as that which is capable of subverting simultaneously the claims of aesthetic monumentality and the power of disciplinarity.

Strolling

In *October Nights* (1852)[10] an originary lack (i.e. *un manque*) is figured as a missed train (*un train manqué*), and the outcome of this critical delay, after three days and two nights of dallying in Paris and the neighboring Valois countryside, will be a missed otter hunt. Between this failed departure (*départ manqué*) and the missed ending, the narrative is structured (if that is the word) by accumulated delay and repeated lack in a way that is foreshadowed, *en abyme*, from the start: having missed his first train because of a lackadaisical approach to scheduling, the narrator also misses the second, having become involved while waiting in the pleasures of flânerie with a friend encountered on the boulevard. The two are thus *anuités*, as they say, "adjourned for the night" with time on their hands, and their response is to fill this potentially endless, Shandyan time of deferral with further flânerie. On the first night this takes the typically Parisian form of strolling the streets in search of a likely place for a late-night supper, interminably putting off the decision until they end up in a low-class dive in the Halles ("chez Paul Niquet"). Thus is launched a narrative in which events, observations, conversations, and subjective impressions follow one another in an aimless, nonteleological and nonhierarchized way — nothing is more important than anything else, nothing advances the narrative toward what is in any case its anticlimactic conclusion.

Engaged in a story that borders on pointlessness, the narrator has a problem to deal with: how to attract and maintain his audience's attention for an account that has no point except its own insignificance. His solution will be an art of temporization, a technique characteristic of paid-by-the-column feuilleton writing which Nerval had already demonstrated, con brio, in "Les Faux-Saulniers" (1850). Temporizing is the check-is-in-the-mail tactic: in lieu of what the audience expects and wants (in this case an ending-oriented story leading to the closure of, as Nerval puts it, either a wedding or a death), a substitute satisfaction is provided, but of such a patently inadequate kind that it generates a whole series of such substitutes. The audience becomes prey to the "just one more" or the "bowl of cherries" syndrome: pointless and deficiently pleasurable as any given narrative moment may be, it offers just enough "satisfaction" to keep the reader reading. There is always hope (which always proves vain) that the next moment will bring a more substantial satisfaction. This is a narrative practice known to us these days through much radio and TV programming; and it has the characteristic feature of producing a strict equivalence between the experience of open, linear temporality and that of desire, structured by lack, as Lacan has it, into an endless metonymic chain of substitute "satisfactions."

It is worth noting that the narrator has rather deliberately chosen to put himself in this situation. If one is invited to an otter hunt in Creil, one can take the Northern railroad direct (even though it describes a long curve that Nerval ascribes on other occasions to real estate speculation: modernity is efficient, but not direct enough to abolish time altogether).[11] It is quite willful, therefore, to choose, as this traveler does, to take the Strasbourg road to Meaux, with the idea of *strolling* through the Valois, traveling by coach to Dammartin, through the forest of Ermenonville on foot for three hours, following the course of the Nonette to Senlis, and from there by coach again to Creil (chapter 22). This is a way of traveling without leaving home—the narrator insists from the start on the proximity of the Valois to Paris—while nevertheless generating something (an *Erfahrung*) to narrate. But as a narrator, too, this willful loiterer has deliberately opted for the difficulties of temporization over the easier, and expected, method of telling a suspenseful story. In this, he says, he is emulating a prolix orator described censoriously by Cicero who cannot say that his client left town without describing him waking, rising, setting forth, taking the right side of the via Flaminia and crossing the bath-house square—and never reaching the port. He has also been inspired by an account of London nightlife by Dickens: "How fortunate the English are to be able to write and to read chapters of observation completely unalloyed by fictional invention. . . . Our neighbors' sense of realism is content with truth in the absolute" (1). But Londoners, the narrator grumbles, are much freer than Parisians: they have a house key ("La clef de la rue" is the title of the Dickens piece) and so can wander their city at night without fear of having to affront a censorious concierge. Our narrator is simply taking for himself *la clef de la rue*, and—since after the first night his story shifts to the country—*la clef des champs* as well.

Expressing disapproval of the hated "portier" as a figure of social authority is not the only risk the narrator knows he is taking. Like Nodier in *Le roi de Bohême et ses sept châteaux*, he imagines the unfriendly review his trivial narrative is likely to draw from an idealist critic (the kind whose doctrine is that "truth lies in falsity" [21]). More alarmingly, he is arrested at Crespy by a gendarme who discovers that the man who culpably misses trains also absent-mindedly leaves his travel passport at the hôtel in Meaux, and who is unconvinced by the story that one might travel from Paris via Meaux to an otter hunt in Creil. Why travel east to reach the north?

Such a loiterly traveler is clearly suspect, and in the nightmare that attends his night in prison, he is hauled before what can only be described as a disciplinary tribunal that reminds him of sitting for the baccalaureate *en Sorbonne* ("the president looked uncannily like M. Nisard; the two assessors resembled M. Cousin and M. Guizot, my old teachers"). They hurl epithets at him: "Realist! *Fantaisiste! Essayist!*" until finally he cracks:

> "*Confiteor! plangor! juro!* . . . —I swear to renounce these works accursed of the Sorbonne and the Institute: from now on I shall write only history, philosophy, philology and statistics. . . . You seem dubious. . . . Very well, I'll write virtuous bucolic romances, I'll try to win poetry prizes and prizes for good morals, I'll write children's books and abolitionist essays, didactic poems . . . tragedies!" (25)

His crime is that of being simultaneously realistic and unserious; in another register, Nerval's passionate apologia in *Aurélia* for the rights of madness against the strictures of psychiatric medicine is foreshadowed here.

For this narrator is no examinee and even less an examiner, and his conversion to disciplined knowledge and structured plots takes place—revealingly enough—only in a dream. A simple observer, an impressionist, he has views, like his friend, *de omnis rebus scibilis*, but his attention span is short and his interest is easily diverted. Like Dante and Virgil, the two friends descend into the night world of Paris: we catch glimpses of various cafés, goguettes, and dives and snatches of slangy, trivial conversation. Brief streetscapes open up ("adultery, crime and weakness jostle without recognizing one another through the deceptive shadows" [10]; "on the right are the leech-sellers; the other side is taken up by Raspail pharmacies and cider-stands" [11]; "what a lot of cauliflower in this street" [14]). The initiatory motif of the descent into the underworld informs us that the nature of true knowledge is at issue, but Nerval's mystic concerns are under wraps here in favor of the practice of flâneur realism. This is not incompatible with the fact that, as the external action shifts to the Valois, the focus of the narrative comes to fall predominantly on the contents of the narrator's mind (for in loiterly texts, the question of the flâneur's identity is always, covertly or overtly, at issue, in view of his self-definition as a man given over, like Baudelaire's "homme des foules," to the exploration of alterity). Thus the nightmare of the third night is preceded on the second by a bad dream in which Fichtean gnomes hammer at the narrator's brain in an attempt to rearrange the deranged structure of his consciousness. But there is also a wonderful page of pure visual impressionism, as the narrator wakes after his disturbed night to sit by the Marne and await his morning coffee, in that absent mood we all know so well:

> People are beginning to come across the bridge; it has eight spans by my count. The Marne is *marneuse*, of course; but at the moment it has a leaden sheen ruffled occasionally by currents from the mills, or, further away, the playful swoop of swallows.
>
>   Will it rain this evening? (20)

The major encounter of this section, however, symmetrical to the fellowship of the narrator with his friend in the first part of the text, is with a group of saltimbanks or strolling entertainers, two Savoyards passing respectively for an Italian tenor and a Spanish dancer, and an alleged "monstre" or freak, a "merino woman" who hails from Venice and whose woolly hair, the narrator speculates, is a genetic throwback to some kind of African ancestry. These folk stand, obviously, for the strangeness of the real in its most everyday manifestations (the flâneur's stock-in-trade), and doubtless also for the tricks of art, since their art—like the narrator's—consists of unstructured, episodic entertainment (first an aria, then a cachuca, then the freak), and appeals to an audience as idle as its performers are shiftless. As the narrator of *October Nights* has a flâneur for his friend, partner, and philosophical alter ego, so the flâneur's own artistic counterpart is the wandering street entertainer, whether saltimbank or conjurer. For the friend was already described in these terms:

> He will stop for an hour at the door of the bird-merchant's store, attempting to understand the language of birds. . . . No group gathers around some work-site or bootblack-seller, no fisticuffs occur, no

> dog-fight happens, without his distracted contemplation taking it in. The conjurer always borrows his handkerchief, which he sometimes has, or the five-franc coin, which he doesn't always have. (2)

The hint of complicity here is unmistakable: if the conjurer engages in sleight-of-hand, the flâneur-narrator is a trickster too, in his way: his art of narrative temporizing "deceives" desire as the *escamoteur* deceives the eye, and the art of programming the reader's or spectator's idle attention, from turn to turn or from moment to moment, is common to both. Not surprisingly, we will find Colette's narrator-protagonist, Renée Néré, among music-hall *artistes*, an *artiste* herself, waiting her turn to take the stage after the performing dogs, the *chanteuse*, and the acrobats.

Touring

While Nerval's narrative starts with a missed train, *The Vagabond* (1910) begins with Renée arriving early at the theater and finding herself "prête trop tôt," ready too soon.[12] She has time on her hands as well, but for reasons and with historical implications diametrically opposed to those of Nerval's flâneur. The latter, in his contempt for schedules, shows himself a belated figure, behind the times; Renée is a New Woman, too early because she is struggling for emancipation from domesticity in a society that, as yet, scarcely has a place for her. Consequently, existence in time is, for her, experienced as a matter of deep insecurity, not only financial but also ontological: "Why are you there, all alone? and why not somewhere else?" she asks herself (4), and later comments anxiously, "How quickly everything changes, especially women" (88). Her problem is not that she is suspect as a loiterer but that she needs steady and honorable work; and if going on tour figures for her what strolling through the city and its near countryside represents in Nerval, the act of travel without leaving home, that phrase now has a negative ring, signifying the inability her anxiety betrays to escape the law of domesticity that imprisons women. For her life in the theater involves difficult compromises that are figured implicitly by her métier as an Apache dancer (the woman brutalized by the male, and performing fluttering steps of attempted escape), and explicitly by the tour through the provinces she undertakes, circling back in due course to Paris: "tourner," for her, is "tourner sur place," "revolving on the spot like my companions and brethren" (67).

There she is, then, ready too early. The consequence is a split identity, but one less metaphysically described than the Fichtean problematic Nerval evokes. Her alternative is between an absurd and lonely existence in pure time ("Why are you there, all alone? And why not somewhere else?") and the personage she sees in the mirror and calls her "conseillère maquillée" [painted mentor] (3), that is, her entertainer's personality garishly made up for performance, a seductive self devoted to entertaining the crowd whose work is the condition for the freedom the lonely self finds at once so precious and so burdensome. It is Renée's need for diversion from this intimate dialogue that accounts for the aspect of the book that most resembles the genre of flâneur realism and situates it as loiterature, despite its novelistic plot: Renée is a steady-eyed, unjudgmental observer of the backstage existence of music-hall performers, their poverty, courage, and pride, their makeshift conditions of life, their colorful language and sometimes easy morality, but also their hard work and devotion to their art—their life of instability that prompts her comment: "How quickly everything changes . . ." *Déclassée* as she is by her employment, Renée shares the flâneur's traditional sympathy for the life of the underclass, along with his ability, as an educated member of the middle class, to represent its color and pathos for a similarly middle-class audience. In this too she is a creature of compromise.

The compromise of her existence becomes a crisis of choice, however, on the occasion of the love affair that introduces narrative interest and plot: will Renée's affair with Dufferein-Chautel, affectionately known as "le Grand Serin" or the Big Noodle, end—as Nerval would phrase it—in marriage? One of the few employment choices available to a "dame seule" is work in the theater, as Renée explains: "What would you have me do? Sewing, or typing, or streetwalking? The music hall is the job [*le métier*] of those who never learnt one" (134)—of those, that is, who have been excluded from the privileges of discipline. Renée, in short, is exploiting for employment purposes the seductive art she learned as a wife (knowing how to use her tears of pain, for instance, to make herself look beautiful). But for that very reason, her theatrical art jeopardizes the freedom of which it is also a condition, exposing her not only to the sexual advances of men (which she knows how to handle) but, more dangerously, to the temptation to return to the security—as well as the pain—of a conforming position in the patriarchal order as a married woman. This temptation is represented by the marriageable Dufferein-Chautel ("he looks married already" [102]), who is drawn to her by her stage performance, with his "ridiculous name, the sort of name for a member of Parliament or an industrialist, or a director of a discount bank" (100), but also with his ready assumption of male authority. Renée knows that she will not necessarily be reduced, as in her previous marriage, to being a kind of go-between in her husband's extramarital affairs; but she is also aware that marriage "turns so many wives into a sort of nanny for grown-ups" (137). Her little dog Fossette (the reference is to a fetching dimple) stands for the strength of the impulse in her to revert to the life of a "submissive bitch, rather shame-faced, rather cowed, very much petted, and ready to accept the leash, the collar, the place at her master's feet, and everything" (120).

Renée, then, has only a choice of compromises: freedom with insecurity, or security with the leash—*and* the opportunity to write. Once a quite successful novelist, Renée's new loiterly, "too soon" existence is one in which, paradoxically, she has no time for writing, since earning a living means being subject to constant distraction and interruption:

It takes up too much time to write. And the trouble is, I am no Balzac! The fragile story I am constructing crumbles away when the tradesman rings, or the shoemaker sends in his bill, when the solicitor, or one's counsel, telephones, or when the theatrical agent summons me to his office for a "social engagement at the house of some people of good position but not in the habit of paying large fees." (12)

Consequently her eventual return to writing, coinciding with her return to Paris, her rejection of the Big Noodle, and her implied acceptance of the loiterly life that is defined by interruption, is—as Nancy Miller has pointed out—the key to the book. Her return is also a renaissance (as her name foreshadows), since the writing to which she returns is not the writing she left behind her in her bourgeois existence. It is the writing, as Miller eloquently proposes, of a "feminist" (and I would add "loiterly") subjectivity, one that has renounced the illusions of the bourgeois self and knows itself "subject to change." Miller rightly emphasizes that the letter of rejection for Dufferein-Chautel that Renée brings back to Paris with her is described as "unfinished" (214). But *because* it is unfinished, and corresponding as it does to the anticlimactic ending of the missed otter hunt in Nerval, this letter cannot signify a resolution of Renée's identity problematic. It means only that, for now, she has chosen between her two compromises and opted for the one that associates independence and freedom with, on the one hand, insecurity and, on the other, the deployment of "feminine" attractiveness, the conditions of her "too soon" existence.

My proposal is that the writing she returns to incorporates a similar compromise and is epitomized in the novel itself: it accommodates the problematic split in Renée's identity in the (mixed) genre of the "loiterly novel," exactly that impure "alloy" Nerval sought to avoid, a compromise between pure observation in the digressive, interrupted flow of a narrative of temporality, and fictional invention, sentimental interest, and the seductions of plot. Such writing indicates that Renée's renaissance derives from her discovery and acceptance of the implications of being "no Balzac." Writing need not ignore interruption but can accommodate to it and incorporate it; it need not have the monumental character of the *Comédie humaine* but can be, in exactly Blanchot's sense, a matter of *désoeuvrement*, of that "crumbling" of the edifice that loiterature as counterdiscursive narrative seeks not to resist or to deny, but to assume and deploy as a tactic of oppositionality—a tactic whose success depends, however, on obtaining the pleasurable assent of its audience.

Part of the compromise Renée invents involves plot, then, but another part involves finding a place in her writing for triviality. Early in the piece, she is tongue-tied when she seeks to represent herself to Dufferein-Chautel, hesitating between her "own *personal* language," which she describes as that of "a one-time blue-stocking," and "the slovenly, lively idiom, coarse and picturesque, which one learns in the music-hall, sprinkled with expressions like: 'You bet!' 'Shut up!' 'I'm clearing out!' 'Not my line!'" ["Tu parles!" "Ta gueule!" "J'les mets!" "Très peu pour moi!"] (77–78). This is exactly the linguistic alloy of writerly distinction and colloquial vulgarity that we discover in the writing of *The Vagabond*, but it is Renée's dancing, as an art of the body ("Nothing is real except making rhythm of one's thought and translating it into beautiful gestures" [41]), that has taught her that it is possible to make art out of the trivial. And as Renée becomes aware when she dances for a society gathering (i.e. in exactly the circumstances she evoked when complaining of the interruptions that constitute the life of an *artiste*), dancing embodies a compromise between the freedom of a woman's body and an art intended to be seductive to the powerful (and specifically to Renée's own former set):

> Is not the mere swaying of my back [*un coup de reins*], free from any constraint, an insult to those bodies cramped by their long corsets, and enfeebled by a fashion which insists that they should be thin?
>
> But there is something more worth while than humiliating them; I want, for one moment only, to charm them [*les séduire*]. It needs only a little more effort: already their heads, under the weight of their jewels and their hair, sway vaguely as they obediently follow my movements. At any moment now the vindictive light in all those eyes will go out, and the charmed creatures will all give in and smile at the same time. (41–42)

By the time she is ready to negotiate her *tournée* with the theatrical agent who stands as another figure of the social (here economic) conditions of Renée's independence (and who is, of course, the personage mentioned in the earlier passage about interruptions), she has lost her linguistic inhibitions—"I have found my voice again and the art of using it, and the right vocabulary [i.e. a suitably salty one] for the occasion" (92)—and it is not accidental that what is at issue here is a contract. Renée's loiterly art will be subject to a contractual obligation—the aesthetic obligation to be "charming" to the bourgeoisie—in a way that is modeled by the financial haggling that governs the limited freedom of her "escape" to the provinces, on tour.

There is a name that might be given to the set of compromises Renée finally opts for, including the compromise formation that is her writing; it is *métier*. In order for a woman to be free of the domestic leash, she must be employed, and *métier* names the only kind of employment for which, as a middle-class woman, she is suited: not the discipline of the factory floor or the professional disciplines of knowledge, but "le métier de ceux qui n'en ont appris aucun," a job one can learn by doing it, under a sort of (pre- or extra-disciplinary) apprenticeship system. For *métier* also names the artistic know-how one can acquire with hard work and under the guidance of a strict mentor, like Renée's partner Brague, from one's actual, "hands-on" contact with the world of the theater: in rehearsal, from observation of the audience, and from watching one's fellow performers. But *métier* finally, in the music hall and perhaps the theater generally, is the art of crowd-pleasing, the tricks of the trade that bring the audience back every Saturday night for more. It designates the theatrical seductiveness Renée must deploy as well as the means of livelihood that ensure her relative independence. In that sense it confirms what Renée's tour also teaches her, that although one can travel without leaving home, it is the impossibility of ever quite leaving "home"—and everything that word implies, for a woman—that governs the degree of travel one can achieve. "I am going away," she writes to Max at the end; but she thinks: "I am escaping, but I am still not free of you, I know it. A vagabond, and free, I shall sometimes long for the shade of your walls" (215).

Cruising

How, then, to "lose oneself in the city"? And what has that to do with knowledge? *Who Was That Man?* has an interesting epigraph drawn from Benjamin: "Not to find one's way in a city may well be uninteresting and banal. It requires ignorance, nothing more. But to lose oneself in a city . . ." I would draw out the implications of this epigraph as follows: if Renée Néré experiences her freedom as solitude and is consequently forced into a compromise with the society that limits that freedom, her problem grows out of igno-rance—ignorance, that is, of any community to which she is connected—the community, say, of other independent women attempting to survive on their own terms. Knowledge of a commu-nity is unlikely, however, to be a disciplinary knowledge, if only because discipline begins by separating its subjects in space, like soldiers on the parade ground, so as to turn them into autonomous individuals. Because it seeks on the one hand to promote "self-reliance," and on the other to instil conformity, discipline is anti-communitarian.[13] And community is therefore likely to be the experience, and the source of identity, of those who are excluded from disciplinary subjecthood.

The model for such people is therefore, in Bartlett's book, the sexual cruiser, seen as one who seeks identity, as knowledge of "self," in a community formed through identification with others, through "losing one's *self*" in a "city." Identity here is not a matter of individuality but of connectedness, in which both self and other, being mutually defining, exist only as members of a community. "I've come to understand," Bartlett writes, "that I am connected with other men's lives, men living in London with me." But he adds: *"Or with other, dead Londoners. That's the story"* (xx). The story, in other words, is not only that personal identity—in this case, for gay men—is indistinguishable from belonging to a community but also that the community extends into the past. Historically, gay identity emerged in London simultaneously with the constitution of a community of gay men; that is why a Londoner living in 1986 is connected with men who lived in 1895, the date of Oscar Wilde's trial. And the reason it is important to establish this historical connection, as the book does, is that in producing Wilde *individually* as a homosexual the trial functioned—in typically disciplinary fashion (i.e. as a kind of examination)—precisely to obscure his membership in a community, and hence to deny the existence of a specifically gay identity as a communitarian phenomenon.

London's present cruising grounds, then, were already cruising grounds a century ago, and the streets have a memory. "What if I rounded the corner of Villiers St at midnight," Bartlett writes, "and suddenly found myself walking by gas-light, and the man looking over his shoulder at me as he passed had the same moustache, but different clothes . . . would we recognize each other?" (xx). In this question of recognition lies the kinship of the historian and the cruiser: the power of recognizing the self in the other makes both historian and cruising man—or, of course, woman—into constructors (for the historian, reconstructors) of community. And recognition is crucial because the social conditions of cruising are such that it cannot be a systematic activity: there is no way of identifying "gay men" unless they identify themselves; they are not available, as gay men, for the kind of disciplinary examination by which "homosexuals" are identified. Cruising can only discover, through recognition, a *covert* community in a *random* way. For similar reasons, the historical cruiser is forced to be an unmethodical searcher, looking for "evidence" (and hoping to recognize it) wherever and however it might turn up.

In this unpredictability sexual and historical cruisers have much in common with the activity of "collecting"; but like collectors, cruisers of knowledge are also driven, obsessive figures, creatures of desire, always in search of one more "item." Because it is driven by desire, there is no end to their work and they are therefore never in a position to systematize finally or definitively what can appropriately be called their "findings," which remain just that: collections of "trouvailles." Between gay cruising literature like John Rechy's *Numbers* or Renaud Camus's *Tricks*, and loiterly history like Walter Benjamin's *Passagenwerk* (a collection of quotations) or Georges Perec's *Je me souviens* (a collection of memories that have the specific quality of being both trivial and nonpersonal, or collective), there are consequently "recognizable" structural and epistemological similarities that imply a generic relationship. Bartlett's book—the record of intense cruising not in Villiers St. but in the British Library—lies somewhere between the two groups. And what is a genre if not itself an assemblage or collection of texts, each "recognizable" in spite of dissimilarities as members of a community—an assemblage carried out, as Anne Freadman insists, as a function of some specific motivation and in a clearly contextualized, situated way?

There is a deliberate rejection in this genre of a certain narrative structure that is itself a structuring of history, and of its implications. Two narrative models are available to gay people, as Bartlett points out (23–24). One is the coming-out story, with its firm narrative structure of "before" and "after," a beginning and an end mediated by a crucial event that has the status of an emergence of truth. A coming-out story can be either individual or collective, and Wilde's coming out—more accurately his involuntary "outing"—functions as both. But the closed structure of such a narrative makes it exclusionary, and Bartlett's study of the 1895 trial demonstrates that the outing of Wilde had as its unacknowledged purpose to silence gay voices that were beginning to be heard, to force back into invisibility and oblivion the community of gay men that had begun to emerge—of "gay men," not just of men with homosexual desires, a distinction that hangs significantly on their communitarian invention of signs of recognition, such as Wilde's green carnation or the moustache in Villiers St. But the cruising story, the obsessive collection of scraps of forgotten history, makes use of just such signs of recognition in order to undo the effect of exclusionary and scapegoating stories constructed by the powers that be. Thus Bartlett notices that men like Arthur Symonds and Edward Carpenter were already, long before him, engaging in the "inspired queenly assemblage of fragments" of gay history (227), and I, in turn, have just pointed out that such cruiser-historians form part of a larger counterdisciplinary epistemological community of (re-)collectors of the past that includes Perec and Benjamin.

The point, then, as Bartlett points out, is that "it never is in all the papers" (125): the official story always needs supplementation by the collector, looking for the forgotten but telling scraps. "What I want are details, details are the only things of interest" (159). "I read texts with the dogged energy that I usually reserve for cruising; I became excited by the smallest hints; I scrutinized every gesture for significance; sometimes I simply stood close and waited for a response" (28). The outcome of working principles such as these is a book whose pages often seem to reproduce the bulletin board in the author's room: "On my wall a handsome face is pasted up next to a fragment from a novel, next to the latest report of an arrest or a persecution" (96); quotations from a range of nineteenth-century sources, personal observations about gay life in modern London, and analytic commentary coexist on the page; a chapter on flowers as recognition-signals includes the story of one Private Flower who was arrested for "cottaging" in the 1830s. Bartlett puts together a portrait gallery of men's faces and a glossary of historical gay slang omitted from the *OED*; he rejoices that at the Wilde trial "the prosecution assembled one of the most extensive and glamorous collections of details about our life" (99), but he also assembles counterevidence of the energy and vividness of gay life in the years between the trial of Boulton and Parks (alias Stella and Fanny) in 1870 and the Wilde trial, in the form of a year-by-year "calendar" of quotations and cuttings that extends over twenty-five pages.

A scrapbook such as this, says Bartlett, is "the true form of our history" (99). Because "our past is continually lost" (59), it is necessary to make good the omissions; "because the clues change" (63) and recognition is therefore always aleatory, no truth claim can be made or conclusions safely drawn. The scrapbook "embodies in its own omissions how we remember and forget our lives. We are always between ignorance and exposure" (99); but in doing so it nevertheless demonstrates that "the past is still with us" (82). Like the cruiser hunting familiar streets that harbor memories of dead Londoners, the scrapbook's demonstration of the proximity of past and present represents another sense in which the loiterer's experience consists of traveling without leaving home. Such *Erfahrung* is exhilarating—but its dependence on recognition also makes its epistemological status dubious, as Bartlett emphasizes. After all, as Oscar Wilde's "composing" of a new identity after 1895 demonstrates, gay men are given to "making it all up as we go along" (170–71); moreover, in a way foreshadowed by Wilde's story "The Portrait of Mr. W. H.," the whole enterprise of the "recollection" of gay culture and community raises the question whether it is perhaps all a fantasy, fueled only by desire. "My father always said, if you're not sure if it's the real thing, then it isn't" (189). And collecting, as an activity of knowledge, has exclusionary implications of its own: it takes place "within a specific economy" (186) of class and privilege and is dependent on one's having "discretionary income" and (something Bartlett does not specifically mention although it is everywhere implied) time and leisure. Who can otherwise afford to spend an idle bank holiday weekend ("I wasn't working, and it was the first good weather of the year") and then return to the library, as Bartlett describes himself doing (125–26)?

What matters here is not the incompleteness of the scrapbook method, or the dubious objectivity of an epistemological "hunt" motivated by desire, or the dependency of this activity on specific social conditions. What does matter is the dubiousness of claims to completeness and objectivity, and of narratives that mask their socially positioned status with implied or explicit truth claims. It is in *not* making such claims, and in making its specific position of enunciation readable in historical, economic, and cultural terms by its careful exploration of the conditions of gay male life as Bartlett knows them in modern London, that this loiterly narrative makes its own epistemological point. In so doing, it makes the point for loiterature in general, whose doubtful reliability in matters of information and whose class ties to the bourgeoisie and its history scarcely need to be indicated. It is not that such features are invalidating, but that their visibility questions the assumptions by virtue of which they might be invalidated. Such assumptions are those of disciplinarity, whose epistemological reliance on examination presupposes the separability of (examining) subject and (examined) object. Claims to dispassionate objectivity rest on such assumptions of separability, assumptions which themselves derive from a concept of individual identity as autonomous, unconnected, not dependent on the alterity of a community in which it is possible to "lose oneself/one's self."

But when Bartlett writes simply: "It's quite true, I am other people" (205), he is echoing flâneur-knowledge that goes back at least to Nerval's "I am the other" (a phrase he scribbled on a portrait of himself), or to Baudelaire's definition of the flâneur (itself derived from Poe) as "l'homme des foules," the man of the crowd.[14] As visible as are the class differences in Nerval's account of Parisian lowlife and Colette's *reportage* on the backstage life of the music hall, there is also a sense of community in these texts—of the community of society's misfits, underlings, and rejects—that draws a line from Nerval's preoccupation with alter egos (the Parisian friend, the saltimbanks), through the comradeship celebrated in Colette's novel, to Bartlett's "I am connected with other men's lives." That statement is embroiled in gendered blindness, just as those of Nerval and Colette are embroiled in the limitations of class, but all of them can be rephrased as: I am connected with other lives.

Although I cannot demonstrate the point at length here (part of the argument is in Werner Hamacher's distinction between *ratio* and *lectio* and elements of another part are in *Room for Maneuver*),[15] I want to enter the claim in conclusion that "reading" is the name that can most appropriately be given to the mode of loiterly knowledge that enacts identity as connectedness and questions the assumptions underlying disciplinary "examination." Where an examiner is focused on an examinee as an other to be dispassionately assessed in terms of a set of disciplinary "norms," the reader is the site of a more intimate and less certain experience—that of a recognition, mediated by much less assured "signs" or "tokens," in which it is through the other that the reading subject becomes known. In reading, the "object" must be recognized as a(nother) subject at the same time as subjectivity is itself experienced, not as in-dividual, but as split, because necessarily produced through that other's mediation.

In Bartlett's text, the narratee is consistently produced as a reader in this sense, because the narrative deploys the pronouns of address, "we" and "you," as pronouns of community, inviting the addressee to confirm the narrator's own recognitions by recognizing in turn, as tokens of gay identity, his various "findings." Earlier loiterly narrators, such as those in Nerval and Colette, are readers of the discourse of the world much like the more familiar Baudelairean flâneur; they are always confronted with a fragmentary text, or a haphazard series of partial texts, that they cannot or do not seek to master, because, in ways both obscure and evident, they have a sense of their own inescapable investment and involvement in the "object," the connectedness of "I" and "not-I." "Always ready too soon," Renée Néré responds by reading: "I'd better open the book lying on the make-up shelf . . . or the copy of *Paris-Sport* the dresser was marking just now with my eyebrow-pencil; otherwise I'll find myself all alone" (3).

If the proximity of city and countryside in Nerval and Colette and that of present and past in Bartlett are the conditions for traveling without leaving home, then reading, as the experience of the proximity of I and not-I, is the paradigmatic form of that loiterly *Erfahrung*. Our theories of reading do not much stress that it is, in essence (but "essence" is not the word), an experience of the inevitably *temporal* constitution of a mediated, and so split, subjectivity—one that knows itself only in and through the other. But temporality is also what the loiterer knows best, and it is inescapably the dimension of experience implied by the contraction of space that conditions travel without leaving home. "With time," reads the first sentence of *October Nights*, "the passion for long trips fades." One might equally say that it is with the fading of the passion for long trips that knowledge, as the *Erfahrung* of time, begins.

Notes

1. Walter Benjamin, "The Storyteller," in *Illuminations*.
2. This essay is partly programmatic and partly exploratory: it is not meant to be exhaustive or even thorough but to introduce a few ideas for discussion. I plan to expand in later work on a number of points that are

made briefly here.

3. See *Narrative Exchanges*.

4. See Ross Chambers, *Story and Situation* and *Room for Maneuver*.

5. I intend the term "counterdisciplinary" to locate the narrative genre that is my subject as counterdiscourse in Richard Terdiman's sense of the word. See his *Discourse/Counterdiscourse*.

6. See *Le récit excentrique*.

7. See Maurice Blanchot, *L'Espace littéraire*. Translator Ann Smock comments on the word *désoeuvrement* on p. 13. See in particular "L'expérience de Mallarmé," 30–42 (trans. 38–48) and "Le regard d'Orphée," 179–84 (171–76). In *Lost beyond Telling*, Richard Stamelman translates *désoeuvrement* as "worklessness" (46).

8. Michel de Certeau, *Arts de faire*.

9. See in particular de Certeau's discussion of tactics as opposed to strategy, 21 (trans. p. xix).

10. All translations are mine, and for the convenience of users of other editions I refer in parentheses to chapter numbers, not pages. On *Les Nuits d'Octobre*, see Ross Chambers, chapter 9 of *Gérard de Nerval et la poétique du voyage*, and Daniel Sangsue, 360–64.

11. On this question, see my *Gérard de Nerval et la poétique du voyage*, 329–30.

12. Page numbers in parentheses refer to the Ballantine edition. I have sometimes silently emended the translation.

13. As my discussion of Bartlett's book will confirm, I do not conceive community either as a matter of conformity (the totalitarian model) or as a contractual phenomenon (between "individuals" and "society"), but as a function of the recognition of self in alterity and so of a mediated play of differences. For theoretical work along these lines, see Miami Theory Collective, ed., *Community at Loose Ends*, work that is itself broadly inspired by Jean-Luc Nancy, *La Communauté désoeuvrée*.

14. See Charles Baudelaire, "Le peintre de la vie moderne."

15. Werner Hamacher, "*Lectio*: de Man's Imperative." More broadly relevant is Michel de Certeau's characterization of reading, in *The Practice of Everyday Life*, as a loiterly practice, like "walking through the city": "to read is to wander through an imposed system" (169).

Bibliography

Bartlett, Neil. *Who Was That Man? A Present for Mr Oscar Wilde*. London: Serpent's Tail, 1988.

Baudelaire, Charles. "La peintre de la vie moderne." In *Oeuvres complètes*. Vol. 2. Ed. by Claude Pichois. Paris: Bibliotheque de la Pléiade, 1976.

Benjamin, Walter. "The Storyteller." In *Illuminations*. Ed. by H. Arendt. New York: Schocken Books, 1969. 83–109.

Blanchot, Maurice. *L'Espace littéraire* [*The Space of Literature*]. 1955. Trans. by Ann Smock. Lincoln: University of Nebraska Press, 1982.

Certeau, Michel de. *Arts de faire* [*The Practice of Everyday Life*]. Trans. by Steven F. Rendall. Berkeley: University of California Press, 1984.

Chambers, Ross. *Gérard de Nerval et la poétique du voyage*. Paris: Corti, 1969.

———. *Story and Situation*. Minneapolis: University of Minnesota Press, 1984.

———. *Room for Maneuver*. Chicago: University of Chicago Press, 1991.

Colette. *The Vagabond*. Trans. by Enid McLeod. New York: Ballantine, 1955.

Foucault, Michel. *Surveiller et punir* [*Discipline and Punish*]. Trans. by Alan Sheridan. New York: Random House, 1978.

Freadman, Anne. "Anyone for Tennis?" In *The Place of Genre in Teaching: Recent Debates*. Ed. by I. Reid. Geelong: Centre for Studies in Literary Education, Deakin University, 1987. 91–124.

Hamacher, Werner. "*Lectio*: de Man's Imperative." In *Reading de Man Reading*. Ed. by Lindsay Walters and Wlad Godzich. Minneapolis: University of Minnesota Press, 1989. 171–201.

Miami Theory Collective, ed. *Community at Loose Ends*. Minneapolis: University of Minnesota Press, 1991.

Miller, Nancy K. "Woman of Letters: The Return to Writing in Colette's *La Vagabond*." Chapter 9 of *Subject to Change*. New York: Columbia University Press, 1988.

Nancy, Jean-Luc. *La Communauté désoeuvrée* [*The Inoperative Community*]. Trans. by Peter Connor. Minneapolis: University of Minnesota Press, 1991.

Nerval, Gérard de. *Les Nuits d'Octobre*. In *Oeuvres*. Vol. 1. Ed. by A. Béguin and J. Richer. Paris: Bibliothèque de la Pléiade, 1966. 77–118.

Reid, Ian. *Narrative Exchanges*. London: Routledge. Forthcoming.

Sangsue, Daniel. *Le récit excentrique*. Paris: Corti, 1987.

Stamelman, Richard. *Lost Beyond Telling*. Ithaca: Cornell University Press, 1990.

Terdiman, Richard. *Discourse/Counterdiscourse*. Ithaca: Cornell University Press, 1985.

2

Generic and Doctrinal Politics in the Proletarian Bildungsroman

BARBARA FOLEY

My topic in this essay is the relationship between form and politics in the left-wing fiction produced in the United States during the Depression. In particular, I wish to examine the usability of the form of the bildungsroman for revolutionary political ends. Many Depression-era writers turned to the developing form of the "collective" novel, as well as to the testimonial form of the fictional autobiography, which was closely tied to the worker-authored "sketch" celebrated in the Soviet Union (Foley). But large numbers of left-wing novelists opted for what critics of the time called "conversion plots" and wrote what were essentially proletarian bildungsromans—accounts of the process whereby a non-class-conscious worker develops into a seasoned and committed fighter for the proletariat. These writers were thus attempting to adapt to radical ends a genre that is often seen as the most typically bourgeois of novelistic modes.

What are the consequences and implications of this choice? Did the "conversion plot" serve proletarian writers well, supplying—as Georg Lukács would argue—a generic model that would dialectically embody the broad contradictions of history in a single concrete instance? Or did the use of the bildungsroman format doom these writers in advance by committing them to an irremediably bourgeois set of assumptions about character and consciousness? Or was form essentially irrelevant, with doctrinal politics or "line" the crucial determinant of political effect in the proletarian bildungsroman? Addressing these issues is important, not only for an understanding of what 1930s proletarian writers were doing, but also for an appreciation of the issues facing other groupings of writers today who are variously termed "oppositional," "marginalized," and "subaltern."

I shall first examine the estimate of inherited narrative forms and the attitude toward "propaganda" in literature that were prevalent among the 1930s Marxist critics. Next, I shall summarize the critique of novelistic realism that has attained widespread currency among contemporary critics. Next will come an analysis of a paradigmatic proletarian bildungsroman, Myra Page's *Moscow Yankee*, followed by a glance at Tillie Olsen's *Yonnondio*, a novel that departs significantly, in both structure and rhetoric, from the standard bildungsroman format. On the basis of this brief theoretical, historical, and textual commentary, I shall offer some conclusions about the relation of generic to doctrinal politics in the proletarian bildungsroman. I shall be navigating some difficult terminological waters, since the two key terms under scrutiny, "bildungsroman" and (especially) "realism," have been subjected to multiple significations. Moreover, while clearly related both theoretically and historically, these two concepts cannot simply be conflated. I attempt to retain an alertness to nuances and distinctions in the deployment of these terms as I draw some general conclusions about the relation of politics to novelistic form.

Those proletarian novelists who turned to the classically realistic genre of the bildungsroman were hardly working against the grain of contemporaneous U.S. Marxist theory about politics and form. Most reviewers and critics writing in the *New Masses* and the various organs of the John Reed Clubs proclaimed themselves agnostic with regard to issues of genre and ideology. To be sure, some cultural commentators, like the editors of *The Left*, the journal of the John Reed Club of Davenport, Iowa, declared that "new forms and techniques must be hammered out to express the fresh substance, the faster tempos and rhythms of the new world order" ("Editorial" 3). Such novels as Dos Passos's *USA* trilogy, William Rollins's *The Shadow Before*, and Clara Weatherwax's prize-winning *Marching! Marching!*—all texts experimenting with innovative styles and structures designed to convey both conflict and totality—were greeted with enthusiasm in the left press (see Schneider, Adler, Basshe). But the literary left never theorized what was "experimental" about these texts or writers or held them up as models. In general, Marxist critics evinced little disquietude that inherited novelistic forms might come into the revolutionary camp trailing the mists of bourgeois ideology. When reviewers found fault with texts written in classically realistic modes—for instance, Grace Lumpkin's *To Make My Bread*, Fielding Burke's *Call Home the Heart*, Jack Conroy's *A World to Win*—they rarely developed a theoretical argument relating politics to genre (see Nadir, Jerome, Le Sueur). Granville Hicks, literary editor of the *New Masses* in the proletarian period, wrote a series of articles called "Revolution and the Novel" in which he argued that the novel form "lends itself to many purposes and all points of view." Even though the novel "has closely corresponded to the rise of the bourgeoisie and has fully expressed . . . the mind of the bourgeoisie," he argued, "it cannot be limited to one class" (19). In Hicks's view, proletarian novelists who opted for the form of the "biographical" novel ran no risk of reproducing bourgeois conceptions of subjectivity or experience.

Indeed, while 1930s Marxists reacted positively to literary experimentation, they generally discouraged writers from using techniques that ruptured narrative illusion in order to call direct attention to political doctrine. Depression-era left-wing criticism is replete with approving references to texts that "weave" or "blend" politics into the tale of a character's attainment of class-consciousness. Contrary to the stereotype of the Communist critical commissar bludgeoning novelists into writing party propaganda, the typical 1930s Marxist critic endorsed an aesthetic of seamless transparency, denigrating texts that engaged in "preaching," "editorializing," or "sloganeering." Even though the critics urged writers to create texts that would be weapons in the class struggle, instilling revolutionary optimism and representing the "way out" from the miseries of capitalism, they chastised novelists who produced "the revolutionary equivalent of the Cinderella formula" (Calmer 17). "Tendentiousness" (a concept taking in a grab bag of rhetorical strategies and devices, from hectoring narrators to pontificating mentors to implausible "conversion" plots) was branded by "Stalinists" and "Trotskyists" alike as "leftist" (see Murphy, Foley). The debates over documentarism, expressionism, and realism that filled the pages of Soviet and German left-wing journals were never fought out on U.S. soil. Indeed, both Brecht and Lukács were relatively unknown to the American cultural left. But insofar as their antipathy to "leftism" led them to embrace a doctrine of showing rather than telling—a kind of left Jamesianism—the American Marxists embraced, if only by default, an essentially Lukácsian conception of realism.[1]

American Marxists of the 1930s would thus have been shocked if they were reincarnated as flies on the wall of a typical 1980s MLA session on the politics of novelistic realism. For the fundamental assumption guiding much—if not all—postmodernist discussion of the classical modes of realism is that they reproduce and support dominant ideology. As distilled in the work of two exemplary theorists, Catherine Belsey and Lennard J. Davis, the postmodernist critique of realism makes three main points. First, realism privileges individual psychology and individual experience. Protagonists presumably serve as synecdoches for their time and place: the intensive totalities projected through the stories of their individual destinies embody in microcosm the extensive totalities of their social worlds. But these protagonists usually turn out to possess intrinsic qualities of "character" that are simply "revealed" through experience: in Catherine Belsey's formulation, "character, unified and coherent, is the source of action" (73). In the classic bildungsroman, as Lennard J. Davis puts it, "the idea that the subject might be formed from social forces and that change might have to come about through social change is by and large absent" (119). Protagonists are routinely portrayed as autonomous moral agents, who end up either "reconciled to" or "pitted against" the social order. Second, realism purports to consider conflicting value systems, but at base it cannot tolerate contradiction. In particular, narrative closure operates as an ideological mechanism guaranteeing that disturbing issues are laid to rest and that competing discourses are subordinated to the text's hegemonic discourse through narrative "inevitability." "The logic of [the structure of classic realism]," Belsey notes, "precludes the possibility of leaving the reader simply to confront the contradictions which the text may have defined" (82). Third, realism co-opts readers into agreement by positioning them as "always already" in concurrence with the politics shaping the narrative. The technique of free indirect discourse (for example, "she came to see that . . .") epitomizes realism's co-optative strategy. A character "realizes" the truth which guides the novel, and to which the reader, in collaboration with the narrator, has been privy all along. The reader is thus, in the Althusserian sense, "interpellated" as what Stephen Heath calls "the unified and unifying subject of [the text's] vision" (85).

The implications of this argument for the proletarian novel should be apparent. The logic of the postmodernist critique of realism is that, hard as they might have tried to make realism serve the ends of a revolutionary politics, the proletarian novelists were headed for failure by their adherence to an intrinsically conservative and repressive mode of writing. The line of political argument explicitly urged in a text—the necessity for militant participation in class struggle, the falsity of petty bourgeois aspirations, even the desirability of communism as an alternative to capitalism—cannot move the reader leftward if it is embedded in a discursive mode premised upon a bourgeois epistemology and bourgeois assumptions about selfhood. The very posture of political certainty encouraged by realistic form produces an effect of ideological closure; if a text wishes to query the existing order of things in a thoroughgoing way, it must instead adopt what Belsey calls an "interrogative" form, one that decenters all putatively authoritative expressions of politics. Despite its posture of confronting and unmasking reactionary idealisms with an unflinching portraiture of "what is," the argument goes, realism turns out to be not an ally but an antagonist to the project of literary radicalism. However left-wing their intentions, proletarian writers who worked in the form of the realistic novel ended up confirming the very world order that they originally set out to oppose.

Not all commentators—on proletarian fiction in particular or on the novel in general—concede that realistic form presupposes naive empiricism or authoritarian control (e.g. Levine). Some critics argue that the novel is in fact uniquely empowered to articulate oppositional discourses. For example, feminist critic Diane Price Herndl, citing Bakhtin's doctrine of novelistic heteroglossia, argues that the novel is historically a "feminine genre" and that "[n]ovelistic discourse achieves a state of non-definability, of otherness, of freedom from hierarchy" (13). Peter Hitchcock, also invoking Bakhtin in his formulation of the "dialogism of the oppressed," writes that "[w]hat is important in theorizing working-class fiction is not form for form's sake, but the *struggles* over form. . . . The interrogative text of which Belsey writes may be antirealist in the classic sense, but nevertheless we should entertain the possibility that such a text may still be realist" (97). Carole Snee takes issue with the "dominant critical practice [which] argues that because the realist novel has been concerned historically with the individual, and its narrative structures operate through one—or a series of—individual consciousnesses, its philosophy is always essentially 'liberal.'" On the contrary: the realistic novel "does not simply at best reveal and interrogate the dominant, unstated ideology, or exist uncritically within it, but can also incorporate a *conscious* ideological or class perspective, which in itself undercuts the ideological parameters of the genre, without necessarily transforming its structural boundaries" (Snee 168–69). H. Gustav Klaus offers the valuable caveat that, while form "is doubtless a carrier of ideology," it is "not the only [ideological] constituent of a text, and it is, above all, not some kind of cosmic, transhistorical category immune to change" (*Socialist Novel* 2).

Nonetheless, most contemporary defenders of novelistic realism qualify their endorsement of inherited fictional modes as potential carriers of oppositional politics. Herndl, it is true—like some other recent celebrants of Bakhtinian dialogism—may proclaim "the novel" an antihierarchical genre *qua* genre. In so doing, however, she greatly oversimplifies Bakhtin, who polemically distinguished Dostoevsky's attainment of a "plural-voiced" novel form with the "monologism" that he saw characterizing all modes of the novel before—and most after—Dostoevsky's time (Bakhtin 5–46). For Bakhtin—if not for all his apostles—"heteroglossia" did not signify protopoststructuralist subversion and free play, but instead the contradictory coexistence of different social discourses within a single text. Hitchcock, a more cautious Bakhtinian than Herndl, concedes most of Belsey's argument about the conservative politics of novelistic realism. Rather than directly defending inherited realistic narrative forms, however, he shifts the ground of the argument, in a Brechtian maneuver, to a redefinition of "realism" itself. Snee admits that a text articulating a *"conscious* ideological or class perspective" necessarily "undercuts the ideological parameters of the genre"—that is, goes against the generic political grain. Klaus, discussing the difficulties posed by the bildungsroman form to socialist writers, notes that the focus on a central hero runs the risk of effacing "the central fact of the class struggle to the lives of individuals" (*Literature of Labor* 127). In short, most present-day advocates of the continuing viability of novelistic realism posit a tension between form and idea: even if a text's doctrinal content may pull it to the left, inherited novelistic conventions will usually pull it to the right. If realistic texts manage to be oppositional, this occurs in spite of, rather than because of, inherited generic tendencies. These critics are anything but reborn Lukácsians.

So far we have been speaking of novelistic realism, or the realistic novel, in general terms. Critics of the bildungsroman, a subspecies of both these larger categories, have generally concurred that this genre is if anything the quintessentially bourgeois form of the novel. Hegel, describing the conventions of the emergent novelistic form epitomized in Goethe's *Wilhelm Meister*, noted that such texts depict "the education of the individual at the hands of the given reality. . . . For the conclusion of such an apprenticeship usually amounts to the hero getting the rough spots knocked off him. . . . In the last analysis he usually gets his girl and some kind of job, marries, and becomes a philistine just like all the others" (quoted in Swales 50). Dilthey, without Hegel's irony, coined the term *bildungsroman* to describe a novel featuring a hero who "enters into life in a blissful state of ignorance, seeks related souls, experiences friendship and love, struggles with the hard realities of the world and thus armed with a variety of experiences, matures, finds himself and his mission in the world" (quoted in Hardin xiv).

Subsequent theorists of the bildungsroman have sought to broaden its ideological scope, noting that the genre can stress conflict over accommodation (Shaffner) and, especially in its modernist variants, can allow for irony and open-endedness (Swales, Sammons). Even the genre's staunchest advocates concede, however, that it is premised upon fundamentally bourgeois notions of self. As James Hardin notes, the great majority of bildungsromans feature accommodation through their depiction of "the intellectual and social development of a central figure who, after going out into the world and experiencing both defeats and triumphs, comes to a better understanding of self and to a generally affirmative view of the world" (Hardin xiii). Even texts that portray alienation or rebellion presuppose a division between self and society, a "confrontation with society" (Steinecke 95). The bildungsroman projects, according to Martin Swales, "a tension between a concern for the sheer complexity of individual potentiality on the one hand and, on the other, a recognition that practical reality—marriage, family, a career—is a necessary dimension of the hero's self-realization, albeit one that implies a limitation, indeed a constriction, of the self" (51). Moreover, the genre is based upon a largely a priori conception of individual identity. As Jeffrey Sammons puts it, "the concept of *Bildung* is intensely bourgeois: it carries with it many assumptions about the autonomy and relative integrity of the self, its potential self-creative energies, its relative range of options within material, social, even psychological determinants" (42). Even when the bildungsroman focuses on society as well as subjectivity, then, it presupposes a "character" possessing intrinsic potentialities who enters an "environment" that either fulfills or restricts his or her individuality. The bildungsroman, which purports transparently to convey the essential qualities of both the self and the world, thus furnishes the textual epitome of "programmatic individualism" (Visser).

What is at stake in this analysis is by now, I hope, clear. If the left-wing 1930s critics are right, the form of the "biographical" novel was ideologically neutral: whether or not a writer successfully conveyed a revolutionary vision depended upon whether he or she adeptly "wove" or "blended" radical politics into the story of the protagonist's "conversion" to class-consciousness. If the post-modernist critics of realism are right, the writers of proletarian bildungsromans were doomed to failure. To test the relative validity of these two hypotheses, we shall now turn to an analysis of two proletarian bildungsromans.

My paradigmatic text in this discussion of politics and form in the proletarian bildungsroman is Myra Page's *Moscow Yankee* (1935). Since I, like other scholars of noncanonical texts, must assume my audience's lack of acquaintance with my material, I shall briefly recapitulate what this novel is about. *Moscow Yankee* is in one sense unusual among proletarian novels in that it takes its hero, Andy, an unemployed Detroit auto worker, to the USSR during the First Five-Year Plan and thus raises directly the issue of socialism. (Almost all U.S. proletarian novels delineate class struggle in the capitalist United States.) In its portraiture of a hero who, through experience and ideological struggle, moves from non-class-consciousness to revolutionary commitment, however, the novel presents an exemplary instance of the "conversion" plot. Moreover, because its politics are so explicit, *Moscow Yankee* brings to the fore important questions about the politics of representation in the proletarian novel. The novel's plot has two main strands. The central plotline deals with Andy's personal growth into a partisan of the socialist USSR. This metamorphosis is effected through three experiences: working on the assembly line at the Red Star tractor plant and becoming a *tovarisch* (comrade) of his fellow worker Sasha; arguing politics with some American Communist expatriates, the white Mac and the black Ned; and falling in love with the winsome young *tovarisch* Natasha, who teaches him that socialist construction is inseparable from changed personal relations between and among people. This personal plot reaches its climax when Andy realizes that he wants to be free of his obligation to his American fiancée, Elsie, who writes him whining consumerist letters and at one point announces that she plans to join him in the USSR. The dilemma is, how is Andy going to free himself honorably from Elsie (who can't be blamed for her low level of consciousness, not being herself a "Moscow Yankee") and end up with his new true love? The key issue raised in the main plot, then, is that of the politics of personal loyalty in the context of class loyalty. The traditional bildungsroman focus upon the individual's maturation through experience is thus invested with revolutionary doctrinal content.

The novel's subplot, which involves two American engineers working in Moscow, addresses the politics of production. The "good" engineer, Boardman, who favors any industrial regime privileging "science, engineering, efficiency," is counterposed with the "bad" engineer, Crampton, who is fixated on "speed, money, costs" (146). The plant's machinery is itself endowed with vital force, being described as a "beautiful, quivering nerve center" (22). The production subplot reaches its climax when some white Russians who are enemies of socialist construction attempt to sabotage Red Star. After a suspenseful chase by Ned, the nefarious activities of the former countess Katia Boudnikova and her entrepreneurial sidekick Alex Turin are thwarted. The key theme raised in the subplot is the necessity for workers' steadfast commitment to building and defending the material infrastructure of the emerging socialist society.

Clearly *Moscow Yankee* raises all kinds of revolutionary politics. But it also offers what many contemporary critics would see as a classic case of realism's antipathy to, and foreclosure of, contradiction. For the two plots are brought to termination not by any political logic or synthesis but by simple narrative juxtaposition. The sense of inevitability accompanying the strong narrative trajectory produces the sense that issues have been resolved, when in fact they have been sloughed over. The suspense and emotional satisfaction deriving from each plotline are displaced onto the other. The main plotline has posed the thesis that the "personal is political" and has argued that socialist construction entails a thoroughgoing fight against traditional notions about gender. There is even a minor subplot about a former prostitute, Zena, who straightens out and regains self-esteem as an assembly-line worker: developing the productive forces, it is implied, also develops human potentiality. Yet Andy is himself let off the hook regarding his personal politics. He never has to decide between Elsie and Natasha, since—somewhat implausibly—near the end of the novel he receives from Elsie a "Dear John" letter, followed closely by a letter from one of Andy's former buddies who tells him that Elsie was a bad lot all along, having been fooling around with one of Andy's other buddies ever since Andy left. At the same time, even though the novel has raised the question of worker control of production, this issue is forgotten amidst the flurry surrounding the threatened explosion of Red Star. When Andy decides to stay in the USSR and do his bit for socialist construction, the actual social relations that socialism entails at the point of production are no longer a point of contention and query in the novel, which ends with Andy happily cuddled up with Natasha and participating in his first Soviet May Day. The personal plot here usurps rather than parallels and interpenetrates the public plot.

It could thus be argued that conventions of bildungsroman narration foster political opportunism in *Moscow Yankee*. Suspense has displaced conceptual argument onto narrative trajectory, thus foreclosing further confrontation with the issue of personal responsibility raised by the Elsie/Natasha plot. Similarly, ideologically coercive (if emotionally satisfying) conventions of romantic closure can be seen to secure Andy's reconciliation with the new society through his discovery of the right love partner. Andy may not have become a "philistine," as Hegel wryly noted of the typical bildungsroman hero; but it would seem that the narrative's focus on "get[ting] his girl" has helped to render moot any further consideration of the question of egalitarianism at the point of production, which was initially addressed in the production plot. Moreover, the bildungsroman's synecdochic presumption that one person's story embodies in microcosm larger social contradictions prohibits skepticism about the typicality of Andy's tale. What Andy "realizes" about the virtues of socialism is what the reader learns—in fact, what the reader is positioned to have known all along, and to have pitied Andy for not knowing. Even though *Moscow Yankee* is, on the level of manifest content, clearly motivated by revolutionary politics, one could argue that the novel's reliance upon inherited realistic plot conventions—in particular, on the individualistic conventions of the bildungsroman—substantially damages, even subverts, the text's political intentions. The *New Masses* reviewer's complaint that the novel ended with a "pink sunset" (Field 26) can thus be attributed—although the reviewer did not say so—not just to Page's utopian politics, but to her option to tell her story through the vehicle of the bildungsroman. According to the postmodernist critique of realism, it is the generic politics of the bildungsroman that undermine the doctrinal politics of communism.

In my view, however, the issue of politics in *Moscow Yankee* is not this simple. For generic politics not only under*mine* but under*line* doctrinal politics in *Moscow Yankee*. Politics are not just a textual phenomenon: the actual line of the 1930s left, specifically with regard both to what was called the "woman question" and to the issue of the role of the productive forces in socialist construction, figures crucially into the opportunistic closure of *Moscow Yankee*. In relation to gender issues, the communist-led left was in some respects the best act in town. There were trials for male chauvinism in the party; women were organized as both workers and housewives; theorists linked women's emancipation to the abolition of classes (see Rosenfelt, Foley, Pitts, and Inman). Yet the left never arrived at an adequate analysis of the political economy of work performed in the home and thus never broke with the capitalist ideological dualism between the spheres of domesticity and production. As a consequence, the 1930s left never consistently repudiated, and in fact frequently reproduced, mainstream ideas about what men and women simply "are." The proletariat was routinely encoded as male in the discourse and iconography of the left; particularly in the post-1935 period of the Popular Front, the legitimacy of the capitalist nuclear family was rarely questioned. When *Moscow Yankee* ends with Elsie turning out to have been a bad girl who wouldn't have benefited from living in Moscow anyhow, and with Andy and Natasha building their Moscow love nest, what is involved is not just an uncritical deployment of conservative narrative conventions. A less-than-revolutionary doctrinal politics about gender both articulates and is articulated by the premise of novelistic realism that character is "given" and that social value is embodied in personal romantic fulfillment.

Similarly, ambiguities in the communist line about socialist construction are reproduced in the production plot's evasion of the issue of workers' control. The formulations of socialism by the 1930s left were contradictory. On the one hand, socialism was a way station on the road to communism; it entailed the creation of new human beings and new social relations, contingent on people realizing their full "species being" by abolishing alienation and taking control over both the forces and the relations of production. On the other hand, even amidst the fervor of the First Five-Year Plan, socialism entailed the full retention of wages, the institution of material incentives (Stakhanovism), the continuing division of mental and manual labor, and other aspects of capitalist social relations. Even though Soviet workers participated actively in socialist construction, the immediate practice of communist distribution—from each according to commitment, to each according to need—was looked down upon as "vulgar equalitarianism," the "psychology of primitive peasant 'communism'" (Stalin 107; Bettelheim). The foreclosure of contradiction that accompanies the "pink sunset" portrait of Andy's "conversion" to socialism at the end of *Moscow Yankee* is thus not simply a function of Page's use of monologic and repressive narrative conventions. The novel's interrupted discourse concerning production relations also reflects the tendency of the entire 1930s left to posit communism as something for the future, and to adopt an attitude toward the building of socialism that was at once mechanistic and voluntarist: tractors plus proletarian enthusiasm would create the new world.

The anomalously "conservative" tenor of the ending to *Moscow Yankee* thus results not from a simple opposition of revolutionary form to radical content, but from a *complicity* between doctrinal and generic politics. The form exerts its most bourgeois influence when and where the text's "line" is least revolutionary. There is, to be sure, a tendency to reproduce dominant ideology built into certain bildungsroman conventions. Larger social contradictions—such as that between capitalist and communist relations at the point of production—can be sloughed over to the extent that the form is focused, finally, on an individual fate and an individual consciousness. Because production relations do not figure as a problem for Andy to confront and resolve, they do not figure in the resolution to the novel. But the bildungsroman form does not itself cause the issue of production relations to be abandoned. One might speculate instead that Page opted to tell her tale as a bildungsroman precisely because she herself saw this issue as "background" rather than as a social and political contradiction crucially determining the nature of Andy's relations with his coworkers.

Yet the political wheel needs to be spun one more time. For the question must then be asked: How damning—from a "left" standpoint—are the conclusions I have reached here? Does the presence of foreclosing and co-optative mechanisms in the novel's form, or of tendencies toward sexism and a doctrine of productive-forces determinism, mean that *Moscow Yankee* loses all its force as an articulation of revolutionary politics? This is a particularly urgent question in the present-day context, when not only the Sunday morning pundits but even many who claim to be on the left are joining the chorus of condemnation of all that has gone forward during the past seventy years under the banner of socialism or communism. I would suggest that despite the many "bourgeois" ideological traces in *Moscow Yankee*, the novel has plenty to say about creating new and better types of human interaction in a new and better type of social order. There *is* inspiration in its message of "I have seen the future, and it works"—not just, I believe, for unreconstructed leftists like myself, but also, as indicated by the novel's largely sympathetic reviews in the contemporaneous mainstream press, to readers closer to the center (e.g. Marsh). Even if conventions of realism co-opt readerly disagreement in *Moscow Yankee*, the reader is positioned to agree that Moscow is a good home to be accommodated to, and that a red factory worker is the ideal bride to effect the protagonist's social reconciliation. The novel's revolutionary message is mitigated but by no means canceled by the text's formal and doctrinal residue of capitalist ways of thinking about, and representing, human potentiality. Even if the postmodernist critics are right that realistic novels coercively position their readers, it is still legitimate to ask whether this coercion is exercised for good or bad ends. Page would no doubt respond that the end justifies the means.

Before closing, it will be a useful contrast to glance at another proletarian novel, one that departs significantly from conventions of narrative transparency while retaining the routine focus of the bildungsroman on an individual's initiation, education, and maturation. Tillie Olsen's *Yonnondio: From the Thirties* takes as its protagonist Mazie Holbrook, a young girl who grows toward selfhood in a context of extreme deprivation, both material and psychological. Because the novel is unfinished (Olsen started but abandoned it in the 1930s), Mazie's development into adulthood is not delineated. But the novel clearly indicates that it was to depict Mazie's growth toward class consciousness; Olsen, moreover, has stated that her protagonist was eventually to become a union organizer (Rosenfelt 399). In its method and plan, if not in its final result, *Yonnondio* is a "conversion" novel squarely within the tradition of the proletarian bildungsroman.

Yonnondio departs from this tradition, however, both structurally and ideologically. The narrative continually intersplices the protagonist's experience and consciousness with those of other family members, particularly her mother and father, Anna and Jim. Mazie's reactions of helplessness and anger when watching Anna being battered by Jim are counterposed with Anna's thoughts; Mazie's feelings of "boundlessness and selfness" (119) during a rare moment of untroubled mother/daughter love are juxtaposed with her moth-er's sensation of inhabiting a "bounded body" (120). Furthermore, both Mazie's and Anna's experiences of Jim's violence are counter-posed with his own confused sense of guilt and powerlessness: "And as he sat there in the kitchen with Mazie against his heart, and dawn beat up like a drum, the things in his mind so vast and formless, so terrible and bitter, cannot be spoken, will never be spoken—till the day that hands will find a way to speak this: hands" (95). Bildungsromans routinely posit the hero's uniqueness and subjectivity as given: even if she or he is affected by social relations, these do not *constitute* her or him. In *Yonnondio,* the relation of self to socius is reversed. Even though Mazie, as a distinct individ-ual, possesses "traits" of curiosity and resilience that equip her to be the novel's "hero," these qualities of "character" are not a priori, nor do they furnish "causes" for Mazie's acts. Rather than an autonomous individual moving through an "environment," Mazie *is* the social relations that encompass her; in a sense, she *is* the working class.

Yonnondio's diffusion of focus away from its protagonist also has an important rhetorical effect: Mazie's growth does not bear the burden of teaching the reader the politics that shape the text. The reader's attainment of greater class consciousness hinges upon him or her inferring general lessons from the totality of the character's experiences. In *Moscow Yankee* the reader's knowledge is contingent upon identification with Andy; if the hero does not come to a definitive position on the question of production relations, neither do we. In Olsen's novel, by contrast, no single character is obliged to "realize" the text's revolutionary doctrine. Even though it is clear that the novel is structured according to the pattern of the "conver-sion" narrative—and it is a significant loss to left-wing literature that Olsen never completed her tale—it is also clear that issues not fully understood by Mazie—or any other character, for that mat-ter—will not therefore be sloughed over. Truth is contained in, but not restricted to, what the hero learns.

Yonnondio manages to project its collectivist politics not only through structural modulations upon the individualistic bildungsro-man plot but also through its bold use of narratorial voice. Whereas in *Moscow Yankee* political values and ideas are left to be conveyed by character development, event, and dialogue, in *Yonnondio* the narrator articulates what the author believes; the text "tells" as well as "shows." Some of *Yonnondio's* devices for producing commentary are conventional; the passage cited above describing Jim Holbrook's incoherent anger, for example, combines tagged free indirect discourse with intrusive omnisicent commentary. While recognizably didactic, the passage remains within the stylistic confines of narrative realism. On several important occasions, however, Olsen abandons standard narratorial omniscience and adopts a free-floating voice that makes no pretension to narrative transparency. For example, when a minor character named Jim Tracy, a coworker of Jim Holbrook, rebels all by himself against exploitation and ends up on a chain gang, the text introduces a long typographically inserted passage in which the voice of an unidentified coworker declares:

> I'm sorry, Jim Tracy, sorry as hell we weren't stronger and could get to you in time and show you that kind of individual revolt was no good, kid, no good at all, you had to bide your time and take it till there were enough of you to fight it all together on the job, and bide your time, and take it till the day millions of fists clamped in yours, and you could wipe out the whole thing, the whole goddamn thing, and a human could be a human for the first time on earth. (79)

In this passage, revolutionary doctrine is conveyed in working-class language. But it is not articulated by a given individual— these are not Jim's thoughts—nor does it emerge as a "natural" consequence of Jim Holbrook's and Jim Tracy's experiences at the point of production. Like the Bolshevik theory outlined in Lenin's *What Is to Be Done?* the call for workers' insurrection in *Yonnondio* is a response to exploitation that comes, epistemologically, "from the outside" (Lenin 374–75). If Olsen's strategy here is "leftist," the term, in my view, warrants not opprobrium—as for most 1930s Marxists—but commendation. The politics of class in *Yonnondio* bypasses economism and projects revolutionism largely because the text has discovered strategic ways of intersplicing "showing" with "telling." As with its dispersal of "character," the novel finds ways to embed the collective in the individual; in its dispersal of narrative author-ity the novel experiments with methods for conveying authorial politics. *Yonnondio* is a bildungsroman, but to a degree it contests the individualistic and transparent premises of the genre.

As in the case of *Moscow Yankee*, however, the political wheel must be spun one more time. For Olsen's achievement in pressing the bildungsroman form to new political limits in *Yonnondio* is not simply a function of her *avant la lettre* experimentation with postmodernist methods for interrogating subjectivity and subverting ideological closure. Olsen's "line" is, on certain crucial issues, also more "left" than that of Page in *Moscow Yankee*. While the plot of *Moscow Yankee* hinges upon a traditional gendered division between a "private" love plot and a "public" production plot, *Yonnondio* continually reverts to the relation between production and reproduction—of people, of social relations, of consciousness. Opportunistic displacement between plotlines is precluded in *Yonnondio* largely because the novel admits to no fundamental difference between labor at the point of production and labor in the home. Moreover, while both novels are radically egalitarian, *Yonnondio* continually stresses the necessity for workers' "fists" and "hands" to break into articulateness. Page's novel leaves unsettled the issue of whether or not eradicating the division of mental and manual labor is necessary to the construction of socialism. Olsen's novel—while set in a context of anticapitalist class struggle that does not require her squarely to address socialist relations of production—still suggests that "a human [will] be a human for the first time on earth" only when workers gain the capacity to speak with something other than their hands. Olsen's experiments with a narrative voice that ruptures realistic illusionism are not merely formal; they bespeak her larger political concern with the new types of articulation that both enable and are enabled by the revolutionary process. As in *Moscow Yankee* there is in *Yonnondio* a confluence of doctrinal and generic politics.

What can we conclude, then, about the adequacy of the postmodernist critique of novelistic realism as applied to 1930s proletarian fiction? How usable were "bourgeois" literary forms to revolutionary writers? As I hope to have suggested here, there is a conservative *tendency* embedded in the classic form of the bildungsroman; Hicks and other 1930s critics were, I believe, in error when they posited that the novel bore no ideological freight from its bourgeois heritage. A proletarian writer like Page, who more or less uncritically adopted the conventions of the genre, reproduced a number of traditional distinctions between male and female, public and private. A writer like Olsen, who worked against the genre's structural and stylistic grain, projected more revolutionary conceptions of potentiality, both individual and social. But, in both cases narrative strategy is inseparable from political "line." While the implication of the postmodernist critique of realism would seem to be that narrative transparency is in and of itself politically "bad," and narrative subversion politically "good," the dialectic of generic and doctrinal politics in the two novels examined here indicates that the relationship between politics and form in the novel is more complicated, more nuanced. Particularly when pressed to adopt experimental techniques to articulate collectivist politics, the traditional "bourgeois" form of the bildungsroman proved usable — perhaps to a surprising degree — by the 1930s proletarian novelist. But even when the proletarian writer acceded to bourgeois ideological pressures of various kinds, emergent left-wing ideas had a stubborn way of making themselves felt and heard in and through the bildungsroman — regardless of the residual forms and discourses that hemmed these ideas in and inhibited their full expression. Amid all the current talk about the unalloyed failures — economic, political, cultural — of twentieth-century movements for class emancipation, it is important to acknowledge the 1930s literary proletarians' often compelling representations of a world by no means powerless to be born.

Notes

1. Brecht's dramatic theory and practice were greeted sympathetically and intelligently in the U.S. left press (e.g. Burnshaw) but did not spark any

polemics. Lukács published in *Partisan Review* an important essay, "Propaganda or Partisanship?" that drew praise from Philip Rahv; Lukács did not, however, function as the locus of any defense of realism in contradistinction to modernism (see Lukács, Rahv). The finer points in Lukács's sophisticated Hegelian defense of realism were not articulated in the American setting, where the best-known spokespersons for Third International aesthetic theory were "official" figures like Bukharin, Radek, and Lunacharsky. Alan Wald, however, remarks that "Angel Flores, who edited *Dialectics* and the Critics Group series, told me on the phone before he died that Lukács was a big influence in his circle" (personal communication).

Bibliography

Adler, Robert. "'The Shadow Before' Is Stirring Novel of Textile Mill Workers." *Daily Worker*, 29 April 1935: 5.

Bakhtin, Mikhail. *Problems of Dostoevsky's Poetics*. Trans. and ed. by Caryl Emerson. Minneapolis: University of Minnesota Press, 1984.

Basshe, Emjo. "Singing Workers." *New Masses* 18 (7 January 1936): 23–24.

Belsey, Catherine. *Critical Practice*. New York: Methuen, 1980.

Bettelheim, Charles. *Class Struggles in the USSR*. Trans. by Brian Pearce. London: Monthly Review, 1976–78.

Burnshaw, Stanley. "The Theatre Union Produces 'Mother.'" *New Masses* 17 (3 December 1935): 27–28.

Calmer, Alan. "The Proletarian Short Story." *New Masses* 16 (2 July 1935): 17.

Davis, Lennard J. *Resisting Novels: Ideology and Fiction*. New York: Methuen, 1987.

Editorial. *The Left* 1 (Spring 1931): 3.

Field, Alice Withrow. "Soviet Tempo in an American Novel." *New Masses* 15 (11 June 1935): 26.

Foley, Barbara. *Radical Representations: Politics and Form in U.S. Proletarian Fiction, 1929–1941*. Durham: Duke University Press, 1993.

Hardin, James, ed. *Reflection and Action: Essays on the Bildungsroman*. Columbia: University of South Carolina Press, 1991.

Heath, Stephen. "Narrative Space." *Screen* 18.3: 68–112.

Herndl, Diane Price. "The Dilemmas of a Feminine Dialogic." In *Feminism, Bakhtin, and the Dialogic*. Ed. by Dale M. Bauer and Susan Jaret McKinstry. Albany: State University Press of New York, 1991. 7–24.

Hicks, Granville. "Revolution and the Novel" (1934). Rpt. in *Granville Hicks in the New Masses*. Ed. by Jack Alan Robbins. Port Washington, NY: Kennikat, 1974. 19–66.

Hitchcock, Peter. *Working-Class Fiction in Theory and Practice: A Reading of Alan Sillitoe*. Ann Arbor: UMI, 1989.

Inman, Mary. *In Woman's Defense*. Los Angeles: The Committee to Organize the Advancement of Women, 1940.

Jerome, V.J. "Toward a Proletarian Novel." *New Masses* 8 (August 1932): 14–15.

Klaus, H. Gustav. *The Literature of Labor: Two Hundred Years of Working-Class Writing*. New York: St. Martin's Press, 1985.

————. *The Socialist Novel in Britain: Towards the Recovery of a Tradition*. New York: St. Martin's Press, 1982.

Lenin, V.I. *What Is to Be Done? Collected Works*. Trans. by Joe Fineberg and Joe Hanna. Ed. by V.J. Jerome. Moscow: Progress, 1961. 46 vols. Vol. 5, 347–530.

Le Sueur, Meridel. "Join Hand and Brain." *New Masses* 16 (9 July 1935): 25.

Levine, George. *The Realistic Imagination: English Fiction from Frankenstein to Lady Chatterley*. Chicago: University of Chicago Press, 1981.

Lukács, Georg. "Propaganda or Partisanship?" Trans. by Leonard J. Mins. *Partisan Review* 1 (April–May 1934): 36–46.

Marsh, Fred T. Review of Myra Page, *Moscow Yankee*. *New York Herald-Tribune Books* (17 April 1935): 20.

Murphy, James. *The Proletarian Moment: The Controversy over Leftism in Literature*. Urbana: University of Illinois Press, 1991.

Nadir, Moishe. "To Make My Bread." *New Masses* 8 (February 1933): 19–20.

Olsen, Tillie. *Yonnondio: From the Thirties*. New York: Dell, 1974.

Page, Myra. *Moscow Yankee*. New York: G.P. Putnam's Sons, 1935.

Pitts, Rebecca. "Women and Communism." *New Masses* 14 (19 February 1935): 14–20.

Rahv, Philip. "Valedictory on the Propaganda Issue." *Little Magazine* (September–October 1934): 1–2.

Rosenfelt, Deborah. "From the Thirties: Tillie Olsen and the Radical Tradition." *Feminist Studies* 7 (Fall 1981): 370–406.

Sammons, Jeffrey L. "The Bildungsroman for Nonspecialists: An Attempt at a Clarification." In Hardin 26–45.

Schneider, Isidor. "Greatness." *New Masses* 20 (11 August 1936): 40–41.

Shaffner, Randolph P. *The Apprenticeship Novel: The Study of the "Bildungsroman" as a Regulative Type in Western Literature with a Focus on Three Classic Representatives by Goethe, Maugham, and Mann*. New York: Peter Lang, 1984.

Snee, Carole. "Working-Class Literature or Proletarian Writing?" In *Culture and Crisis in Britain in the Thirties*. Ed. by Jon Clark, et al. London: Lawrence and Wishart, 1979. 165–92.

Stalin, Joseph. "Interview with Emil Ludwig." *International Literature* 2–3

(1932): 104–8.

Steinecke, Hartmut. "The Novel and the Individual: The Significance of Goethe's *Wilhelm Meister* in the Debate about the Bildungsroman." In Hardin 69–96.

Swales, Martin. "Irony and the Novel: Reflections on the German Bildungsroman." In Hardin 46–68.

Visser, N.W. "The Novel as Liberal Narrative: The Possibilities of Radical Fiction." *Works and Days* 3 (1985): 7–28.

3

Narratives of Bourgeois Subjectivity in Mozart's *Prague* Symphony

SUSAN MCCLARY

The recapitulation of the finale of Mozart's Symphony No. 38 (the *Prague*, 1786) begins quite innocuously with the return of the playful tune that serves as protagonist for this movement. At this point, we might well become complacent: our experience with other such pieces may lead us to expect little more from what remains of the movement than the reiteration of themes and a grand conclusion. But after a mere thirteen bars, the proceedings are rudely derailed by a blast from the brass and timpani.

Principles of formal propriety for this period dictate that new materials not intrude into a composition so late in the game. And, as it turns out, the outburst is not entirely extraneous: we can trace it back to the development section, where it repeatedly obstructed the progress of the principal theme. Thus we might explain the event in the recapitulation by arguing that the business of developing had not quite been completed within the segment of the piece devoted to development, so that it necessarily spills over into the section usually concerned with consolidation.

But the blast also recalls a more distant referent: the symphony's introduction is repeatedly disrupted by a similar configuration, which is not so much resolved as sidestepped by the comedic affairs of the opening movement. Its reappearance here at the eleventh hour, after all the turmoil ought to have subsided, represents quite literally a return of the repressed. Indeed, the eighteenth-century topos here invoked is the *ombra*, a stock image long associated in opera with the shadowy supernatural.

Moreover, this moment resembles the one near the end of *Don Giovanni* where the foreboding *ombra* that opened the overture suddenly breaks in on Giovanni's revelry to announce the arrival of the statue.[1] That Mozart was writing the *Prague* Symphony and *Don Giovanni* at the same time encourages the comparison, even though there are crucial differences—most obviously, the sinister music in the opera announces Giovanni's impending doom, whereas the symphony's finale recovers its playful character for an affirmative conclusion. But as in *Don Giovanni*, the symphony's finale suffers the intrusion of the militant materials from the introduction into what appears to be an extremely secure context. In neither instance can purely structural accounts suffice. Like the parallel occurrence in *Don Giovanni*, this disruption in the *Prague* may tempt us to appeal to narrative for explanations.[2]

While an earlier generation of critics were happy to write in narrative terms about such tensions in Mozart's instrumental music,[3] musicologists of the last thirty years have focused almost exclusively on its formal dimensions. Many critics today prefer to hear his music as the manifestation of perfect order, and their analyses consequently strive to account for that order, which is presumed to stand outside or beyond the realm of mere signification.[4] Disruptions are demonstrated not truly to have been disruptions at all, but instead sophisticated strategies in voice-leading, discernible by those who have studied advanced music theory. Moments of apparent conflict, such as the one that occurs in the last movement of the *Prague*, are not so much explained as explained away.

In the last few years, however, the issue of narrative in instrumental music has reemerged in musicology and has sparked a lively theoretical debate. On the one hand, scholars such as Anthony Newcomb, Lawrence Kramer, and Fred Maus—all of whom focus on questions of musical signification—have begun to demonstrate how narrative procedures often informed nineteenth-century instrumental music.[5]

The other side of the debate has been most forcefully articulated recently by Carolyn Abbate.[6] Abbate objects to narrative accounts of most instrumental music in part because they usually fall short with respect to both musical and historical specificity: that is, as the plotline proposed by the critic takes on its own momentum, details of musical construction (especially those that do not advance the cause of the plot) are often ignored; and insofar as the narrative scenarios suggested by critics tend to fall into a few stereotypical patterns, crucial differences between moments in musical style are obliterated. In short, narrative accounts, while perhaps attractive as crutches, lead us away from the piece of music and its cultural particularities.

These objections need to be taken very seriously, even if—especially if—the *Prague* tempts us to appeal to narrative. I propose that narrative impulses began to influence compositional procedures in the late eighteenth century—that narrative is not simply imposed from the outside by critics who lack analytic sophistication, but that it is often integral to the rationale of the music itself—and that these impulses correspond to extremely important concerns emerging in other areas of European culture at that same moment in history.

By suggesting that Mozart's instrumental compositions may have narrative dimensions, I do not mean to imply that he engages in what later became known as programmatic music (in which a title or accompanying scenario indicates explicitly the framework to be employed in listening), but rather that he often introduces significant narrative inflections into his formal procedures. In other words, the structural order and balance celebrated by so many analysts are indisputably present in his music, but so are other elements—such as the event described at the beginning of this paper—that raise the kinds of questions typical of plot-oriented media.[7]

As Terry Eagleton has demonstrated, this tension between formal and narrative impulses is among the most fundamental characteristics of bourgeois culture. In *The Ideology of the Aesthetic* (1990), Eagleton explains how the theories of art that emerged in the 1700s served as one of the sites where the emerging bourgeois class worked through many of the dilemmas it confronted as it attempted to carve out a new *modus operandi*. Significantly, many of the principal aestheticians of the day were also leading political theorists, and these two domains—art and the public sphere— were understood quite self-consciously in the same terms.

In both realms, attention was focused especially on questions of the self. Previous eras had seemed to bestow markers of identity such as class at birth; but with increasing opportunities for upward mobility, intellectuals and artists began to concentrate on the process of self-generation, with its attendant rewards, but also its responsibilities and anxieties. Thus eighteenth-century aestheticians, like political theorists, typically deplored the rigid conventions of the *ancien régime* and advocated free individual expression. But at the same time they recognized that private feelings without objective form fail to be intelligible, just as groups of individuals acting according to their own separate whims produce chaos. Structure, therefore, was deemed indispensable to the new art and to the new society; yet the structures that made identity viable had to seem now as though they were the result of internal necessity, motivated by ongoing trajectories of becoming, rather than of the surrender to outside authority. Eagleton writes: "If the aesthetic comes in the eighteenth century to assume the significance it does, it is because the word is shorthand for a whole project of hegemony, the massive introjection of abstract reason by the life of the senses. What matters is not in the first place art, but this process of refashioning the human subject from the inside, informing its subtlest affections and bodily responses with this law which is not a law" (42).

Much of what Eagleton writes concerning aesthetics and bourgeois ideals would sound quite plausible if we were dealing with Beethoven.[8] But Mozart? Even though Beethoven too worked under aristocratic patronage for much of his career, we tend to associate Mozart far more closely with that institution. Our accounts of Mozart often assume that he faithfully reflected in his music the sensibilities and interests of his patrons, that he accepted unconditionally the constraints of his employment as he composed. Thus our critical readings of Mozart's music typically emphasize its courtly dimensions: its noble grace and formal balance.

We have no evidence that Mozart had any interest in class politics per se. Yet even if he did not identify his plight with those of other nonaristocrats, he frequently bridled at having to submit to those who had economic authority over him.[9] Moreover, he had a healthy regard for his imagination, which permitted him to inflect in such unexpected ways the *galant* style that surrounded him. And if we delve beneath the polished surfaces and assuring reconciliations that characterize the public veneer of Mozart's music, we often find him wrestling with precisely the tensions Eagleton analyzes as characteristics of late eighteenth-century bourgeois culture.[10]

Mozart's music could scarcely have avoided the tensions that preoccupied his particular historical moment, for they were already implicated in the formal procedures he had inherited before he even touched them. In other words, the narrative impulses of his music are not truly "extramusical": they emerge from the premises of the most fundamental of his musical materials—tonality and sonata.

The brand of tonality that developed in Italy over the course of the seventeenth century traces something like the familiar quest narrative, whereby identity (the tonic key area) is established, destabilized through excursions into other keys, and eventually regained (fig. 1a). In most music of the 1600s, this pattern of beginning, middle, and end is best explained by rhetorical models—which is, in fact, how theorists of the day accounted for effective musical organization. So long as the expected series of events proceeds relatively unimpeded, narrative seems not be at issue.[11]

FIGURE 1

a: Tonal Trajectory

   Tonic (1)   »   Key X   »   Key Y   »   Key Z   »   »   »   1

b: da Capo form

A	B	A
1 » X » 1	Y » Z	exact repetition of A

c: Binary Form

   (repeat)   (repeat)
   ‖: 1 » X :‖: X » (Y) » 1 :‖

d: Sonata

        Exposition   (repeat) Development Recapitulation (repeat)
   ‖: 1st key/theme (1) » 2nd key/theme (X) :‖ ‖:   X » Y » Z » ‖1st (1) » 2nd   (1) :‖

As the eighteenth century approached, the onrushing flamboy-
ance of early tonality became domesticated, in part through stan-
dardization, in part through the rise of various formal schemata
that served to contain and channel its extraordinary vitality.[12] The
da Capo aria that dominated aristocratic opera seria during the
1700s, for instance, operates according to a principle of nested
symmetries: the opening section presents the tonic, moves to a
closely related key, and returns to reestablish the tonic for closure;
a middle section moves through contrasting areas; then the opening section returns intact to insulate the unstable middle section,
to restore both tonic and the initial affect (fig. 1b).[13] The linear
thrust of earlier procedures was thus radically reconstrued: eighteenth-century formal designs continued to draw on tonal energy,
but they kept tight control over its potentially unruly qualities
through hierarchically arranged patterns of structural repetition.

Sonata procedure—a new formal means of articulating the tonal
background—began to appear in the mid-eighteenth century, and
it became the principal organizing schema in most instrumental
genres for over a hundred years. Like most other structural procedures of the 1700s, sonata depends heavily on formal conventions. But the exuberant rhythms of opera buffa animate this
procedure, infusing it with dynamic energies reminiscent of tonality

before its formal containment. Thus sonata resulted from a fusion between the symmetrical structures of the eighteenth century and a newly invigorated, somewhat rebellious tonal impulse. The history of this genre has been played out along the fault lines between these virtually incompatible elements.

On the one hand, sonata procedure developed not from the kinds of baroque movements that unfold through principles of linear progress, but rather from the staid binary form of the courtly dance (fig. 1c). Thus, while its opening section moves dramatically to the point of the first modulation (on the dominant or relative major), this section must then be repeated. Likewise, the second half—which contains the series of contrasting keys as well as the return to tonic—is reiterated. The dynamic impulse contributed by the tonal dimension of sonata is effectively held in check by such formal imperatives (fig. 1d).

Sonata procedure itself adds yet another structural device that weighs against progressive narrative: the section articulating the return to tonic (recapitulation) grows to mirror in both length and sequence of events the opening half (exposition). And as bipartite dance forms become rather more tripartite in their distribution of functions, issues of architectonic balance begin to inform the process, as they do in da Capo arias. Textbook diagrams of sonata sometimes resemble a static classical building, with symmetrical wings buttressing a middle section.

But on the other hand, certain other aspects of sonata intensify the dynamic forces that fuel it. Composers began to mark the openings of sonata movements with idiosyncratic themes which are deployed as though they were protagonists. Moreover, the second key area in the exposition started to rival the tonic in duration, and it often brought with it its own themes and affects. The relationship between first and second key areas varies from piece to piece: the sense of uniform agency typical of Baroque music may be maintained if both keys are articulated with the same theme; or the two may establish a crucial dramatic dichotomy, either complementary or antagonistic.[14] The tensions between these two aspects of the exposition are not immediately resolved;

rather they spill over into the middle section, which destabilizes and develops thematic materials as it proceeds through its series of distant keys.

Thus far (if we count the repetition of the exposition as something like an instant replay that allows us to witness once more the move from tonic to secondary key), the process could be regarded as linear.[15] Moreover, the development leads back eventually to the dramatic return of tonic and opening theme for recapitulation and closure. But at the point of recapitulation, principles of formal balance suddenly come to the fore, since the central business of this section is to reiterate the events from the exposition. Unlike the return in the da Capo aria, however, the recapitulation is not a mechanical reiteration of a previous self-contained section. The tensions raised by the dynamic contrast of the exposition are resolved only in this concluding section, in which all materials typically confirm the tonic. Thus the recapitulation serves as a literal "capitulation" to formal convention, but also as narrative telos—as the site of reconciliation for all the dramatic conflicts that made the movement seem idiosyncratic.

As it attempts to satisfy both the demand for formal symmetry and also the desire for unimpeded progress and free expression, sonata manifests in its musical premises the tensions Eagleton describes.[16] In some movements, structural exigencies appear to prevail over the particularities of the process. Others privilege the more dynamic aspects of sonata, so that something like a narrative trajectory rather than a predetermined set of conventions seems to motivate the movement's central events. Neither of these solutions, of course, can be entirely consistent: the energies whipped up by the process always threaten to overflow the bounds of the form, making containment seem a bit arbitrary; and narrative inflections—while they may encourage us to hear some of the important junctures of movements in terms of linear causality—do not influence the many passages where conventional musical processes dominate.

But in any case, sonata is never merely a form imposed from the outside. Because it captures so well the dilemmas surrounding identity and dynamic change in the bourgeois era, sonata becomes the central arena in music where such issues are explored, fought through, and negotiated. Whatever the solution in any given movement, the tensions between energy and stasis inherent in the procedure remain—just as they remained unreconciled in the social sphere. Yet music's malleability always suggests that a possible answer to the great puzzle is just around the corner. This is why generations of musicians continued to hack away at sonata rather than inventing thoroughly new procedures, once the frustrations of sonata became apparent. We can tell a good deal about what was most important to each artist, each moment in history, by observing where the compromises occur, what gets sacrificed, and what is preserved at whatever cost in sonata-based constructions.[17]

Mozart's narrative inflections in his instrumental music operate simultaneously on two fronts. First, he sometimes enacts resistance against the musical signs of aristocratic absolutism and against the social constraints that manifest themselves in music as formal conventions. In other words, the revolutionary impulse that becomes far more explicit in Beethoven is detectable not only in Mozart's operas such as *The Marriage of Figaro* or *Don Giovanni*, but also in some of the instrumental music.[18] The emancipatory narrative recounting the emergence of a new variety of self-sufficient (bourgeois) individual here begins to make its appearance.

At the same time, Mozart can be heard exploring a set of issues that seem at first glance to be more private: the construction of an integrated self in the face of both the desire to remain in an infantile state of blissful coextension with the mother, and the threats and demands posed by patriarchal law. In "The Image in Form," Maynard Solomon proposes a psychoanalytic model for addressing such issues in Mozart's music, manifested in Mozart's proclivity for dark undercurrents that often threaten to break through his affirmative surfaces. While accepting much of Solomon's Freudian schema, I would like to qualify it a bit.

First, rather than regarding Freud's account as the universal experience of early development, many theorists now contend that important aspects of this model are particular to males and to the bourgeois era.[19] This explains in part why Mozart and Freud could both arrive at similar constructions, why we latter-day bourgeois still are hailed by it, and why musics of other places and times seem not to work according to such precepts.

Second, even if such an experience of subjectivity were commonplace, European composers did not see it as a suitable topic for musical representation until about Mozart's time. We might relate this set of issues to Mozart's own struggles with his father for adult identity. But Mozart certainly was not the first composer to be burdened with a domineering father. He does happen, however, to have been composing at a time when the ordeals of the inner self as it aspires to maturity had become paramount in European culture—not only in literary genres such as the *Bildungsroman*, but also in music.[20] These "private" issues turn out, in other words, to be at the center of *public* discourse in the late 1700s: we need not read Mozart's pieces as revealing personal secrets.

To some extent, these two narrative strands—emancipation from aristocratic/patriarchal authority and the self-generation of a seemingly autonomous identity—are similar stories. And many of the cultural artifacts of the late eighteenth and nineteenth centuries merge the two. The kind of self celebrated by the psychologically preoccupied novels of this time is a specifically bourgeois subject— a subject who must learn how to negotiate successfully in a world in which class status and masculinity must constantly be won anew, how to prize yet compartmentalize sentiment, how to overcome and repress the contradictions required in achieving selfhood.[21]

For on the one hand, the liberation and *Bildung* agendas of this historical moment need to show the generation of the new breed of subject step by step—a feat that requires that we first meet him as a vulnerable, relatively unformed being and that we witness him become something other than what he was, even though such a process often involves severe crises.[22] But on the other hand, this same subject needs desperately to believe in his immutable integrity; consequently, the traumatic narrative of emergence is disavowed at the very moment it succeeds. The increasingly "organic" aspects of such narratives are designed to imply that the seeds of success were present in the subject from the start, that identity owes nothing to contingency but is (regardless of conflicts in the manifest content of the story) always already guaranteed.[23]

Mozart's music also resides uneasily between these positions, as he takes up and works through the same thorny issues.[24] If he increasingly inflects his musical procedures with narrative drama, he also puts increasing effort into the "purely musical" relationships within his compositions. Many of his constructs try to sustain the fiction that we can have it both ways—narratives of becoming and structures of immutable being at the same time. It is, I believe, for this reason that we who still cling to many of these same fictions gain such solace from his music.[25] Yet the contradictions are quite apparent, even in Mozart.[26]

The adagio that opens the *Prague* Symphony fulfills the functions typical of slow introductions in this repertory, in that it arouses our expectations for what follows.[27] To use Edward T. Cone's terminology,[28] an introduction serves as an extended rhythmic upbeat that releases its accumulated tension only with the arrival of the allegro and the securing of the tonic key area. It exists prior to the beginning of the movement's sonata procedure; and although its relative instability may seem to propel us causally forward into the movement's exposition, it need not share actual materials with the remainder of the symphony.

Mozart's adagio turns out to be more integral to the unfolding of the symphony than usual, for—as we realize in retrospect—it introduces in the course of its fantasia-like meanderings many of the topoi, motives, and dilemmas that pervade the remainder of the piece.[29] It begins conventionally enough, with grand, sweeping gestures invoking the French overtures of Louis XIV, the absolutist monarch *par excellence*. Both the presence of trumpets and timpani and their favored key of D major underscore the opening's aristocratic (and potentially military) associations.

Somewhat incongruously, this majestic pronouncement is followed by quiet, staccato pitches creeping up through the tonic triad, as though to some other place. The F-sharp at the peak of the ascent is met by the full orchestra blaring out an unexpected, deceptive harmony that diverts us away from D major to B minor. Apparently unfazed, the strings echo the diversionary tactic and arrive on G major; the winds do likewise and take us even further afield, to E minor.

Instead of unfolding rationally to establish the tonic D major, the continuation from the bold opening triad simply spirals off into what is marked—for the moment at least—as unintelligibility. Recall that Eagleton speaks of aesthetics as "this process of re-fashioning the human subject from the inside, informing its sub-tlest affections and bodily responses with this law which is not a law." This musical passage seems to have escaped the old law, only to indulge in feelings that do not yet have any "objective" form to regulate them.

After a pause, the strings take us back to D, but into the very different affective realm of *Empfindsamkeit*—the highly stylized tenderness of mid-eighteenth-century bourgeois sensibility. In contrast to the absolute certainty of the opening, this section (mm. 7–13) proliferates sighs, languid melodies, exquisite harmonic inflections (once again to E minor), and chromatic meltdowns, all over a hesitant accompanying figure.

One could associate these gestures with "femininity" as it was construed in musical codes of the time. Certainly this section represents a more intimate, gentle mode of discourse than the public spectacle heralded by the opening. But an important feature of the middle-class *male* subject was his sensitivity, even his will-ingness to display tears.[30] Thus we could read this moment both as feminine and also as a function of masculine interiority. More-over, given the appropriation of sentiment by bourgeois males as evidence of their moral superiority to the noblemen they aspired to displace, we might read it as pertaining to class as well.

At last, in measure 12, we are prepared for a clear diatonic cadence. True to its melancholic predisposition, however, the phrase ends instead on a sigh and a deceptive cadence, which is echoed in the winds. But this is exactly the same move that diverted the movement from D and its aristocratic bearing in the first place. The full orchestra suddenly bursts in, as though picking up where it left off before the tender bourgeois episode we have just enjoyed. Indeed, Mozart banks on our having enjoyed this episode so much that it returns, gently wresting the controls back from G major, which the trumpets and drums had asserted, for a second attempt at a cadence on D.

The sentimental dalliance of this material, however, is not allowed to subvert the composition—at least not without a proper battle. At this point, the trumpets and drums return with a vengeance, in the guise of the *ombra* topos. The benign D major of the beginning is disfigured into a grim D minor, made all the grimmer by a military tattoo in the timpani. As in measure 3, the strings sneak up through the triad presented, now intensified with pleading turn figures. Each would-be arrival is met by a new orchestral chord, to which the cowering strings conform—yet from which they apparently seek escape.

The series of chords at first seems almost arbitrary—the exercise of absolutist authority. But the chords are not truly random: after leading us through a number of flat-laden keys related to D minor, they lead back inexorably to a dominant pedal anticipating a cadential arrival in that key. The chords also turn out to be the ones dictated by the constraints of those signs of aristocratic might, the natural trumpet and timpani: in order to sound with their full acoustical force, these instruments can play only the pitches D and A. Yet these restrictions become the most terrifying evidence of their power over the discourse, as they legislate that all motion be confined to accommodate their own severe limitations.[31]

In the final bars of the introduction, motivic fragments from the *Empfindsam* section return, their former mobility now imprisoned by martial alternations between D and A, their sweetness rendered pathetic by the minor-mode context. Once again, both class and psychoanalytic readings seem plausible, as absolutist or patriarchal order thwarts the emergence of another kind of agent: one that exhibits such characteristics as flexibility, curiosity, tenderness, and dynamic motion—namely, a bourgeois subject. Yet its very sentimentality seems to have hampered it from successfully evading the static law of the aristocratic Father.[32]

I have chosen thus far to highlight those elements in the score that would enhance a narrative approach. But most of my musicological colleagues would select rather different details— those that demonstrate that an iron-clad sense of musical order underlies all the discontinuities and violent ruptures I have privileged. And they would, of course, be perfectly justified in doing so. For instance, those digressions to B, G, and E near the beginning are soon folded back into normalcy. Every musical detail can be understood as operating within an autonomous musical domain of harmonic, melodic, contrapuntal, and rhythmic relationships.

Yet I would view an entirely formalist account as reductive. Mozart presents within this introduction a bewildering array of culturally significant affects and topoi that seem virtually to *demand* a story, a justification for materials that are not yet rationally deployed. The economy that we expect of aesthetic objects of this period—especially Mozart's—requires something more by way of explanation. Why have we been subjected to this jumble?[33] If we have faith that these fits and starts were purposeful, the continuation of the symphony will reward our expectations. Rather than choosing between strictly formal and strictly narrative accounts, it seems critical to acknowledge that Mozart is operating continually in both registers, and to see this tension as perhaps the most important aspect of content in this work.

The first movement of the *Prague* enacts marvelously the construction of the subject, from timid beginnings to a degree of confidence comparable to—if vastly different from—the autocratic gestures of the introduction. If we examine the clues we already have been given, we might know in advance something of what will constitute an appropriate answer to the opening section, for the orchestral forces deployed at the outset will probably be used again—in part for the sake of balance, but also (on a much more pragmatic level) to have made the hiring of all those musicians worthwhile. In other words, despite its exceedingly modest debut, the subject of the first movement must eventually grow to fill the very large shoes of its predecessor.

The inauguration of the allegro's subject is singularly inauspicious: while the solo D in the first violin delivers the tonic pitch foretold by the introduction, it does so hesitantly, in quaking syncopations. The other strings enter with tentative, inverted harmonies that hover between consolidating D as tonic and inflecting it as a function prepared to resolve to G major, the passive, subdominant side of the key. So insubstantial is the first violin that the lower parts may be heard as the melodic line, a line that strives twice to rise before it descends to the first genuine cadence we have had thus far. At the moment the lower strings begin their descent, the first violin emerges from its paralysis with a small motive of its own and joins in the arrival.

The first theme of the exposition contrasts sharply with what has preceded it, yet it draws heavily upon figures that Mozart already has set forth. The syncopations of the opening, for instance, had been established in the final measure of the adagio; the turn in measure 43 had already marked the tormented ascents between oppressive blasts from measures 17–27; and the tendency to deflect inward to G major or B minor—rather than pushing dynamically toward the self-confirmation of tonic and dominant—had occurred repeatedly in the introduction.

But even if its genetic materials can be traced to the adagio, the identity of this thematic unit is woefully insecure, given its ambivalence with respect to pulse, phrasing, direction, key, and even which line counts as the tune. Nevertheless, it does succeed in pulling together enough rhythmic and harmonic momentum to achieve the tiny triumph of a cadence, an occasion hailed with a fanfare by the whole ensemble—brass, drums, and all. This burst of approbation encourages the theme to repeat itself, leading to a second cadence and the beginning of the theme's progress toward self-realization.

Skipping ahead to the end of the movement, we find that the process concludes with a victorious apotheosis of this first theme. It has been duly transformed to occupy its role as confident adult: its parts are inverted so that the yearning gesture originally in the lower strings now serves unequivocally as melody, while the stammering syncopations have developed into constant eighth notes that press dynamically forward to the final cadence. This, then, is the telos, the goal toward which the movement strives: the confident coming-to-power/coming-of-age of a subject whose advent can be detected in retrospect in the introduction, who begins his journey unaware of his own resources, and who eventually works through his own potentialities to become fully actualized.

More than most Mozart movements, this one seems determined always to generate new ideas out of materials already presented: consequently, the development of the self-sufficient subject seems constantly at stake. For instance, the harmonic motion of measures 51–54 is accomplished by the motive of measure 42 laid end to end; the turn figure inverts and the syncopations become aggressive to produce the vigorous sequence beginning in measure 55; and even the halting redundancies of measures 9 and 39–40 are embraced and mobilized in the jubilant arrival on the dominant in measures 63–71.

But if the movement as a whole pursues a trajectory of linear development, it does not do so simplistically. The emancipation from aristocratic/patriarchal control is only one feature of the story here enacted; even more crucial is the question of what kind of subject the emergent self will be. As though addressing precisely these concerns, Mozart problematizes various critical moments in the unfolding of the movement—the moments where the narrative and structural components of the composition are most likely to pull in opposite directions. These include most obviously the second key area and the requisite return to opening materials for recapitulation.

Although formal procedures had not yet become frozen into the schemata theorized later, the second key area was even in Mozart's time a moment when contrasting thematic materials most often appeared, in order to heighten the tonal dichotomy fundamental to the dynamic process.[34] In this movement, however, Mozart installs his contrasting key with yet another enactment of the emergence of the first theme. Its identity thus is stamped on this site where integrity might have been threatened, and although a contrasting theme occurs presently in this new key, the terrain of this key is already defined as belonging to the protagonist — especially as the increasingly empowered opening subject returns to serve also as closing material.

The second key area offers a new set of challenges to our subject. First, it turns out that to cadence *on* the dominant is not the same as to be *in* the dominant, nor does self-proliferation of imitative patterning guarantee security. The enterprising sequential passage beginning in measure 82 seems to intensify identity, yet it rushes headlong into a tonal crisis — the first suggestion of violence in this otherwise rather playful context. It is as though the dominant had been won too easily, without the struggle such a step necessarily entails. The brass and timpani return to set out an unyielding pedal on D; and it is only with tremendous effort (the bass shoving up through a chromatic scale) that A major is regained — *earned* this time rather than simply assumed as the next step in the convention.

This process — the sustained D in the brass, the chromatic bass leading eventually to an arrival on A — resonates with the crisis of the introduction (mm. 16–28). In the introduction, the arrival served as containment; here in the exposition, it represents hard work, success, and the opening of new terrains. Instead of smacking into the dominant as though conquering it, the escape from D deflects deceptively onto F-sharp, from which position the harmony floats down graciously into A major. Only now, in this carefully circumscribed realm, does another thematic unit appear.

This unit is not, of course, altogether new: it is related affectively — even through melodic profile and accompaniment pattern — to the lyrical materials that first appeared in measures 7–12 of the introduction. Unlike the principal theme, which constantly overflows expected phrase boundaries, this second theme unfolds complacently in symmetrical four-bar groupings. It luxuriates in sensitive chromatic inflections, then repeats itself in the melancholic coloring of A minor. But at the moment of cadence where the minor mode might have established itself, the major intercedes and brings us back—at first tenderly, and then by the energetic sequential motives that first brought us to the dominant—to the triumphant opening theme.

We might regard these contrasting materials as representing another force, perhaps—as in the introduction—aligned with femininity.[35] Yet it seems that Mozart has taken great pains to situate them within a domain bracketed firmly at both ends by the principal theme. Moreover, they too display the legacy of the introduction: they resemble the motives that worked in opposition to the tyranny of the brass but were too weak to prevail. Here in this context—after the principal theme has laid the public foundation for its unimpeded continuation—it becomes possible to indulge in tenderness, in depth of feeling without the fear of destruction from the outside. Form has begun to structure feeling.

To be sure, sentiment soon devolves into melancholy and threatens to undo the confident facade achieved during the first section of the exposition. Thus the sudden turn to major in measure 112 sounds like a conscious decision not to continue in that vein. But this detour into sensitivity makes the eventual triumph of the principal theme seem all the more palatable, for we have witnessed not only the battle of self-development waged in the public sphere of motivic construction, but also the realm of subjective interiority: the spiritual depth demanded of the new bourgeois male.

The recapitulation is a bit different. Adorno has made us aware of the problematic nature of formal recapitulations: the conventional demand that a movement return to its original key and thematic materials two-thirds of the way through the piece would seem to destroy the illusion of ongoing narrative development that became such a central concern of nineteenth-century culture.[36] Beethoven tended to display his rebellion against the external requirements of formal conventions quite dramatically, and the entry into recapitulation is often the site for his most resistant maneuvers. In contrast with Beethoven, Mozart sometimes seems to accept the constraints of formal convention without a struggle. But in the *Prague*, the moment of recapitulation is inflected narratively rather more than one would expect.

The development section itself is one of the most intensively combinatorial passages in Mozart, as he works through a series of motives, each put into canon-like imitation with itself and in superimposition with the others. The one moment that had seemed to stand outside the subject—the huzzah that greets its first presentation in measure 43—unexpectedly provides the motive (originally a simple countermelody to the brass fanfare) that pervades its development section. Once all these ideas have been explored sufficiently, Mozart channels the tension through a linear buildup into what sounds initially like the recapitulation. We have heard precisely this buildup and resolution before, however: it is a repetition of the passage that first arrived on the dominant. And this is exactly what happens here—we begin not on tonic but on A major.

Notwithstanding its problematic key, the principal theme begins confidently; but within a couple of measures it becomes hesitant and lists toward D minor. The melancholy shadings of the second theme are recalled, as well as the sense of entrapment over the A pedal at the conclusion of the introduction. The motive that had dominated the development so aggressively now fades into mourning and reveals its affinity with the lyrical motives of the second theme. But it gradually builds momentum and drives into the actual recapitulation in measure 208.

Once again, this presentation on A of the principal motive serves as a foil, to demonstrate the follies of premature assumptions. Just as the easy arrival on the dominant had to be discarded and properly achieved in the exposition, its reappearance in the movement's most critical juncture makes the return to tonic seem earned rather than mechanical. To be sure, the recapitulation satisfies formal expectations; yet Mozart designs his strategies to suggest that it is motivated not by convention, but by the demands of this narrative of becoming.

Mozart also problematizes the security of D major itself after it returns. In measure 217 (after the celebratory fanfare), the theme indulges in chromatic inflections and moves unexpectedly into B-flat major. It is as though the first theme is sufficiently confident that it can incorporate some of the flexibility of its more private side into its public presentation. This move requires a renewed struggle if the identity of D major is to be regained: thus the crisis that built toward the second theme in the exposition can be repeated *as though of internal necessity*, and the lyrical themes themselves serve as welcome dramatic contrast rather than blind repetition.

The movement ends with the consolidation of identity: the principal theme occurs twice in its triumphal form, inflected with the chromaticism of the second theme, permitting the two to reach a kind of synthesis at the end. Unlike the rigid, aristocratic gestures of the introduction, the subject that has fully emerged by the conclusion of the movement is dynamic, its motives carefully balanced among its central figure's yearning, sensitivity, and confident ability to enact closure. And like the bourgeois individual whose characteristics the movement so closely resembles, it appears to be autonomous—self-reliant and self-generated.

To some extent, the narrative closure enacted by this opening movement seems to render subsequent movements superfluous. This is, of course, a central formal preoccupation of the nineteenth century: when narrative components appear to motivate structural unfolding, the usual four-movement series becomes an embarrassment. Beginning most clearly with Beethoven, composers attempt to refashion their narratives so that the finale serves as closure for an entire cycle of interrelated movements.

While Mozart often creates affinities among his movements, one rarely finds evidence of cyclicism per se. Yet he rarely pushes his narrative inflections as far as he does in the opening movement of the *Prague*; and in this piece, some of the dilemmas confronted more vehemently by Beethoven begin to emerge. The most obvious instance of cyclical interdependence in the *Prague* occurs in the passages of the closing movement mentioned at the very beginning of this paper, where the patriarchal authority left behind in the introduction suddenly returns in full force.

The exposition of the presto drops few clues that anything troublesome might be forthcoming. Its principal theme is sprightly and confident from the outset; it does not seem to demand a narrative of becoming, for its identity is already secure. To be sure, the exposition goes through the paces expected of it, and it recalls superficially some of the tensions of the first movement—the modal shifts and chromatic inflections similar to those in the allegro recur, as does a triumphal transformation of the sprightly opening theme. But the doubts that confronted the subject of the earlier movement appear to have been transcended: the crises that appear in the exposition of the finale sound like tempests in teapots.

The development section alters that state of affairs, however, as it opens with the notorious blast from the brass and timpani. As in the introduction, the protagonist here follows the harmonic dictates of the blasts—yet its impish energy tends to mock the seriousness of those autocratic pronouncements. And after four brass interjections (none of them, incidentally, particularly disruptive harmonically), the subject just dances off. The remainder of the development is devoted to working out the implications of the principal theme itself. After some clever feints and dodges, it enters into the recapitulation in measure 216. The business at hand would seem to be the reiteration of the sequence of events in the exposition and final closure on the tonic.

Scarcely has the D major recapitulation begun, however, when the aristocratic blast reenters, now in earnest—in G minor. The theme itself might be said to have provoked this harsh intervention, for it had just pivoted off teasingly (and apparently irresponsibly) toward G major. As in the introduction and development, the theme follows dutifully the dictates of the blasts, even as it appears to be attempting to sneak away. Suddenly in measure 244, the protagonist seizes the powerful voice of the brass and timpani, but compels it now to conform to the finale's principal tune. It marshals those forces through to the arrival on the dominant in measure 260, at which point the puckish second theme group emerges unscathed.

Something like this particular crisis with the brass and timpani had already occurred in the exposition. But it was not at that time explicitly affiliated with the symphony's introduction. What Mozart accomplishes in the finale's recapitulation is the confrontation that had been postponed since the first movement's exposition began. For while that movement successfully demonstrated the generation of the self, it did so without referring to the traumas that had preceded it. The theme in measure 37 of the opening movement simply turns its back on the introduction's painful struggle over authority. But if we have been paying close attention to the implications of that opening movement, we may feel as though we have been waiting for the other shoe to drop—as we are throughout the apparent frivolity of *Don Giovanni*.

As in the opera, the symphony's nightmares are realized when the repressed refuses to remain buried and returns to interrupt the proceedings. However, this composition is far more comedic than *Don Giovanni*, and the return offers the opportunity for the emergent subject to demonstrate that he has in fact achieved the aristocratic father's strength and stature without also taking on his more autocratic tendencies. Power has been transformed from prohibition to dynamism. Yet one more crisis occurs (mm. 307–17) before the end—again brought on by an ill-advised approach to G; but, as was the case in the parallel moment in the exposition, it is quickly laid to rest and is superceded by playful triplets, trills, and a final statement of the theme, which has appropriated the brass-and-drum fanfares to its own glory.

If only the outer movements were at stake, I would be inclined to follow primarily the political implications of this narrative trajectory: the emergence of a bourgeois sensibility out of aristocratic oppression. But it was a slow movement that inspired Maynard Solomon's psychoanalytic inquiries, and the middle movement of the *Prague* too invites a reading that draws us into the private sphere (which is no less publicly articulated).

The andante is in G major. This follows convention, for the subdominant had long been a common choice for slow movements. But this key also ties in with some details of the framing movements. Recall, for instance, that the principal theme of the allegro has a tendency to lean passively toward G—a tendency that has to be overcome repeatedly in favor of forward motion. And the central crisis in the finale is precipitated by an attempted move to G—a move that brings down all the prohibitive weight of the Law. In other words, the key of G seems to be desired yet forbidden—by external forces and also by the subject's own imperatives for dynamic progress and self-sustained identity.

As the second movement begins, this realm becomes topically more specific. The movement presents a kind of pastoral, in that its rhythms are those of the siciliano and its melody (doubled in "sweet" sixths) occurs over a tonic pedal, in the style of a musette. It displays a tendency toward its own subdominant, stressing the nostalgic atmosphere already suggested by the references to antiquated and rustic types.[37]

The altered inflections that had already appeared in the introduction and first movement proliferate here, producing an affect of heightened sensitivity. A chromatic scale seems to lead toward the first implied cadence in measure 4, only to overflow with excess bounty through the measure to the beginning of the next phrase. This next phrase turns out to be a repetition of the first, but intensified by still more inflections and yearning suspensions. Measure 8 brings in a contrasting idea—a tiny staccato motive moving timidly in sequence. Gradually its baby steps acquire greater confidence and lead back into the embrace of lush suspension chains related to the opening material, rounding off the first section.

This nostalgic landscape of plenitude corresponds to images not simply of "the feminine," but, more specifically, of "the maternal." This is so not only because of the semiotic associations with which Mozart engages in constructing this tableau, but also because of the conflicted way this material operates within the movement's structure. A successful representation of infantile coextension with the mother would require that the static quality of this opening be maintained indefinitely; in fact, the movement's sequence of events implies that this dreamy stasis is precisely what is desired.

· 87 ·

Alas, the movement is indelibly stamped with its own historical moment—the late 1700s—and the procedures of that time necessarily bring dynamism along with them. The andante can be intelligible only if it participates (however reluctantly) in the teleological processes of tonality and sonata. In contrast to Movements I and III, which seem to rely on narrative inflection to overcome the nay-saying oppression of the brass, this interlude resists change and must be forced into narrative (the by-product of separation) by harsh interventions. It seems to cling to the fixed image of preoedipal bliss; yet reality keeps breaking in, disrupting the peace and pressuring the movement to participate both in the progressive dimensions of late eighteenth-century ideology and in the traumas of maturation.

The first disruption happens in measure 18, where the cocoon of G major is suddenly shattered by loud B octaves, introducing an imperious E-minor passage. As in the introduction to the symphony, a struggle ensues as the more gracious elements emerge and move through a chain of sighs toward D major, then D minor. The louder forces break in again on B-flat, and when the sighs return, it is over an A pedal—again as at the end of the symphony's introduction. The sixteenth-note runs that had spelled plenitude at the beginning of the movement circle within this minor-mode context as though lost, until they are marshalled toward a cadential arrival on the dominant, D major. The second key area restores the musette, suspensions, and baby steps from the opening passage. At measure 45, they participate briefly in a minuet, as though they have moved to a more external, social terrain. A crisis in measure 51 threatens to destroy the illusion, but it is defeated and maternal peace seems to reign at the end of the exposition.

If in the other movements the Law of the Father seems to prohibit growth, here it is generative, as it destabilizes the domestic inertia and nostalgia into which the subject seems all too happy to regress. The kinds of identity forged in the outer movements could not emerge if the pastoral were permitted to survive. Thus we hear this landscape through a glass darkly—we get glimmers and half-forgotten memories, but access back to the experience itself is heavily mediated by noise and interference. As Solomon has written so eloquently:

> Such music is expressive of a preverbal, preoedipal state of symbiotic fusion of infant and mother, a dual-unity matrix that constitutes, under favorable circumstances, an infancy Eden of unsurpassable beauty, inexpressible love, and ecstatic merging, but also a state completely vulnerable to terrors of separation, loss, psychosis, and even fears of potential annihilation; moreover, a state that inevitably terminates in separation, which even under the most favorable circumstances leaves a residue of mourning and engenders a desire to rediscover anew the blissful sensation of undifferentiated fusion with the mother. (10)

In the development section, Mozart inscribes the opening tableau on three successive pitch levels (mm. 64–83), as though he were trying to find a way to reconstitute and inhabit this Edenic memory. Each time it disintegrates after a few measures. At last the baby step motive is forced to undergo a stormy development; and although it eventually finds its way back for the recapitulation, the pastoral is henceforth indelibly marked by a history of violent struggle. Again, Eagleton locates this structure within its historical context:

> The subject of the sublime is accordingly decentred, plunged into loss and pain, undergoes a crisis and fading of identity; yet without this unwelcome violence we would never be stirred out of ourselves, never prodded into enterprise and achievement. We would lapse back instead into the placid feminine enclosure of the imaginary, where desire is captivated and suspended. Kant associates the sublime with the masculine and the military, useful antidotes against a peace which breeds cowardice and effeminacy. Ideology must not so thoroughly centre the subject as to castrate its desire; instead we must be both cajoled and chastized, made to feel both homeless and at home, folded upon the world yet reminded that our true resting place is in infinity. It is part of the dialectic of the beautiful and the sublime to achieve this double ideological effect. (90)

Mozart presents in this movement an adult's reminiscence of an experience that might be foundational to subjectivity but that can never actually be regained. He knows you can't go home again. And thus we return to the public sphere of the finale where identities can seem to be consolidated through struggle, but where traces of that interior world occasionally surface to balance the more aggressive qualities of self-generation.

In the decades that followed Mozart, these tensions between structure and narrative in musical composition became increasingly more vexed—as they did in the social arena of the nineteenth century. The containment so admired during the Enlightenment lost credibility, and the notion that the subject conformed to formal dictates from internal—rather than external—necessity came to appear deluded. Thus, beginning with Beethoven, the forms of the eighteenth century were subjected to sustained attack.

As his career proceeded, Beethoven called into question virtually every aspect of sonata that still operated according to unexamined convention. He cast aside traditional tonal backgrounds in favor of idiosyncratic progressions derived from his own materials; he bashed away at the boundaries separating self-contained movements until they became interlocking segments of overarching narrative entities; he protested *within his music* against what he marks as the external "necessity" of recapitulation.

Yet even as he shattered the relative complacency of sonata's conventions, Beethoven put more and more energy into the illusion of rigorous motivic integrity. The split that opened up in the 1810s between the forms required for intelligibility and the desire for narratives of ongoing self-generation became increasingly exacerbated, parallel with the same dilemmas raging in the social world.[38] Many of Beethoven's successors accepted the terms of the struggle, and a kind of metanarrative unfolds over the course of the nineteenth century in which the contradictions of sonata become ever more pronounced until they break down at the beginning of the twentieth century.

Mozart is usually regarded as speaking to us from a prelapsarian moment before certainty collapses into relativity, before—in Karl Marx's words—all that is solid melts into air. Because Mozart was writing at a time when optimism in the emergent bourgeois subject was still warranted, he was able (like eighteenth-century aestheticians and political theorists) to present the possibility of a solution without seeming to compromise himself. As Karol Berger has described it:

> It is rather the characteristic sense of life of the pre-revolutionary or better pre-Terror Enlightenment (Kant's view of history comes to mind as another example of the same trust which similarly escapes the charge of naiveté because it is tempered by the same awareness of the possibility of tragedy), a *Lebensgefühl* so utterly absent from the art for such a long time now that we cannot but hear in Mozart's music a voice from a very distant and alien past.[39]

Mozart's music strikes a balance between formal constraints and sensitivity, between the conventions that make his music publicly intelligible and the marks of individuality that cause his adherence to those conventions to seem self-determined. Yet the contradictions in subjective formation that eventually proved unsolvable can be detected even here. Is identity guaranteed by narrative coherence? by motivic integrity? by formal propriety? What is the relationship between interiority and the feminine (or the maternal)? Does trafficking in this terrain render the subject vulnerable? How does one strike a balance between interiority and public objectivity in the construction of the self?

By indicating how these concerns inform even his most affirmative compositions, I may be undermining that image of universal, perfect order that makes Mozart the darling of festivals. But I hope to be clarifying how his music, far from holding aloof from the struggles of his day, contributed compelling early models for how bourgeois subjectivity might be constructed in the face of both oppressive authority and the temptation to regress into nostalgia.

Notes

1. See the comparison between the introduction to the *Prague* and the overture to *Don Giovanni* in Allanbrook, 198.

2. In "Music as Narrative," Fred Maus has argued that *all* movements from this repertory—even those that follow the norms—invite narrative readings (17–18). I concur with him and will later suggest that the conventions themselves already have narrative implications. But for now I focus on anomalies that seem to demand special explanation.

3. Jens Peter Larsen, for instance, described the *Prague* as a Manichaean battle between good and evil. See Larsen, 188.

4. For a fuller discussion of this tendency to reduce Mozart to principles of order, see my "A Musical Dialectic from the Enlightenment."

5. See Newcomb, "Once More 'Between Absolute and Program Music'" and "Schumann and Late Eighteenth-Century Narrative Strategies"; Kramer, *Music as Cultural Practice, 1800–1900* and "Musical Narratology"; and Maus, "Music as Drama" and "Music as Narrative." I have examined some of the ideological premises of the narrative schemata of nineteenth-century music in my *Feminine Endings*.

6. Abbate, especially chapters 1 and 2. Abbate wants to restrict the word "narrative" along lines prescribed by Paul Ricoeur, who demands as one of his criteria a sense of past tense. She thereby eliminates from consideration most instrumental music. This definition seems unnecessarily narrow, for it disqualifies not only music, but also plays, films, and many other media that are regularly discussed in terms of narrative strategies.

7. See Leo Treitler's elegant narrative reading of the slow movement of Mozart's Symphony No. 39 in "Mozart and the Idea of Absolute Music," in his *Music and the Historical Imagination*, 176–214. Treitler, however, seeks to locate Mozart's instrumental music within the category of "absolute" music: that is, "autonomous instrumental music that is essentially musical because it is not determined by any ideas, contents, or purposes that are not musical," or music that is "not conditional upon the associations—cultural and personal—that language necessarily carries as its historical baggage" (177). I argue that Mozart's music likewise is burdened with "historical baggage."

For helpful theoretical discussions of plot in literature, see Brooks and Chambers. Brooks and Chambers (and also White) deal with narrativizing as a crucial feature of nineteenth-century culture.

8. It is surely no coincidence that many of the discussions concerning instrumental music and narrative focus on Beethoven (see, for example, Maus, "Music as Drama" and "Music as Narrative," Hatten, and Kramer, "Musical Narrativity"). Yet only Kramer addresses the historical context that predisposed Beethoven to narrative strategies.

9. See the appraisal of Mozart and his social relations in "The Rebel," chapter 7 of Stafford's *The Mozart Myths*, 177–206. See also Pestelli, 142–48.

10. Eagleton points out that Kant, one of the foremost aesthetic theorists of this movement, manifests many of the same ambivalences with respect to class politics as does Mozart.

11. See Bonds for a study of how eighteenth-century theorists conceived of musical form. See also, however, my discussion of how narrative elements break into Bach's Brandenburg Concerto No. 5 in "The Blasphemy of Talking Politics," 21–41.

12. For a discussion of how formal devices begin to regulate the opera aria in the late seventeenth century, see chapter 10 of Rosand. Opera seria itself was a rule-bound attempt at salvaging the spectacularity of opera while purging it of the excesses it had exhibited during its phase as public entertainment in Venice.

13. Indeed, this final section is not even notated. The middle movement concludes with the designation "da Capo" (from the top), and the first section is performed again exactly as before, except with the addition of improvised ornaments.

14. Second themes that pose threats are rarely found before the nineteenth century, when dilemmas involving alterity begin to emerge at the very time the liberal project begins to be threatened from below—by those who must be kept in subordinate positions, such as workers, ethnic aliens, women, and femininity itself. By contrast, the eighteenth-century sonata usually focuses on the viability of the subject per se: its freedom of activity, its depth of feeling, and its capacity for consensual interchange.

15. Some theorists at the time found the repetition quite problematic, even from the point of view of rhetoric. Grétry, for instance, wrote in 1797: "A sonata is an oration [*discours*]. What are we to think of a man who, dividing his discourse in half, repeats each half? 'I was at your house this morning; yes, I was at your house this morning to talk with you about something; to talk with you about something' . . . I speak above all of the long reprises that constitute the halves of an oration. Reprises may have been good at the birth of music, at a time when the listener did not comprehend everything until the second time around. I know that an oration is often divided into two sections; but without a doubt, one does not present each one twice." Quoted in Bonds, 130–31.

16. Lawrence Kramer draws on Jacques Derrida's notions of force and structure to make a similar argument in "'As If a Voice Were in Them': Music, Narrative, and Deconstruction," *Music as Cultural Practice*, 176–213.

17. Eagleton, 107: "The aesthetic is a kind of fictive or heuristic realm in which we can suspend the force of our usual powers, imaginatively transferring qualities from one drive to another in a kind of free-wheeling experiment of the mind. Having momentarily disconnected these drives from their real-life contexts, we can enjoy the fantasy of reconstituting each

by means of the other, reconstructing psychical conflict in terms of its potential resolution."

18. For a similar argument, see Rosen, 325.

19. Eagleton also argues this position throughout his book. See also Chodorow and Benjamin.

20. For a discussion of how the Kantian categories of the sublime and beautiful are defined in terms of patriarchal law and the mother's body respectively, see Eagleton, 90–93. See also the quotation from Eagleton below.

21. For discussions of how the work of bourgeois social formation was accomplished in the novel, see Moretti and Armstrong.

22. I am using masculine pronouns deliberately because the narratives inscribed in most such stories involve male protagonists. Jane Austen's works foreground women who must learn how to negotiate between the social world and their own subjectivities, but those tensions are quite distinct from both those in novels by male authors and those in Mozart's narratives. This is not to suggest that women listeners cannot identify with the male protagonists in either literature or music, but only to acknowledge important historical differences.

23. See Ballantine, "Beethoven, Hegel and Marx," *Music and Its Social Meanings*, 34: "Where, in the earlier style, a piece evolves on the basis of what is already there at the beginning, in the later it gropes ever towards a new formulation, one not given but latent within an original contradiction: it strives to become what it is *not*, on the basis of what it *is*." Ballantine specifically includes Mozart in "the earlier style," yet what he says applies to certain of Mozart's later compositions, especially the *Prague*. See also chapters 6–8 of Meyer.

24. For other discussions of Mozart along these lines, see Subotnik, "Evidence of a Critical Worldview in Mozart's Last Three Symphonies," *Developing Variations*, 98–111; and Slavoj Zizek, *The Sublime Object of Ideology*, 188–90. I have also benefited from reading Christine Bezat's Foucauldian account in "The Order of Things in the *Prague Symphony*."

25. Moretti calls the late eighteenth-century Bildungsroman "classic," because it typically tries to reconcile tensions. Compare Agawu: "Mozart can disrupt a nominally secure conventional tonal world, knowing all along that such disruption is illusory, that the security guaranteed by a closed, hierarchic tonal structure remains an immutable law. This is artistic play of a subtle and alluring kind" (83). Later novels by Stendhal and others insist on the fundamental impossibility of reconciliation, as do many nineteenth-century composers beginning with Beethoven.

26. For an example in which the contradictions seem quite exposed, see my "A Musical Dialectic."

27. The remainder of the article presents a reading (by no means the only one feasible) of the *Prague* Symphony. I have tried to describe the music in such a way as to assist those who cannot read notation, but the reader must consult a recording or score in order to follow the arguments. While performances differ radically, the recording by Nikolaus Harnoncourt on Teldec comes closest to projecting what I describe.

28. Cone, 24–31.

29. Strangely enough, Charles Rosen comments on how little the introduction has to do with the remainder of the piece. See his *The Classical Style*, 347.

30. See Caplan. Even as late as *David Copperfield*, tears served as an index of masculine sensitivity. For an account of the cult of eighteenth-century sensitivity in Germany, see Ford, 33–37.

31. On connections between the limitations and semiotics of the natural trumpet, see Walser, "Musical Imagery and Performance Practice in J.S. Bach's Arias with Trumpet," 63–69.

32. See Ford, 34–35, on the political passivity of German *Empfindsamkeit* and even *Sturm und Drang*. See also Szondi, "*Tableau* and *Coup de Théâtre*: On the Social Psychology of Diderot's Bourgeois Tragedy," *On Textual Understanding and Other Essays*, 115–32, for a discussion of how eighteenth-century sentimentality stands as a substitute for genuine action: "[A]s long as the middle-class spectator wants to feel pity in the theater, the model hero of bourgeois tragedy will be the helpless victim of an absolute ruler's arbitrary power. . . . Or, conversely, as long as the bourgeoisie does not revolt against absolutism and make a bid for power, it will lie solely for its emotions, bewailing in the theater its own misery" (132).

33. For an examination of the relationships between topics and formal structure in this introduction, see Agawu, 17–25. Agawu is reluctant to refer outside the music and its immediate codes; he explicitly insists on "reference without consequence" (38). Indeed, he seems to want to read works from the height of the Enlightenment as perfect instances of what Fredric Jameson disparages as the "blank parody" — the mere "playing with signs" — of postmodernism. Along with Eagleton, I believe there is far more at stake here, that the references do have consequences — both within the domain of the composition and in the realm of social formation.

34. For eighteenth-century confirmation of this point, see Bonds, especially 98–102.

35. I am drawing here (as is Mozart) on the codes that circulated on the operatic stage. In some sense, it does not matter whether we regard this passage as a feminine Other or as the privatized, domestic dimension of the subject.

36. Adorno wrote extensively on this dilemma in many disparate

places. An insightful narrative account of his various arguments is presented in Rose Rosengard Subotnik, "The Historical Structure: Adorno's 'French' Model for the Criticism of Nineteenth-Century Music," pages 206–38 in *Developing Variations*.

37. For more on the topical associations of the siciliano and musette, see Allanbrook, 44 and 52–54. She writes: "The siciliano is closely identified with the pastoral genre; Sicily is, after all, the Italian Arcadia. . . . [I]t often bears an affect of nostalgia and resignation, passions naturally attendant on memories of a better world" (44).

38. See my "Narrative Agendas in Absolute Music." See also Eagleton for a metanarrative of how these tensions develop within aesthetic theory, and Moretti for how they develop in the later *Bildungsroman*.

39. Berger, 28. Moretti observes the same change in the contemporaneous *Bildungsroman*.

Bibliography

Abbate, Carolyn. *Unsung Voices: Opera and Musical Narrative*. Princeton: Princeton Universty Press, 1991.

Agawu, Kofi. *Playing with Signs: A Semiotic Interpretation of Classic Music*. Princeton: Princeton University Press, 1991.

Allanbrook, Wye Jamison. *Rhythmic Gesture in Mozart*. Chicago: University of Chicago Press, 1983.

Armstrong, Nancy. *Desire and Domestic Fiction: A Political Hitory of the Novel*. Oxford: Oxford University Press, 1987.

Ballantine, Christopher. *Music and Its Social Meanings*. New York: Gordon and Breach Science Publishers, 1984.

Benjamin, Jessica. *The Bonds of Love: Psychoanalysis, Feminism, and the Problem of Domination*. New York: Pantheon, 1988.

Berger, Karol. "The First-Movement Punctuation Form in Mozart's Piano Concertos." Paper delivered at the conference "Current Issues in the Interpretation of Mozart's Instrumental Music." Stanford University, 1991.

Bezat, Christine. "The Order of Things in the *Prague Symphony*." Unpublished manuscript, 1990.

Bonds, Mark Evan. *Wordless Rhetoric: Musical Form and the Metaphor of the Oration*. Cambridge, MA: Harvard University Press, 1991.

Brooks, Peter. *Reading for the Plot: Design and Intention in Narrative*. Cambridge, MA: Harvard University Press, 1984.

Caplan, Jay. *Framed Narratives: Diderot's Genealogy of the Beholder*. Minneapolis: University of Minnesota Press, 1985.

Chambers, Ross. *Story and Situation: Narrative Seduction and the Power of Fiction*. Minneapolis: University of Minnesota Press, 1984.

Chodorow, Nancy. *The Reproduction of Mothering: Psychoanalysis and the Sociology of Gender*. Berkeley: University of California Press, 1978.

Cone, Edward T. *Musical Form and Musical Performance*. New York: Norton, 1968.

Eagleton, Terry. *The Ideology of the Aesthetic*. Oxford: Basil Blackwell, 1990.

Ford, Charles. *Cosi? Sexual Politics in Mozart's Operas*. Manchester: Manchester University Press, 1991.

Hatten, Robert. "On Narrativity in Music: Expressive Genres and Levels of Discourse in Beethoven." *Indiana Theory Review* 12 (1991): 75–98.

Kramer, Lawrence. *Music as Cultural Practice, 1800–1900*. Berkeley: University of California Press, 1990.

———. "Musical Narratology: A Theoretical Outline." *Indiana Theory Review* 12 (1991): 141–62.

Larsen, Jens Peter. "The Symphonies." In *The Mozart Companion*. Ed. by H.C. Robbins Landon and Donald Mitchell. New York: W.W. Norton, 1956. 156–99.

McClary, Susan. "The Blasphemy of Talking Politics during Bach Year." In *Music and Society: The Politics of Composition, Performance and Reception*. Ed. by Richard Leppert and Susan McClary. Cambridge: Cambridge University Press, 1987. 13–63.

———. *Feminine Endings: Music, Gender, and Sexuality*. Minneapolis: University of Minnesota Press, 1991.

———. "A Musical Dialectic from the Enlightenment: Mozart's *Piano Concerto in G Major, K. 453*, Movement 2." *Cultural Critique* 4 (1986): 129–69.

———. "Narrative Agendas in Absolute Music: Identity and Difference in Brahms' Symphony No. 3." In *Music and Difference*. Ed. by Ruth Solie. Berkeley: University of California Press. 1993. 326–44.

Maus, Fred. "Music as Drama." *Music Theory Spectrum* 10 (1988): 65–72.

———. "Music as Narrative." *Indiana Theory Review* 12 (1991): 1–34.

Meyer, Leonard B. *Style and Music: Theory, History, and Ideology*. Philadelphia: University of Pennsylvania Press, 1989.

Moretti, Franco. *The Way of the World: The* Bildungsroman *in European Culture*. London: Verso, 1987.

Newcomb, Anthony. "Once More 'Between Absolute and Program Music': Schumann's Second Symphony." *19th-Century Music* 7 (1984): 233–50.

———. "Schumann and Late Eighteenth-Century Narrative Strategies." *19th-Century Music* 11 (1987): 164–75.

Pestelli, Giorgio. *The Age of Mozart and Beethoven*. Trans. by Eric Cross. Cambridge: Cambridge University Press, 1984.

Rosand, Ellen. *Opera in Seventeenth-Century Venice: The Creation of a Genre*.

Berkeley: University of California Press, 1991.

Rosen, Charles. *The Classical Style*. New York: W.W. Norton, 1972.

Solomon, Maynard. "The Image in Form." Paper delivered at the conference "Current Issues in the Interpretation of Mozart's Instrumental Music." Stanford University, 1991.

Stafford, William. *The Mozart Myths: A Critical Reassessment*. Stanford: Stanford University Press, 1991.

Subotnik, Rose Rosengard. *Developing Variation: Style and Ideology in Western Music*. Minneapolis: University of Minnesota Press, 1991.

Szondi, Peter. *On Textual Understanding and other Essays*. Trans. by Harvey Mendelsohn. Minneapolis: University of Minnesota Press, 1986.

Treitler, Leo. *Music and the Historical Imagination*. Cambridge, MA: Harvard University Press, 1989.

Walser, Robert. "Musical Imagery and Performance Practice in J.S. Bach's Arias with Trumpet." *Journal of the International Trumpet Guild* 13 (1988): 63–69.

White, Hayden. *The Content of the Form: Narrative Discourse and Historical Representation*. Baltimore: Johns Hopkins University Press, 1987.

Zizek, Slavoj. *The Sublime Object of Ideology*. London: Verso, 1989.

4

The Ethics of Forms: Taking Flight with *The Wings of the Dove*

WAYNE C. BOOTH

When I accepted the assignment to "do an essay for our volume, one that will combine theory with practical criticism," I felt no compunctions about undertaking once again a task that thousands of us perform annually: raiding a book for critical purposes. I would simply do a careful "ethical" critique of some major novel. Then I thought over those I would like to read again, chose *The Wings of the Dove*, and began my first re-reading in about three decades of a novel that I remembered as impressive but more formidable than lovable.[1]

Long before the middle of the book, however, the reading had forced me to ask how my project would appear to the master of moral subtleties. I had of course promised him that I would try to obey his commands—that I would do my best to surrender to whatever the book demanded of me before drawing back and becoming the professional critic: I would struggle to understand before pursuing any *over*standing. But of course I was still driven by the assignment to look for my point of critical entry.

The story I found myself meeting, however, threatened to condemn that assignment. The touching account of Milly Theale's betrayal seemed to nag me about the fundamental difference between those like Kate Croy who comfortably use others, and those like Milly who know how or learn how to find their life by living with and even for others.[2] Whatever I might finally say about this novel, I could be sure that it was not written to be *used*, to be reduced to a counter in some critical economy—even mine. It was written to *be*, or to *act*, or to *teach*, or to make us *see*—choose your own critical view of what novels are written for, but do not, if you want to enter Henry James's drawing room, say that his elaborate tales are written to be used a century later by this or that critic with an ax to grind. I was being reminded, in short, that no other moral fault, in James's rich display of faults, is given more attention than reduction of beauty or truth or goodness to market value.[3]

Yet in the way the story is told I seemed to find a confirmation of my project: James-the-old-intruder was inviting me to turn my attention away from the story of Milly and Kate and Merton to attend to his idiosyncratic way of telling it—a way not all that idiosyncratic by standards of our time but radically so in his. As I went on reading, more and more slowly, sometimes exasperated by James's subtlety, deflected from the "story" by his many reminders, explicit and implicit, of rhetorical manipulations, I soon realized that I was caught between two seemingly contradictory demands:

> "Don't use me, because like every other thing of beauty I am not to be turned into a commodity."

> "Do use me critically, just as my author 'uses' me by calling your attention to his blatantly manipulative way of telling his story."

Indeed that second demand at times seemed almost explicitly directed to Wayne Booth, the lifetime practitioner of point-of-voyeurism. The full strength of this demand will perhaps not be fully intelligible to those who have not read at least one of James's late novels. For any such who happen to have stumbled upon me here, and also for readers who, though they have read *The Wings of the Dove*, find that their memory of its details is as dim as mine was a few weeks ago, I offer in the apendixes two sorrowfully simplified summaries: first of what I shall call "the raw chronology" (what Gérard Genette calls "story" and some narratologists have called the *fabula*, what my mentors used to call the "material plot") and then of what we can call, adapting James Phelan's terminology, "the actual progression" (what Genette calls the "narrative" or "narrative discourse"). I assume that many readers will find those appendixes simply unreadable, but I am convinced that only in attending to what they reflect can one appreciate both the full powers of James's "late" way of composing and also the *ethical* pressures that thinking about such complex powers can exert.

My question thus became, as I carried through with my determination to face James down if he could not answer well: Is your presentation of these seemingly contradictory reading demands of any great value to me, one of your devotees? In the terms I raise in *The Company We Keep*, are you really good company, in the sense of being my true friend, working for my weal?

The Many Kinds of Reading

To address the question properly, we must back up and underline the complications that make ethical questions about narrative methods extraordinarily difficult.

In the first place, the question as put won't do. It should not be, "Is this novel, is this implied Henry James, *my* true friend?" Who but Wayne Booth cares about that? The question should be, "Is this novel, when given its full head, a true friend potentially to all readers who read it with any care?" And that question thrusts us into the facts about diverse readers and readings. Are they not unlimitedly various? Can anyone these days deny that the effects of *The Wings of the Dove* will vary from reader to reader, and for each reader from reading to reading? Do we not hear, as we pursue ethical questions, a strongly ethical demand from several critical camps that we celebrate diversity and deliberately ignore or violate the work's own demands? Since the phrase "the work's own demands" is itself absurd, I can hear some critical friends saying, the only ethical stance is to pursue freedom of spirit, or sharpness of perception, or political awakening, all in the name of the deepest of all truths: there is no fixed truth anywhere, and—even more certainly in an uncertain world—there are no single certain readings.[4]

Yet if one wants to talk about the ethical value of a work *in general* and not just about what it has done to or for any one reader, one can hardly reject all concern for what it seems to ask every reader to do—not just "me" but "us"—regardless of how strongly we may want to emphasize what we can do *to* it.[5] In short, the serious ethical critic is always faced with two tasks, not just the one that earlier ethical critics performed in describing *the* moral health or disease of any one work. To talk about the ethical powers of a work as being actually in the work, regardless of readers' differences, is one thing. To talk about a work's actual ethical effects is quite another. Can the two tasks in any way be reconciled?

I think they can be, if we distinguish three kinds of reading that we all practice.

We all engage, at least at times, in readings that I shall call "reading-with": the reading we do when we simply accept what seem to us the obvious demands of the text. The title is, say, *Poirot Investigates*, and the author is Agatha Christie. The cover calls her "The Unsurpassed Mistress of Mystery," and the title page adds a picture that includes some pearls and some blood. We know that a murder will occur, that Poirot will encounter many suspects and some fools who are confused by them, and that the book will end with the murderer exposed. No problem here, unless we are determined *not* to read-with: we know we have a specific kind of whodunit and we read for the mystery and for the mystery alone. Or let's say that the title is *The New Awakening*, described as "A Novel"; the publisher is Virago Press, a publisher noted for its feminist endeavors. In the opening pages a stupid cruel husband is shown mistreating a mousy wife; at the end the wife is—in one way or another—no longer a mouse; she's awakened at last. Again no problem: we read *for* that moment of liberation. Or we pick up a book with the title *Merovingian Art from 500 to 751*, or *Plato's Epistemology*, or *Cognitive Science: A Synthesis*; the publisher is, say, Cambridge University Press, and we find, on reading, that the title's generic promises are roughly fulfilled. No problem: we read the book in the same spirit shown toward the others; we cooperate. Of course each of these readings will be in one sense entirely different: we "hear" radically different questions and answers. But all such reading is the same in one crucial respect: we never question—if we go on reading at all—the terms of the contract clearly specified by the work's emphasis on its own genre. We rely—even the least sophisticated *and* the most critically up-to-date among us rely—on our past experience of genres, slotting in the new work until and unless we bump into powerful violations of generic expectations. We can even say that two readers who read the "same" text in entirely opposed ways, one as a tragedy, say, and the other as a comedy, are still reading it "in the same way," for our purposes here, so long as each of them thinks the reading is reading-with.

Stories that we read-with (putting aside for now scientific and scholarly and political discourse that is not overtly storied) come in three sub-types: (a) those that so clearly invite a probing of *meanings* that most or all readers agree that the invitations are "there on the page"; (b) those that so clearly seem to be "just story," just plain gripping event-after-event, that only highly motivated critics bother to find meanings in them; and (c) those that seem happily to respond both to readers looking for profound meanings and to those who hope for a gripping experience of story. Aesop's and George Orwell's tales are of the first kind: they demand, if we are to read-with them, that we think about (and then perhaps talk about) meanings, ideas—the relation of the story to "life." With or without moral tags attached, readers have to work hard to avoid seeing a moral point in an Aesopian fable. The second kind—"Puss in Boots" and most murder mysteries and thrillers like *Jaws*—in effect asks us *not* to worry about meanings: "Just keep moving, if you hope to enjoy me in my primary being."

If tales all fell clearly into these first two kinds, the life of the critic would be simpler. But most do not. A great deal of our critical energy has always gone into making sense of the third kind (surely the largest pile): those that allow readers to move in either direction while *believing* that they are reading-with. Nothing the story-centered reader encounters disrupts the story: it all seems to be just "what happened." Yet everything the meaning-centered reader encounters supports or invites a given interpretation of meanings.

Readers of popular fiction generally read-with; they just assume that they have the second kind of work (type b) in hand, and they suppress all concern for meanings. For them, as for me early in my reading life, that becomes the only kind of reading. They usually do not re-read, and even when they do they are likely to make their second time through pretty much like the first; they—we critics in some of our moods—seek simply to renew the original pleasure. As Peter Rabinowitz and Janice Radway have both argued, this kind of reading has been either ignored or condemned by modern criticism, and the pleasures and profit derived from such rapid, "unreflective" but deeply engaged reading-with have been almost universally underrated by critics while being exploited by commercial authors.[6] It is for some recent critics as if the only way to make reading such works worthwhile is to go to the opposite extreme, what I'll call "reading-against."

The reader who reads-against sets out to find in the text whatever it does *not* promise or invite to, whatever its author presumably never intended but unconsciously either allowed in or specifically banned. There are several terms on our critical scene for this fashionable kind of reading: "strong," "resistant," "deconstructionist," "anti-intentional" and so on. For many critics, as I have already suggested, this could be called "the only intelligent" or "the only ethically defensible" type of reading. My central question here can be thus rephrased: As I impose my ethical question on *The Wings of the Dove*, am I reading-against or reading-with?

The third type is not quite a blend of the other two, though it at first looks like that. It is what some of us do when, after having had a rewarding experience that we think of as reading-with (whether simply "for story" or for multiple meanings), we decide to go back and re-read, trying either to deepen or clarify the experience, or to discover how the author managed to achieve the results we love, or why he or she did not achieve such results. We might call this "critical reading," were it not that most readers-against see their kind of reading as the only really critical kind. For want of a better term, call it "critical re-reading."

Such reading again comes in different kinds, depending on our critical interests. For now, we need only distinguish re-reading that probes for deeper *meanings* and re-reading that probes for an *understanding of structure*—the principles that determined the author's act of composition. Re-reading for meanings is often conducted as if the novel might just as well have been written backwards; re-reading for structure, in contrast, cares deeply about every flashback, every foreshadowing, every expansion or contraction of the raw events, every shift of point of view.[7]

Sometimes critical re-reading, whether for meaning or for architecture, can lead us to deplore our having read-with on the first go: we've been had. Why did we not see these vile meanings that the author obscured or never suspected, or these structural flaws that the author concealed? But often such re-reading can lead instead to heightened admiration, especially when it is assisted by other readers who see qualities we had overlooked.

Responding to Explicit Invitations

We now have three kinds of stories and three ways that they can be read—with two subclasses of critical re-reading. Whether we find this complexity annoying or not, I would claim that I did not invent it—that it is thrust upon us by the explicit and implicit invitations that various works offer to any attentive reader. Works "try" to tell us, in myriad ways (quite aside from their authors' statements outside the text) not only what genre to place them in when reading-with, but also whether they will be more rewarding when the reading-with leads us to re-read critically. Note that in this scheme it is in principle impossible for any work to invite us to read-against its full being, however chaotic or anti-intentionalist that being might be. At the most negative, all a work can do is invite us to read-against generic expectations that we *mistakenly* thought appropriate.

A. C. Bentley's *Trent's Last Case*, for example, starts out as if asking to be read entirely "with," as a whodunit. But as Trent's solutions to the crime are successively undermined, even the first-time reader is invited—or could one say "forced"?—to move to critical re-reading: "Just what is the genre here? What have I foolishly taken for granted in reading earlier detective fiction? What, indeed, does this surprise ending, with its explanation of the book's title, say about fiction, about detective fiction, about the relation of stories to life, about truth . . . ?"[8]

Though it would be absurd to expect Bentley's novel to invite us to read-against its every stroke, it is not absurd of *us* to read-against it and ask questions not on its list, most notably questions that are raised in the second kind of critical re-reading, reading for architecture: "Just how did you put this together? What is your architecture here? Did you do the best possible job in ordering the parts, in handling point of view, in expanding or contracting scenes?" To ask those questions of *Trent's Last Case* is to read-against, even when, as I have discovered in this case, to do so increases one's admiration for the writer. The book responds to my questions about its architecture, but it does not itself raise them, just as it invites no questioning of its own ethical value. (Note that most "formal" critics in the past—including me—have assumed that to appraise structure and technique is to read-with. It has taken me decades to realize that to ask *Macbeth* "Why did Shakespeare begin you just this way?" or "Why did he prolong the Porter's scene?" is to read-against *Macbeth* even though Shakespeare usually—not always—stands up brilliantly to such questions.)

The Invitation to Attend to Architecture

When we ask of *The Wings of the Dove* first what kind of reading it "wants," and second whether that kind is ethically constructive, the answer to the first question is clear: anyone who has as much as dipped into this novel, reading-with it, will feel as I did a pressure to re-read-critically—that is, to combine the first and third kinds of reading. What is more, that pressure will be toward thinking not only about moral and philosophical meanings but to think about construction. Many a fine novel—for example, any one of Jane Austen's—resembles Bentley's in this respect, never even hinting at questions about structure; *Pride and Prejudice* invites critical re-reading, but only the kind that attends to a deepening of moral insight. *The Wings of the Dove*, in contrast, openly demands that we attend precisely to its author's act of composing.

What it does not even hint at is the kind of question I am asking here: Is it really good for us—as readers, as creatures in the world—or even for the art of fiction, to spend hours, days, months, reading-with James's explicit invitations and finding ourselves practicing a highly intricate kind of critical reading, the kind that generations of critics since Percy Lubbock have now exhibited? He never for a moment questions—and he always implies—the superiority of the kind of experience he struggles to provide. In his commentary outside the novels, he does occasionally claim explicit ethical value to what he calls his "method." But within the novels themselves he only implies it, never states it.

But surely we have a right—more clearly in this decade than in any earlier time—to read-against and demand an answer: Have the hundreds of thousands of hours and millions of words spent on the *art* of fiction, fiction as *poetry*, fictions as well-wrought urns, exemplified a kind of life worth living? Many an exasperated reader has answered no, both with respect to such novels and to the criticism they inspire.

If the answer for me were not in some sense yes, I obviously would not waste my time by adding to those millions here. But the details of the answer are not at all obvious. To put the matter as sharply as possible, shouldn't I be spending my time on some more self-evidently worthwhile form of life: working for aid to starving Africans, say, or tutoring deprived children, or—closer to home— becoming a media critic? Here I am, in my early seventies, as sure of my own coming death as Milly could be of hers—though not quite as sure about the timing—and I spend a large slice of my remaining time trying once again to appraise the gift James has offered to share with me. Does that make sense at the deepest levels of meaning to which we can probe? Why do this rather than enjoying the latest Dick Francis or Sue Grafton romp?

James's Plans in Prospect

In the planning stage of *The Wings of the Dove*, James not only ignored our present "reading-against" question; for a long time he did not even talk about the "how" of telling. We can never know what really went on in his mind and heart as he worked and reworked his plans in his notebook. But what he *said* he was up to was not the construction of meanings or anti-meanings, whether metaphysical, psychological, political, religious, or ethical; nor was it about clever play with chronology and point of view and proportions. Rather it was all about finding a powerful story, an action, a plot to be read-with *as story*. That task for him, as for all story tellers, involved first the discovery of what characters of a given kind would do to one another, and why.

In short, he began not with an "idea" at all but with a "situation." This was never for James a static picture, a mere "image," as some have suggested; the words I have put in italics in the following passage show just how much his mind is on the need for action, for narrative movement, rather than on doctrine or how to draw out the right tricks from his copious trick bag:

> . . . the *situation* of some young creature . . . who, at 20, on the threshold of a life that has seemed boundless, is suddenly *condemned* to death . . . by the voice of the physician? She learns that she has *but a short time to live*, and *she rebels*, she is terrified, she cries out in her anguish, her tragic young despair. . . . She is like a creature *dragged shrieking to the* guillotine—to the shambles. The idea of a young man who *meets her*, who, knowing her fate, is terribly touched by her, and who conceives the idea of *saving her* . . . [perhaps by offering her] the chance to *love* and *to be loved*. . . . But the young man is *entangled* with another woman . . . and *it is in that that a little story seems to reside*. I see him as having somehow to *risk something* . . . *to sacrifice*

something in order to *be kind* to her. . . . the anecdote, which I don't, by the way, at all yet *see* [James's italics], is probably more *dramatic* . . . on some basis of *marriage* . . . marriage with the other woman, or even with both! The little *action* hovers before me as abiding, somehow, in the particular *complication* that his attitude (to the girl) engenders for the man, a *complication culminating in some sacrifice . . . or disaster*. (*Notebooks* Nov. 3, 1894)

And on he goes, through pages of planning, toward the discovery four days later (Nov. 7, 1894) that his "little action" requires

the man's *agreeing with his fiancée that he shall marry the poor girl in order to come into her money and in the certitude that she will die and leave the money to him* [James's italics]—on which basis . . . they themselves will at last be able to marry.

James then tries out more and more possibilities for plot—well over 2,500 words with not one word about anything but "my story pure and simple."

Three months later, re-reading his speculations, he finds them good—and suddenly introduces for the first time an ethical note that relates to my main point here. This story will do something *for him*, something that "compensates" him for five years of "bitterness," "wasted passion and squandered time," "unspeakable . . . tragic experience," "long apparent barrenness," "suffering and sadness intolerable": the "story" is "strongly, richly there; a thing, surely, of great potential interest and beauty and of a strong, firm artistic *ossature*."[9] Note that what it will give to him—the gift to his ethos, as we might put it, to stress the ethical note—is the gift of discovering the right "ossature," the right bone structure for his story: after years of barrenness, he can at last once again tell a story worth telling.

It is hard to tell here whether James is thinking of the compensation as granted by the story emerging—the "what," the raw chronology—or by the "how," the lessons he has learned, through the painful years, about the art of dramatic "showing" through scenes in order to create a beautiful "actual progression." Just what the ossature of any story is can always be hard to determine. But it is beyond question that the beauty he is probing is the beauty of a well-constructed story—one that will engage readers in an "ossature" that inextricably combines the "what" and the "how."

His Plans in Retrospect: The Preface

That's where his mind still dwells nearly fifteen years later when, fresh from re-reading and revising the work, he writes his long, detailed "Preface." He begins as before with the firm bone structure of the *action*. For several pages one finds, as in the notebooks, nothing whatever about meanings. It is again all about an action, the action of Milly's "struggle"—of the young woman's "disintegration," of the "act of living," of the "battle," of how the "process of life gives way fighting," of how his heroine will be "dragged by a greater force than any she herself could exert," "contesting every inch of the road," of a "catastrophe determined in spite of oppositions," of the "drama" of her wresting "from her shrinking hour . . . as much of the fruit of life as possible," and of the drama of her opponents' "promoting her illusion . . . for reasons, for interests and advantages, from motives and points of view, of their own" (5, NY vii–viii).

But he soon shifts to the topic not mentioned in the notebooks: the "how" of the story's telling, and the effects of the "how" on the reader. This topic, perhaps even less fashionable in 1994 than the topic of what makes for good raw chronology, he celebrates in loving and prolonged detail, as if to say, "Just think, dear reader, of the problems I faced, and of the hitherto unimagined solutions they led me to!"

Since my subject inescapably expands itself from the effects of reading "the novel itself" to the issue of reading and writing the kind of criticism it leads us to, I must dwell a bit on this material that a few critics may still want to call "extrinsic." The great point, he says, was

> that if in a *predicament* she [Milly] was to be, . . . it would be of the essence to create the predicament promptly and *build it up* solidly, so

that it *should have for us* as much as possible its *ominous air* of awaiting her. . . . One begins so, in such a business, by looking about for *one's compositional key*, unable as one can only be to move till one has found it. . . . [T]hough my regenerate young New Yorker [Milly] . . . should form my *centre*, my *circumference* [those who observe and exploit her] was every whit as *treatable*. Therefore I must trust myself to know *when to proceed from the one and when from the other*. (7, NY x–xi; all italics mine except for the word "engaged")

Then, following an account of how not using serialization set him free to "begin as far back" and as far "behind" Milly's own story as he wished, James celebrates just what opportunities freedom from editorial constraints granted him. It yielded

the pleasure of feeling my divisions, my proportions and general rhythm, rest all on permanent rather than in any degree on momentary proprieties. It was enough for my alternations, thus, [of point of view and locations in time and space] that they were good in themselves; it was in fact so much for them that I really think any further account of *the constitution of the book reduces itself to a just notation of the law they followed*.

There was the "fun," to begin with, of *establishing one's successive centres* [*in order to*] . . . *make for construction*, that is, to conduce to effect and to provide for beauty. (8, NY xii; my italics)

There followed from this fun the anguish of not being able to carry out his plan as fully as hoped. He "mourns" at some length, viewing the "gaps and the lapses," the "intentions that, with the best will in the world, were not to fructify" (9, NY xiii). He specifies the "gaps" (some of which seem very strange to me, since in my reading they were not felt as gaps at all). But then he recovers his confidence: each piece is, after all, "true to its pattern, and . . . while it pretends to make no simple statement it yet never lets go its scheme of clearness." After citing proof of his own clever strategies, particularly his consistency with point of view and his tact in withholding intimate scenes that other novelists would have provided, he turns to stronger self-praise, disguised as a criticism of the disportionate length of the two "halves" of the work:

For we have time, while this passage lasts ["the whole Venetian climax"], to turn round critically; . . . we have time to catch glimpses of an economy of composition . . . interesting in itself: all in spite of the author's scarce more than half-dissimulated despair at the inveterate displacement of his general centre. . . . The latter half, that is the false and deformed half, of "The Wings" would verily, I think, form a signal object-lesson for a literary critic bent on improving his occasion to the profit of the budding artist. (7, NY xviii)

The invitation here to turn one's attention from Milly's sad/happy fate to James's rhetoric could not be more open. And he goes on, a bit boastfully, about the tricks he plays to divert the reader who accepts the invitation into his games.

This whole corner of the picture bristles with "dodges"—such as he [the critic? myself, in 1994?] should feel himself all committed to recognise and denounce—for disguising the reduced scale of the exhibition, for foreshortening at any cost, for imparting to patches the value of presences, for dressing objects in an *air* as of the dimensions they can't possibly have. (12–13, NY xviii–xix)

Though James is probably sincere in his regret about the faulty proportions of the two "halves," he is also rightly proud of his skill with "dodges," disguises, foreshortenings, and illusion-producing. His strongest self-congratulation is reserved for the constructional inventions of volume 1:

I recognise meanwhile, throughout the long earlier reach of the book, not only no deformities but . . . a positively close and felicitous application of method, the preserved consistencies of which, often illusive, but never really lapsing, it would be of a certain diversion, and might be of some profit, to follow. (13, NY xix)

I quote at such length—perhaps about a twentieth of what James writes about the story's architecture in the preface alone—in order to emphasize not only his notion of the ideal author, the genius of form, but also his picture of the ideal reader: a reader who, like the imagined critic who could teach other authors how to do it, finds that to "read-with" requires critical attention to the pleasures of compositional subtlety.

Asking whether a particular move is a fault, he says, "distinctly not"—not for the careful reader:

> (Attention of perusal, I thus confess . . . is what I at every point, as well as here, absolutely invoke and take for granted; a truth I avail myself of this occasion to note once for all. . . . The enjoyment of a work of art . . . is greatest, it is delightfully, divinely great, when we feel that the surface of the work, like the thick ice of the skater's pond, bear[s] without cracking the strongest pressure we throw on it. The sound of the crack one may recognize, but never surely to call it a luxury.) (14–15, NY xx–xxi)

And back he goes to a demonstration of what he wants his ideal reader to do: place the strongest possible pressure on the "thick ice" to discover just why his subtle way of "driving portents home" (15, NY xxi) by transforming raw chronology and point of view will resist cracking under the weight. And he concludes after much more on similar points with a cheerful lament that space does not allow him to say as much as he would like to say about the novel's construction!

The novel itself fulfils James's hopes for this kind of attention—does so, that is, for any reader who is willing to read-with its invitations. So we can now bring our ethical pursuit to a head by asking, bluntly, how we are to value all of what many from the beginning called mere artificiality, fussiness, and even elitist destruction of the true value of "story"? Should we not after all join his brother William, a habitual reader-against, in calling it perverse?

> You've reversed every traditional canon of story-telling (especially the fundamental one of *telling* the story, which you carefully avoid) and have created a new *genre littéraire* which I can't help thinking perverse, but in which you nevertheless *succeed*, for I read with interest to the end many pages, and innumerable sentences twice over to see what the dickens they could possibly mean. . . . (Norton 458)

Or do we allow the master to have his way with us—and then praise him for having offered an ethical gift in requiring us to attend not just to the *what* of the story but to the *how*?

"The achieve of, the mastery of the thing"

So far as I can discover, our question has never been addressed except in a most perfunctory way—either in the form of brusque expressions of annoyance like William's or brief praise for the "poetry" of James's novels. What more can one say, other than "I like it" or "I detest it"?

The full effect is of course beyond summary; it can be known only to those who have succumbed to the master's demands and followed his steps as he takes them, with or without the assistance of his guidebooks. Indeed the *full* effect, for the serious critic, can come only for those willing to follow step by step a detailed comparison echoed inadequately by my appendixes. (Surely I can talk at least one or two of you out there into tackling them?) Only someone who has gone through that can then face the full force of the question: Was that good for you?

My own response to this late, late Henry James, in spite of some frustration along the path of this essay, can best be described as gratitude. I was myself surprised by just how powerfully this great implied author, purged entirely of the daily pettinesses that we know the "real" James was capable of in his "declining" years, affected me. I had spent a lifetime arguing that implied authors are always not only different from but *to some degree superior to* their makers, purged of whatever those makers took to be their living faults. I was therefore not surprised to find myself engaged with a "James" who was the most "Jamesian" figure I had ever met—even compared with his other late novels. What was a bit surprising was the gratitude I felt for one more experience with the "fussiness."

"James" has invited me to re-create under his tutelage a beautiful structure—not just *any* abstract structure but a structure of beautifully realized human creatures highlighted miraculously by the artist. He offers me the chance to pretend, for the duration of my reading, that I too live "up there" with him, able not only to appreciate what he has done but to do it myself. Nobody, including James himself, has ever lived for long in this empyrean: sharing not just the intensity and depth and wit and wisdom of other fine artists but the special precise attention to getting it all right—to creating it all better than anyone else could, even given the same "materials."

We can explain something of this power if we examine the more important steps he took that were by no means necessary, given the raw chronology he finally arrived at for the story of Milly, Kate, and Merton. (Readers who have never read the novel might do well to read my detailed summary in Appendix A.) Their story could be told in innumerable ways, without violating its factual and moral intricacy. It could, for example, be told as a simple chronological melodrama of two lovers plotting for the fortune of a dying woman and ending with the ambiguities and beauties of this novel's ending. Even if we decided to tell essentially the story that James tells, no longer just the story of Milly that he first planned but with as much emphasis on Kate and Merton as we now have, we still could make many un-Jamesian choices.

METAPHORIC EXTRAVAGANCE

Turning instead to what he actually did, we could dwell on his "choice" (though by this time in his career he could hardly choose differently) to bestow on all of his main characters a metaphoric and imagistic gift that is totally beyond what any "real" characters like Milly and the others could exercise. They all *think* in elaborate characteristic metaphor and imagery, and they needn't have done so. One could take this book and cut out every one of the passages that begins "It was for him *as if* . . ." and one would still have a readable story (in one sense a more readable one).

Of all the marvels that would be lost in such a cutting, the one most pertinent here is the effect on the reader of having to sort out just who is responsible for each metaphor or image. There is a "dialogue" of different imaginations here, producing a "polyglos-sia" that makes the effect that Bakhtin attributes to Dickens seem simple by comparison; indeed even Bakhtin might see Dostoevsky as at least rivaled here, if not surpassed. It is a dialogue that requires us to attend to each stroke, alert to the distribution of responsibilities.

That James sees his own allocations of metaphor in something like this light is revealed in a marvelous passage where he plays with three imagists at once: Kate, Milly, and the narrator. It occurs in Venice (VII. ii) when the two women are reveling in their successes among the British socialites and at the same time relish-ing those moments when they can "put off their harness" and their social "masks," and relax together (I feel uneasy about what the ghost of James will want to say about my intrusive commentary in the right-hand column):

These puttings-off of the mask

there is no hint that this image would be used by either of them: it is the narrator's alone

had finally quite become the form taken by their moments together . . . whenever, as she [Milly] herself expressed it, she got out of harness.

an image all three share

They flourished their masks, the independent pair, as they might have flourished Spanish fans;

the narrator alone again

clearly this "as" belongs to the nar-rator alone

they smiled and sighed on re-moving them; but the gesture, the smiles, the sighs, strangely enough, might have been sus-pected the greatest reality in the business.

"strangely enough" to whom? we have to ask by now. The narrator

seems to hear our question and re-
plies:

Strangely enough, we say, for
the volume of effusion in general would have been found by
either on measurement

aha!, so "we" say it!

presumably, then, they didn't get
around to measuring?

to be scarce proportional to the
paraphernalia of relief. It was
when they called each other's
attention to their ceasing to
pretend, it was then that what
they were keeping back was
most in the air.

in the air for them? Certainly not
in this form, because neither knows
all of what the other is keeping
back

There was a difference, no
doubt, and mainly to Kate's advantage: Milly didn't quite see
what her friend could keep
back, was possessed of, in fine,
that would be so subject to retention; whereas it was comparatively plain sailing for Kate

is this metaphor Kate's? probably
not

that poor Milly had a treasure

quite possibly Kate's way of think-
ing of Milly's secrets?

to hide. This was not the treasure of a shy, an abject affec-
tion . . . it was much rather a
principle of pride relatively bold
and hard, a principle that
played up like a fine steel
spring at the lightest pressure
of too near a footfall.

at last one that is surely Kate's, her

self-conscious picture of what will happen if she presses too close to the truth of Milly's illness: a steel trap will be sprung; the hunter will become the hunted

Thus insuperably guarded was the truth about the girl's own conception of her validity; thus was a wondering pitying sister

"sister" is in fact an ironic metaphor here, because Kate is much more than a "wondering pitying sister"

condemned wistfully to look at her from the far side of the moat she had dug round her tower.

Kate's image? Probably not, since Kate would not want quite to think of herself as laying siege to an enemy's castle; but like all the others, James's image has become ours, in our pity for the besieged Milly

Certain aspects of the connexion of these young women show for us,

Yes, for us; again the two central characters are shut out!

such is the twilight that gathers about them,

his and ours, not theirs

in the likeness of some dim scene in a Maeterlinck play; we

ah, yes, we!

have positively the image, in the delicate dusk, of the figures so associated and yet so opposed, so mutually watchful: that of the angular pale princess, ostrich-plumed, black-robed, hung about with amu-

lets, reminders, relics, mainly
seated, mainly still,   *all ours, and possibly Kate's*

and that of the upright restless
slow-circling lady of her court
who exchanges with her, across
the black water streaked with
evening gleams, fitful questions
and answers (VIII.iii, 261–62,   *ours and definitely not Milly's.*
NY II.138–39).

And so "we" go on observing Kate circling Milly ("like a pan-
ther"), "with thick dark braids down her back, drawing over the
grass a more embroidered train." Under James's tutelage we extend
the Maeterlinck play to include Milly's confidante, Mrs. Stringham.
"We" come to know more about both of these hearts than either
knows, even about herself, and we thus read the relatively literal
apologia for Kate that follows with an awareness totally different
from what it would have been without the elaborate metaphor (262–
63, NY 140–41).

Metaphors by their very nature require greater creative energy
in the receiver than straight talk. They risk more; many a reader
will just get off the metaphorical boat and condemn the clumsy
author. But when they work, they bind us to the author—in this
case all three "authors"—with no route for escape.

SILENCES

Another requirement on our creative powers is even more powerful—what might be considered the opposite of rhetorical ampli-
fication: suppression, silence, deliberate omission from the narration of crucial events in the raw chronology. The most revealing of
these suppressions of what other novelists would have considered
essential is his silence about what happens when Densher is at long
last invited back to the *palazzo* for a final interview with Milly.
James's friends and critics objected to that omission, just as he
himself had rebuked H. G. Wells, decades before, for failing to

dramatize the crucial courtship scene between lovers in the novel *Marriage*.[10] But once one has been tuned to vibrate on James's inimitable wavelength, the effect can be an enormous stimulation of the imagination. I have found myself working over that omitted scene again and again, imagining the lovely frail girl who has dressed herself up, perhaps for the last time, in order to present to the man she loves a courageous and inoffensive front. I am helped in these reconstructions by the hints Merton later gives to Kate:

> "Did she receive you—in her condition—in her room?" [Kate asks].
> "Not she," said Merton Densher. "She received me just as usual: in that glorious great *salone*, in the dress she always wears, from her inveterate corner of her sofa." And his face for the moment conveyed the scene, just as hers equally embraced it. "Do you remember what you originally said to me of her?"
> "Ah I've said so many things."
> "That she wouldn't smell of drugs, that she wouldn't taste of medicine. Well, she didn't."
> "So that it was really almost happy?"
> It took him a long time to answer, occupied as he partly was in feeling how nobody but Kate could have invested such a question with the tone that was perfectly right. (X.i, 362, NY II.328–29)

We have no good critical vocabulary for the ethical effect of having one's mind preoccupied with all this "perversity" in the telling: piling up obtrusive metaphors, deliberate excision of "essential" parts, to say nothing of obsessive transformations of point of view. How can I express my conviction that it is good for me to be required to go through all this, and to know that if I return with similar attentiveness to the other late novels I'll be invited to similar—but always fresh—re-creations? I have no doubt about it myself—I who am so much inclined to preoccupations of far less defensible kinds. My ultimate defense, if I could ever fully work it out, would have something to do with what happens to the "back of my mind," during the waking hours before and after returning to the desk to wrestle with this recalcitrant work. Its scenes and languages and puzzles form a running accompaniment while trimming my beard and showering, while paying bills, while driving. In other words, it has made me over—in James's direction.

Of course none of this kind of questioning could be considered significant if we once lost the belief that some ways of spending our lives are better than other ways: Why should it matter how I conduct my waking dreams, especially when they are only "at the back of my mind"? But if any value judgments about ways of living make sense, then those authors (and composers, and painters, and so on) who subtly lead us to live moments of high creative intensity even when we are not directly engaged with their works are indeed among our truest friends.

As Milly says to the obtuse and bewildered Lord Mark, "One can't do more than live." "And you don't do anything?" he asks in his confusion. "I do everything," she replies. "'Everything's *this*,' she smiled; 'I'm doing it now. One can't do more than live.'" She is acting, she says, under the great surgeon's advice—

> the best advice in the world. I'm acting under it now. I act upon it in receiving you, in talking with you thus. One can't, as I tell you, do more than live."
> "Oh live!" Lord Mark ejaculated.
> "Well, it's immense for *me*." (VII.iv, 272, NY 155)

It's immense for us too. Though we may not put quite as much emphasis on expensive rococo surroundings as James and Milly seem to do throughout the novel, we live in the greater richness James provides, both in taking in his moral probing of how Milly and Kate and Merton behave and in the discovery that we have been led to create and re-create all that, both while reading and long afterward.

The part of this new life that explicitly wrestles with James's self-chosen constructional task would be described in conventional terms as "formal" and hence "aesthetic." But obviously here the aesthetic task has become deeply ethical. To *get the craft of it right*, to keep the ideal of the highest excellence constantly before one as a demand to *do it better* than what at first seemed merely good, so that those who travel with us—our readers—will get it right too: that is the ethics of craft. It required of James courage, persistence, and a willingness to risk hearing once again from his brother a gentle mocking of his results. It required, in sum, a kind of conscientiousness that fuses morality and the love of beautiful form. And it requires of us an echo of those virtues.

The beautiful thing is that—in contrast with Milly's luxurious purchases—ours are in unlimited supply: there is no zero-sum game here. Our "possession" of these gems never diminishes the supply; indeed, the more lovers such works find for themselves, the better, since talking with other lovers about the treasures "appreciates" their value.

Are not the hours we spend sharing with James and his readers—at least when we are at our best—hours that James might well have had the surgeon add to the remedy he offers Milly? If she was to *live*, why did the doctor fail to order her to spend some time reading the novels of Jane Austen or George Eliot, perhaps, or even, in a postmodernist reflexive ploy, *The Wings of the Dove*?

Appendix A:
The Chronological Story

Until you have tried to summarize the real action of any one of the late James novels, you don't know just how complex his plots are. When one looks at the summaries provided in any of the reference books, what is most striking is how little evidence they provide about what really happens. The mere outline of how, say, a nondescript "Kate" lies to and seeks the fortune of an equally nondescript "Milly" cannot tell us whether the lie was noble or base, and it thus gives us no notion of what the story is really about—of how we are made to hope for, or fear, or in any way enjoy a given resolution. As Martha Nussbaum insists in her account of The Golden Bowl, *the moral meaning of any one choice—whether to lie, whether to seek a fortune—is found only within the full specificity of circumstances and characters, not in any one principle allowing or forbidding lying or pursuing a fortune.*

The following summary is only slightly more useful than the kind I have just condemned. But at least it hints at what I think James was striving for in his elaborately ethical probing: How should one live one's life? What forms of perception and behavior can be justified, in the face of the ultimate fact of tragically early death?

Kate Croy, beautiful and talented and morally sensitive daughter of an impoverished and unscrupulous English gentleman, is urged by her widowed sister, helplessly poor and burdened with four young children, to cultivate their rich aunt, in the hope that Kate might relieve their poverty both by marrying rich and by receiving some of the aunt's fortune. Kate at first resists, sensing all the ways in which truckling to her aunt will infringe on her freedom and violate her principles. But after falling in love with Merton Densher, a highly attractive, witty, intelligent London journalist with little income, and experiencing—in a trial period living at her aunt's—some of the genuine amenities of life that are made possible only by money, she realizes just how essential it is *to her* not to marry poor. Living with her aunt while Merton is in America on an assignment as a journalist, she meets her aunt's guests, two Americans, one an orphaned but rich young woman, the beautiful, innocent, generous-hearted Milly Theale, the other Milly's devoted and intelligent confidante, Susan Stringham, a former schoolmate of the aunt.

Kate and Milly become friends, and we learn that Merton and Milly have met and become friendly in America. Milly and Susan Stringham learn that Milly has an incurable illness, one the fatal effects of which can only be postponed by living life to the hilt—and especially by loving and being loved.

When Kate learns of the illness, she sees the chance both to obtain a fortune for herself and Merton and at the same time to do a favor to the dying Milly: she persuades the reluctant Merton to pay court to Milly, hoping that Milly will leave her fortune to him on her death. To make the scheme work—Merton only gradually realizes the full nastiness of it—they must of course continue to deceive everyone, especially Milly, about their own engagement: the world must believe that although Merton has indeed been in love with Kate, Kate now feels nothing for him and he is thus perfectly free to shift his affections to Milly. The highly intelligent, courageous—indeed in most respects admirable—Kate proceeds on a course of openly lying to Milly, even while acting in every other respect as Milly's most intimate and loving friend. Merton himself, while attending regularly on Milly, assuages his confused conscience by scrupulously refusing ever to tell an actual lie; he simply exercises his natural charm on her and thus allows the deception to proceed.

For some time their plot seems to be working: Milly becomes radiantly happy as she lives her waning life fully in a Venetian palazzo, courted, as she has increasing reason to believe, by the most charming young man she has ever known. A far less charming suitor, Lord Mark, a bland, empty-hearted moral nonentity who has been one of the vulgar aunt's candidates for marriage to Kate, arrives in Venice to win her hand. He also has learned of the fatal illness and worked out his own plan to obtain Milly's fortune through a kind of "death-bed marriage"; he makes his crude proposal to Milly and she politely and firmly refuses him. Meanwhile Merton, who has been "courting" Milly daily, though with no formal statement of intentions, is becoming increasingly uneasy about the various moral issues in his situation: he is doing all this for Kate, assuming her love for him, but what proof does he have of her love? Does she really love him enough to justify the whole plot? He insists that to prove her love she must "come to him," in his apartments rented specifically for that purpose, and the ravishingly beautiful creature, who really does love him, comes, for one night. She then returns to London, leaving him to continue his false courtship until the girl's death.

Lord Mark, having learned that Kate and Merton are in fact engaged, gets his revenge for Milly's refusal by telling her, basely, of the whole base scheme, and Milly is devastated: she "turns her face to the wall," refuses ever to see Merton again, and prepares to die. Susan, her confidante, desperately trying to save her, attempts to persuade Merton to go to her and deny the engagement to Kate, but this is a lie he refuses to tell. ("We *are*," he later moans to Kate, when she wonders, back in London, why he didn't go ahead and tell Milly that they were *not* engaged, "We *are*, my dear child, I suppose, still engaged" [X.i, 323]). He simply waits, day after day, hoping—by now more fully caught up in Milly's beautiful spirit than he can acknowledge to himself without acknowledging that he has behaved like a "brute"—that he might see her again. She finally relents, for reasons we do not learn, and invites him back for one last meeting—which we are not privileged to witness.

The final events—all of book X, considerably more than a tenth of the whole novel and, along with book V, much the longest in the book—consist entirely of Kate's and Densher's wrestling with what all this is to mean for them—how they are to live with what they have done and with what it has meant for Milly. And it is all from Densher's point of view. For several weeks he does not even visit Kate—though he still assumes their engagement. When they do meet he has received a letter from Milly, intended to be received on Christmas Eve; he has chosen not to open it except in Kate's presence. But Kate throws it into the fire, and Merton resists the impulse to rescue it and discover what Milly would say to him at the end. They soon discover, from lawyers, that a part of what she would have said is that she is after all making him, in a splendidly magnanimous gesture (or perhaps an act of revenge against Kate? we are never to know for sure just how much Milly has inferred), her heir. Learning of this, Kate is exultant: their scheme has worked. They have the money they need to marry, and they have it with Milly's blessing. Merton, however, having been awakened to a fully moral perception of the whole experience, tells Kate point-blank (or as point-blank as anyone ever tells anyone anything in this novel) that he will marry her only if she'll join him in repudiating the money; on the other hand, she can have the money—without him. She says that she'll take him, without the money, if he can swear that he is "not in love with Milly's memory." Since he refuses to do that, they separate, aware that the whole experience has changed them both and—we are left to assume—made their marriage an impossibility. We are left to speculate: Will Kate take the money? Will she marry someone as awful as Lord Mark? Has she been morally destroyed or perhaps deeply enlightened by what has happened? Readers have—for reasons that should be obvious—shown much more curiosity about her fate than about Merton's.

Appendix B:
The Story-as-Told
(The Narrative, the Discourse)

These notes might be taken as a step toward that critical act that James hoped some "literary critic" would undertake, "bent on improving his occasion to the profit of the budding artist." Or perhaps it is only a failed try at demonstrating the "attention of perusal" that he claims he wants, at every point, absolutely "to invoke and take for granted."

Page numbers are to the New York edition. Italics indicate James's operations with time scheme and points of view. (Abbreviations: M, Milly; MD, Merton; K, Kate; S, Susan Stringham; L, Mrs. Lowder [Aunt Maud]).

I.1: *Inside Kate (K)*, at age 25, for all of book I. She turns for rescue from her isolation first to her father, after living for one winter with her Aunt Maud (L). Is she already in love with Merton (MD)? (21 pp.)

I.2.: *Inside K*, living at aunt's, chronologically *before* I.1. Sees value of material things for her. Torn by "bond of blood" (32).

After chapter 1, we see, in interview with sister Marian, that Marian is obviously willing to *use* K (34). Marian warns against MD, because he means poverty for them both.

II.1.: *Inside MD*. His patient waiting for K, *before* chief events of book I (back to p. 47). The appeal of his "mind." We learn that they met *before* her mother's death: *4 pages on their first meeting, then encounter on railroad, 54. Inside both K and MD, back and forth a bit about courtship; in other words, they are "together" for a while.*

Inside K, with L for a while *after* I.1, about Mr. Croy.

K walks with MD, *with point of view alternating again,* moving to MD *alone* (61–74). K tells MD of I.1 and I.2; long discussion of the morality of Mr. Croy and K: K's self-described "small stupid piety" (71); "I do see my danger of doing something base" (72), but "I shall sacrifice nobody and nothing" (73). They plan to work on L. (27 pp.)

II.2: *Inside MD,* waiting for L. Made to *see* the meaning of wealth (4 pp.!). 6 pages of scene with report to K. MD called to America (86). *K and MD mixed point of view,* long conversations about selves and prospects, leading to engagement (95), then plans for dealing with L, letters, talk about planned deception.

Note that this concludes 100 pages, one seventh of the book, with what, from one point of view, is "only" background! Of these pages, about half are "inside" K, but much of book II is also about her, as seen through MD. Such expansiveness obviously explains James's lament about his "misplaced middle," but he understates the effect the misplacement will have in centering our emotions on K.

III.1: *Inside Susan Stringham (S). Retrospective account* of Milly's [M] earlier life: as princess, as heiress of all the ages (to 120, 18 pp.). M's view of the Alps as of the universe (through S's eyes). S's view of M's promise. *Note that we've had no real scene through this chapter, no developed conversations.*

III.2: *Inside S still, talking with M about MD.* First hints of early dying (134–45). *Note that we've had almost 150 pages with no inside view of M, who was originally at the center of James's conception!*

IV.1: *Inside M for first time,* talking with Lord Mark at a dinner party, which actually took place a *short time after III.2* — time enough for M and S to be welcomed fully by L. M baffled by all the changes. Thinks of K, a "wonderful creature." Only a very few comments from the author's own voice (159). M speculates about Lord Mark and K — clear that she herself cannot consider him as a possible mate (163). M accepts herself as a "quantity" — someone whose life has real importance (166).

IV.2: *Inside S,* speculating on their social successes, with occasional glimpses "inside" M. K and M together shop etc. (*point of view mixed, making them seem really together*). K is puzzled at not hating M for her money (176). K explains London society to M. M on K: not "brutally brutal" (182).

IV.3: *Inside both M and S, though mainly M: they are REALLY together.* They discover that the Londoners know MD (185). *Inside M* (187 and following): M increasingly aware of how much K keeps back. K's sister warns M about MD (193). Long discussion between M and S about MD and K. (10 pp.)

V.1: *Mostly inside M,* almost entirely with Lord Mark, S, L, at Matcham: culture laid on heavily, dramatizing M's "felicity" but also her puzzled speculation about K and Lord Mark. "She was somehow at this hour a very happy woman and a part of her happiness might precisely have been that her affections and her view were moving as never before in concert" (215–16). We have meanwhile been "told," in various ways that the "concert" is misguided, the felicity doomed.

V.2: *Inside M.* She is shown a Bronzino portrait said to look like her—"with her slightly Michael-angelesque squareness, her eyes of other days, her full lips, her long neck. . . . And she was dead, dead, dead." Thinking thus, M weeps—she is aware of her own mortality, yet feels that she "can never be better than this," that nothing will ever "be so right again" (211).

K then probes her about her health, M meanwhile reaching out to K for friendship: "I absolutely trust you." M asks K to go with her to see the surgeon, Sir Luke Strett. (*James is hitting hard on the dramatic irony by now, with no character knowing everything that others know.*) (12 pp.)

V.3: *Inside M.* Accompanied by K, she goes to Sir Luke Strett. Interview not shown, but she comes out from it strengthened. 3 pages of speculation about it with K. Then 2nd interview with the doctor (K not in attendance); the doctor is authoritative, sympathetic, but highly oblique: tells her she has a "great rare chance" to *live*, while implying, quite clearly, that she will soon die. (15 pp.)

V.4: *Inside M, 8 pages of interior monologue* ("several hours worth" about her situation, about whether K has told S, about why S is not more inquisitive about her health, etc.

K rushes to her in the evening to find what the doctor has said; to M she looks suddenly the way she must look when she (K) is looking at MD, and she infers—correctly, of course—that the two of them must have a "connexion" (257). She dissembles her illness to K, saying mainly, "I'm now to go in for pleasure." K makes heavy assertion of her loving desire to help—*more dramatic irony.* (13 pp.)

V.5: *Inside M.* L probes her for knowledge about whether MD has returned from America. M further senses that K and MD have a connexion, because she can read in K's eyes that MD has come back from America. (11 pp.)

V.6: *Inside M.* K instructing M about the ways of the world, claims she is "giving away" everything, including herself. But of course she is not: *more dramatic irony.* K tells M Lord Mark has shifted his goal from K to M. K: You should drop all of us, including me: "Oh, you may very well loathe me yet!" M arranges for S to learn of her illness through the doctor (286). *Intense foreshadowing*: M increasingly seen as "dove," with others as predators. (12 pp.)

V.7: *Inside M.* National Gallery. M surprises K and MD together; K covers brilliantly. M only partially deceived: she believes it is indeed a liaison, but, she thinks, one based on MD's love of K, with K indifferent. Left alone with MD, she slowly works through her feelings for him and her anxiety about what the doctor has told S. Our attention at the end of volume 1 is entirely on M, a total contrast from opening of this volume, where we were entirely interested in and concerned for K. (14 pp.)

VI.1: *Opens with privileges inside both MD and K, moves mainly "into" MD*, who is suffering sexual deprivation and is puzzled by K, who says her cleverness has grown "infernal." He does not know K's plans. (12 pp.)

VI.2: *Inside MD*. K still is not telling him her full plan; he is still frustrated about their physical separation. Two long intense embraces, partial physical satisfaction. Long discussion of how to deal with L. K hints at her plan: he should "lead M on," because K has a "beautiful plan," which she does not reveal. He wonders why she will not "come" to him. The chapter is all about her plan. (15 pp.)

VI.3: *Inside MD*. At Lowder dinner, watching the "drama" performed by L and K. A sustained account of gossip about M. Society mocked at length, as they turn M into a "Christian maiden, in the arena, mildly, caressingly, martyred" (42). L needles MD about his time in NY with M. He wonders how much K knows, "though it was not until much later on that he found himself, in thought, dividing the things she might have been conscious of from the things she must have missed" (42). MD's rising sympathy for M, friendship with S. More *foreshadowing* about what MD is to learn later: "These things were of later evidence" (46). (16 pp.)

VI.4. *Inside MD*. After dinner. MD and K discussing M. (10 pp.!) "What you want of me," MD says, "is to make up to a sick girl." MD meets Lord Mark (56), but we quickly are with MD and K alone as he puzzles through K's obliquities, for a full 7 pages. K: you and M are both my "victims." MD: "Then if anything happens, we [MD and M] can console each other" (63). *(Thus an explicit promise of what's to come.)* Briefly MD with S. (23 pp.)

VI.5: *Inside MD*. Visit to M. MD's speculation about the rights and wrongs of what he's doing. (12 pp.!) Then conversation with M. She says she'd "do anything for K." He is stricken: "He was *afterwards* to say to himself that something had at that moment hung for him by a hair" — that is, he'd almost blurted out his secret (85).

More conversation, more signs that MD finds M touching and charming. More introspection (2 pp., 88–89). 6 pages of talk between MD and K, culminating with his agreeing that everything must be left in her hands. (27 pp.)

VII.1: *Inside M. Long retrospect* to luncheon after the National Gallery (far back in V.5), and S's observations of K at that time, while MD and M were talking. What did the doctor say? S and M "fused" in loving understanding, supported by giving inside views of both and thus *fusing point of view* (103). S sees the "light" — M's chances with MD. (7 pp.)

Inside S: (transition of point of view, 106) to scenes with L, plotting for M and MD. (13 pp.!) (total of 22 pp.)

VII.2. *Inside S for 3 pages, then inside M* with the doctor. (8 pp.) Makes it clear the doctor thinks her the best person in the world; *foreshadowing* of Venice. (10 pp. on this: *It's puzzling why James spends so long within the doctor's perspective, even though this chapter is comparatively short.*)

VII.3: *Inside MD*, settling into Venice, surrounded by women. Then the *author's own voice* for a bit, with K and M "putting off masks"—but not really. See pp. 116–19 above.

  Back to M's point of view, first alone, wandering, then with Lord Mark. (14 pp.)

VII.4: *Inside M.* Lord Mark's proposal and rejection (20 pp.!), concluding with entry of MD.

VIII.1: *Inside MD.* An entire chapter of MD's moral musing: thoughts about what it means to take private apartments in order to make love to K, and about how she is manipulating him. (16 pp.)

VIII.2: *Inside MD.* Resentful of getting nothing for all the fuss, he exacts from K her agreement to come to him for a night of love. His thoughts are packed with moral speculation: he knows he is becoming corrupt. (16 pp.)

VIII.3. *Again Inside MD.* MD's rising fondness for S, love for M. M's big party for the doctor. K for the first time is "wanting in lustre," in MD's eyes. M a dove. MD and K, with MD still dense about the plan, but he finally realizes "I'm to marry her" and get the money. He agrees, only if she'll "come." (28 pp.!)

IX.1: *Inside MD*, living with aftermath of the night of love. Musing on his daily visits to M. M (naively? subtly?) tries to draw him out about why he is staying—a fairly long scene between them. (8 pp.) He is visibly trapped between two motives. (16 pp.)

IX.2: *Inside MD.* MD is turned away by M after twenty days of conversation with her. Long speculations about his moral position. Sees Lord Mark in the square. After 3 days S comes to him. (18 pp.)

IX.3: *Inside MD.* S pleads with him to rescue M by denying Lord Mark's claim. *Scene entirely in direct conversation.* MD "moans." (23 pp.)

IX.4: *Inside MD.* The doctor comes, tells MD he should now visit M again, at her request; MD says he will. A great burden is lifted. (15 pp.)

X.1: *Inside MD*, for whole of X. MD and K: Why didn't he lie? (350). He is stupefied. (20 pp.)

X.2: *Inside MD.* He and L. (*No clear function of this final time with L?*) MD: "Something has broken in me." 6 pages with K, she thinking mainly of the cash, of their "success."

X.3: *Inside MD.* Longing for news, goes to the doctor's. He has received M's final letter, but has not opened it. Scene with L, coming from the doctor. He goes to Brompton Oratory, to pray (361).

X.4: *Inside MD* at K's sister's. Lord Mark is back living with L. MD challenges K: "How in the world did he [Lord Mark] know we're engaged?" (12 pp.)

X.5: *Inside MD*. Still at sister's, dusk falling, moving to showdown. K answers challenge: Lord Mark figured it out. K on her father. Though main attention is on MD's rising moral clarity, considerable sympathy is aroused for K, as in book I. K burns M's letter, MD resists temptation to rescue it. (11 pp.)

X.6: *Inside MD*. The inverted battle over the cash: his ultimatum, either me or the cash, not both. He'll marry her still, "as we were" but "We shall never be again as we were!" (14 pp.)

    Note that all of book X is from Densher's point of view. The novel has become his moral battle.

POSTSCRIPT

Such a summary, combined with Appendix A, provides only a beginning on the kind of appreciative analysis that would do justice to the full achievement of James's creation. But perhaps a comparison of the two appendixes will be enough to suggest my grounds for the following prediction:

If, a hundred years from now, there is any sensitive historian of ideas still practicing, nothing about us will seem more absurd than our repeated undervaluing, with our reading-against, of what great authors do as they create their works. Here we have James working away month after month, at the height of his imaginative powers, making thousands of subtle, highly "personal" choices each day during the hours when he is most alive, most of those choices quite consciously directed to fulfill highly articulated and conscious intentions. And here on the other hand we find a fair number of half-baked critics, schooled in critical dogmas and unschooled in how to reconstruct the vast created edifices built by the great, pronouncing their ostensibly egalitarian dogmas about there being "no such thing as intrinsic merit." Every lover of the high achievements of any art — of classical music or jazz, of mystery writing or sci-fi, of painting or satirical cartooning — should rise up in anger about the debasement of the world that occurs when people pretend that it's all one great heap of equivalent stuff.

Notes

1. Many readers have found *The Wings of the Dove* exasperatingly difficult. In this matter, though not in his rather lukewarm final evaluation, William James speaks for us all when he says, in a letter to Henry in the fall of 1902, that he had to read "many pages, and innumerable sentences twice over to see what the dickens they could possibly mean." I must have encountered fifty moments when I had to stop, puzzled, and then choose for a pronoun the most likely antecedent (Norton 458; in my citations throughout, the first figure will refer to the Norton edition, the second to the New York edition).

2. My pages here could be filled with quotations about "use" versus "living." Milly's story is in large part her gradual discovery of how Kate Croy, Merton Densher, Lord Mark, and Mrs. Lowder would use her. As she begins, for example, to experience the lionizing of the clever but vulgar socialite, Mrs. Lowder, "it came up for Milly that Aunt Maud [Mrs. Lowder] had something particular in mind. . . . Mrs. Lowder made use of the moment: Milly felt as soon as she had spoken that what she was doing was somehow for use" (161, NY 263–64).

3. In James's works it's not easy to say which is worse, reducing people to *objets d'art*, as Gilbert Osmond in *The Portrait of a Lady* uses the wonderful Isabel, finding her "as smooth to his general need of her as handled ivory to the palm," or exploiting others for financial gain, as Kate and Densher use Milly here. I wonder whether my "use" of this novel would be more blameworthy, for James, if I were being paid a fortune for it. If the payment entailed my saying what I knew would harm someone I would become one of his worst villains.

4. Melvyn New has neatly exposed the self-contradiction exhibited by many a "proof" of unreadability. His central text is *Tristram Shandy*, and to me he succeeds in annihilating any interpretation that says: "*Tristram Shandy* wonderfully undermines all claims to a clear single reading — except mine" ("Sterne and the Narrative of Determinateness"). Of course there are some novels since Sterne's that do deliberately attempt to frustrate every attempt at a single interpretation, including the attempt to prove that they frustrate . . . , etc. (My favorite example is Nabokov's *Pale Fire* — see Peter J. Rabinowitz, "Truth in Fiction: A Re-examination of Audiences.") But their existence does not establish any ethical demand that we should read other works as totally indeterminate.

5. In chapter 4 of *The Company We Keep* I present a detailed case for the inescapable *potential* powers of works themselves. In practice not even the most aggressive theorist denies those powers, just as I of course do not

deny that a novel's powers will fail with readers not prepared to discover them.

6. Janice Radway, "Reading the Romance." The qualities and dangerous powers of popular fiction, when millions in a given culture "read-with" it, are explored by Claudia Roth Pierpont, in "A Study in Scarlett." Her chief subject is *Gone With the Wind*, but she helps explain why other blockbusters—*Uncle Tom's Cabin* and *Ivanhoe*, for example, get themselves "read-with" by so many, while yet others, aimed equally at a popular market, fail.

7. By far the most devoted and persuasive reading of this kind I've encountered, addressed to one novel alone, is Gérard Genette's tracing of Proust's maneuverings, in *Narrative Discourse*. To me it is unfortunate that Genette for the most part protects himself from the task of direct evaluation, but implicit in his loving attention is one grand judgment: *Remembrance of Things Past* is a great achievement. Even though his kind of detailed tracing is not today in the forefront of criticism, a fair number of "narratologists" are practicing the sympathetic attention to structural choices that it requires. I find even more interesting a variety of efforts to combine ideological interests—Marxist, Freudian, feminist, ethical—with the closest possible attention to authors' achieved forms; in other words, these studies have combined reading-with and reading-against without destroying the works considered. I document several of these—Barbara Foley's, James Phelan's, Peter Rabinowitz's, David Richter's—in the notes to my "The *Poetics* for a Practical Critic" (esp. nn. 15 and 29). But others are emerging, especially Mary Doyle Springer's work on the "feminist" prophecies of Wallace Stevens (a book forthcoming); see also her "Closure in James: A Formalist Feminist View." Another group of scholars are moving from what might be called the opposite side: starting with ideological questions and finding them best answered by close reading. The most impressive volume I've found pursuing this direction, published since completing this essay, is *Famous Last Words: Changes in Gender and Narrative Closure*, ed. Alison Booth. All of the "feminist" essays Booth commissioned attend closely to *intended* forms, most of them in ways that might well have impressed James. The one most relevant here, however, is by Stephen D. Arata: "Object Lessons: Reading the Museum in *The Golden Bowl*" (199–229). Many of Arata's points about the ethical effects of reading that great book could be incorporated here. But of course he does not mention the ethical effects on *him* of pursuing his critical task, or on *us* of reading the results.

8. A first-class introduction to the conflicts between the ethical demands of given genres and the ethical interests of implied authors is given by Peter Rabinowitz in "'Reader, I blew him away': Convention and Transgression in Sue Grafton," in A. Booth, *Famous Last Words*.

9. All quotations here from the *The Complete Notebooks of Henry James*, 102–7, 114–16.

10. In "The Younger Generation," as quoted in *Henry James and H. G. Wells: A Record of Their Friendship, Their Debate on the Art of Fiction, and Their Quarrel*, 190–92. An excellent brief defense of James's silence in the palazzo scene is given by Mary Doyle Springer in *A Rhetoric of Literary Character: Some Women of Henry James*, 162–63, 165–66.

Bibliography

Booth, Alison, ed. *Famous Last Words: Changes in Gender and Narrative Closure*. Charlottesville, VA: University of Virginia Press, 1993.

Booth, Wayne C. *The Company We Keep: An Ethics of Fiction*. Berkeley: University of California Press, 1988.

———. "The *Poetics* for a Practical Critic." In *Essays on Aristotle's Poetics*. Ed. by Amelie Oksenberg Rorty. Princeton: Princeton University Press, 1992. 387–408.

Genette, Gérard. *Narrative Discourse: An Essay in Method*. Trans. by Jane Levin. Ithaca: Cornell University Press, 1972.

James, Henry. *The Complete Notebooks of Henry James*. Ed. by Leon Edel and Lyall H. Powers. New York: Oxford University Press, 1987.

———. *The Wings of the Dove*. New York: Scribner's, 1909.

———. *The Wings of the Dove*. Norton Critical Edition. Ed. by J. Donald Crowley and Richard A. Hocks. New York: Norton, 1978.

———. "The Younger Generation." *Henry James and H.G. Wells: A Record of Their Friendship, Their Debate on the Art of Fiction, and Their Quarrel*. Ed. by Leon Edel and Gordon N. Ray. Urbana: University of Illinois Press, 1958.

New, Melvyn. "Sterne and the Narrative of Determinateness." *Eighteenth-Century Fiction* 4 (1992): 315–29.

Nussbaum, Martha G. "Flawed Crystals: James's *The Golden Bowl* and Literature as Moral Philosophy." In *Love's Knowledge*. New York: Oxford University Press, 1990.

Phelan, James. *Reading People, Reading Plots: Character, Progression, and the Interpretation of Narrative*. Chicago: University of Chicago Press, 1989.

Pierpont, Claudia Roth. "A Study in Scarlett." *New Yorker* 31 August 1992: 87–103.

Rabinowitz, Peter J. "Truth in Fiction: A Re-examination of Audiences." *Critical Inquiry* 4 (1977): 121–41.

———. "Against Close Reading." *Pedagogy as Politics: Literary Theory and*

Critical Teaching. Ed. by Maria-Regina Kecht. Urbana: University of Illinois Press, 1992.

Radway, Janice A. *Reading the Romance: Women, Patriarchy, and Popular Literature*. Chapel Hill: University of North Carolina Press, 1984.

Springer, Mary Doyle. *A Rhetoric of Literary Character: Some Women of Henry James*. Chicago: University of Chicago Press, 1978.

_____. "Closure in James: A Formalist Feminist View." In *A Companion to Henry James Studies*. Ed. by Daniel Mark Fogel. Westport, CT: Greenwood Press, 1993. 265–82.

5

Picturing Spectatorship

JUDITH MAYNE

Textual analysis is one of the most important theoretical and practical legacies of 1970s film theory. Recent film theory has moved, as Kaja Silverman has argued, from semiotics to psychoanalysis, with attendant shifts in the notion of the subject, and the changing dimensions of textual analysis in film studies reflect that shift. If Christian Metz's early semiotic analysis in *Film Language* was concerned with specifying the conditions of coherence in narrative film, Raymond Bellour's notion of coherence had far more to do with the "subject" of the film, the ideal yet always imaginary spectator to whom coherence is addressed ("Le blocage symbolique"). Indeed, fictions about the film spectator have shaped the development of textual analysis in film studies, and in that sense textual analysis engages centrally with spectatorship, with the various components of vision, identification, and pleasure that have characterized the way film viewing is constructed.

In the last decade, the field of film studies has undergone considerable shifts, and the theoretical pronouncements of the 1970s, particularly those having to do with psychoanalysis, have been reexamined and sometimes ridiculed. It may well be true that textual analyses of the 1970s relied too exclusively on the formal and technological aspects of the cinema, and therefore gave exclusive signifying authority to the individual film and ignored the complex nature of the cinematic institution. And by exploring in exhaustive detail the signifying structures of the individual film, textual analysis created film texts that had only the most remote connection with the ways in which films are actually received (an issue which has not been ignored by practitioners of textual analysis; see Bellour, "Le blocage symbolique"). Textual analysis might also be criticized for resurrecting the old dichotomy of text and context, privileging the former and ignoring the latter.

The textual analyses that have become "classics" of film theory are virtually all performed on classical Hollywood films: Stephen Heath's detailed reading of *Touch of Evil* ("Film and System"), Raymond Bellour's analyses of a number of films by Hitchcock, especially *North by Northwest* ("Le blocage symbolique"), Thierry Kuntzel's analysis of *The Most Dangerous Game* ("The Film-Work"). While these analyses are different in scope, they share an emphasis on understanding a classical film narrative as a system of interweaving oppositions, a system that is threatened and restored, corresponding to the overall movement of plot, narrative, and *mise-en-scène*. Virtually without exception, the "threat" has something to do with Woman. The classical Hollywood system thus excavated by textual analysis is located at the intersection of structuralism — concerned with the various codes that make exchange possible, a privileged mode of which is the exchange of women; and psychoanalysis — concerned with the various ways in which sexual difference is displaced, denied, or otherwise negotiated.

At the same time, textual analysis in film studies is marked by the transition from semiotic studies of narrative, concerned with the overall modes of coherence and stability in the text, to post-structuralist studies, concerned more with what exceeds or puts into question those very modes of coherence and stability. While this shift has influenced virtually all areas of contemporary theoretical endeavor, the changing status of textual analysis in film studies nonetheless represents a particularly important area of inquiry. For the classical Hollywood film, the preferred object for textual analysis, is the kind of dominant, transparently realist text which would, in a classical structuralist analysis, lend itself quite easily to the discernment of a series of predictable patterns. But through the lens of poststructuralism, classical film puts into question the very notion of a dominant text, realist or otherwise. The influence of Roland Barthes' detailed analysis of "Sarrasine," a novella by Balzac, in *S/Z*, cannot be overestimated in this context. Just as the classical narrative cinema would appear, in structuralist terms, to be perfectly "readerly," so it would acquire, in poststructuralist terms, a "writerly" status informed at the very least by a notion of "limited plurality."

When described in the somewhat "classical" structuralist terms of opposition and resolution, one could assume mistakenly that textual analysis is concerned with form and structure in a purely aesthetic or thematic sense. In truth, textual analysis in film studies was linked with psychoanalysis, particularly insofar as theories of the subject were concerned; and to a lesser extent with Marxism, particularly insofar as the Althusserian notions of symptomatic reading and interpellation were concerned. Despite the efforts of many theorists to separate absolutely the "subject" from the "viewer"; that is, the "position" from the "body," some slippage occurs, and as a result one of the legacies of textual analysis is a notion of the film viewer as held, contained, or otherwise manipulated by the mechanisms of a cinematic institution which finds its most succinct expression in the various textual strategies of delay, resolution, and containment which engage the spectator. The psychoanalytic and ideological ramifications here are fairly obvious, in both cases connected to a concept of regulation.

The legacy of psychoanalysis for textual analysis has been ambiguous, due in part to an unfortunate tendency to collapse the unconscious with ideology, to tame the unconscious and transform it into another predictable crisis of male subjectivity. Yet a far more pervasive and important psychoanalytic influence is the assumption that whenever a structure is created or imposed, something is repressed. The process of textual analysis therefore is the attempt to retrace the evolution of structure and its attendant process of repression. The assumption is that the film text functions for the spectator in much the same way that Freud saw works of art, as particularly condensed instances of unconscious processes, desires, and fantasies. At the same time, this particular psychoana-lytic influence was mediated by Althusserian Marxism, specifically insofar as "symptomatic readings" were concerned—for instance, the assumption that within any structure there remains a symptom of what has been repressed or marginalized.

I note above the importance of the concept of spectatorship for textual analysis of the classical Hollywood cinema. There has been considerable debate in film studies about whether the "spectator" in spectatorship is the subject of the film, the viewer in the movie theater, or both (see Bergstrom and Doane). I find the notion of spec-tatorship most productive when textual analysis attends to the spaces between the various "positions" one can deduce by analyzing the narrative patterns of a film, and to the hypothetical responses of viewers, which are never adequately understood as pure "positions." I want to explore the relationship between textual analysis and specta-torship by focusing on a particular case study, the trope of portrai-ture and its narrative function in a 1945 film directed by Albert Lewin, *The Picture of Dorian Gray*. Like many of the films that have been immortalized (at least within film studies) through textual analysis, this film demonstrates a visible and foregrounded preoc-cupation with spectatorship. To some extent, of course, *all* films do; the advantage, however, of analyzing a film so visibly preoccupied with spectatorship is obvious, since it is an opportunity to observe how the classical cinema creates a narrative about itself, how it en-gages in self-reflexive myth-making. *The Picture of Dorian Gray* is also interesting in that in order to designate a space for viewing, it must engage with potentially controversial material, the most obvious being the gay persona of Oscar Wilde and the gay implications of the novella upon which the film is based. It is not my purpose here to enter into the question of censorship and the impact of the production code on this film, although it is worth noting that one of the most interesting developments in textual analysis of recent years is the exploration of the interaction between film texts and industry texts. Indeed, critics like Mary Beth Haralovich, Lea Jacobs, and Annette Kuhn have suggested that censorship was a dynamic, complex relationship, and not one of simple negativity.

The director of *The Picture of Dorian Gray*, Albert Lewin, directed only six films, and all of them demonstrate a peculiar blend of the Hollywood commonplace and the excessive (particularly true of *Pandora and the Flying Dutchman* [1951]). In his *A Biographical Dictionary of Film*, David Thomson says of Lewin's films that "arty aspiration showed like a teenage slip" (347). *The Picture of Dorian Gray* is both exceptional and typical; exceptional in that it has obvious pretensions to artistic sensibility and upper-class mores, and typical in that it reflects a core structure evident across a wide range of classical Hollywood films. The question of typicality is a nagging one for textual analysis, although the question may have more to do with excessive claims for an analysis than with the film under scrutiny. The use of textual analysis to find "a" subject position that typifies "the" classical cinema is both futile and pretentious. Rather, individual films—which are always a blend of the typical and the exceptional—offer, through the lens of textual analysis, a series of hypotheses about the varieties of spectatorship. *The Picture of Dorian Gray* may lean a bit more toward the exceptional than the typical, but the figures of spectatorship drawn in the film find parallels in other films.

It is not my intention to engage in a detailed textual analysis of the film. In any case, textual analysis is less a matter of exhaustiveness than of strategy—the recognition, say, that a detail which might initially appear insignificant provides a perspective from which other seemingly insignificant details suddenly emerge in another kind of coherence, or that within the large oppositions that form the overall structure of the film, there is nonetheless a pressure, a sense of something always at the horizon or on the edge of the opposition. It would of course be ludicrous to assume that what I, in the name of film theory and academic film studies, see in my reading of an individual film is necessarily what any and all spectators will see. Unfortunately, ludicrous or not, some practitioners of textual analysis do seem to assume that the critic uncovers an unconscious of the text, and that the unconscious of the viewer is inscribed in the text. While the notion of a textual unconscious is crucial to the development of film studies, the

necessarily metaphoric implications of that assumption are frequently lost. For texts may inspire unconscious responses, but they
don't "have" an unconscious—only people do.

In Oscar Wilde's 1891 novella, a triangle connects three men—
Dorian Gray, a handsome aristocratic young man; Basil Hallward, a
painter; and Lord Henry Wotton, an idle aristocrat who assumes a
tutorial role of sorts in relationship to Dorian. The novella opens as
Basil puts the final touches to his portrait of Dorian. In the presence
of both Basil and Lord Henry, Dorian makes his fatal wish: "If it
were I who was to be always young, and the picture that was to
grow old! For that—for that—I would give everything!" (42). Influenced by Lord Henry's philosophy, Dorian pursues pleasure for its
own sake. During an outing to a London slum, he happens across a
theater where Shakespeare is being performed. The star of the
show is a young actress, Sibyl Vane. She possesses an uncanny gift
for performance which is highlighted even more by the incompe-
tence of her colleagues. Dorian immediately falls in love. When he
brings his two male friends to observe Sibyl's talents, however, she
is wooden and dull.

Sibyl later explains that since she found love with Dorian, she is
no longer capable of performing well. That is, having found "art" in
the realm of everyday life, she can no longer produce it. Dorian
promptly abandons Sibyl. She commits suicide, after which Dorian
begins to degenerate—in several senses of the word. But the
changes in Dorian's life are manifested not in his own body, but in
Basil's portrait of him. Dorian eventually shows Basil the transformed portrait, and then murders him. While attempting to
destroy the painting, Dorian himself dies. His body finally records
the changes previously visible only in the painting, while the
painting is restored to its original state.

Even though Wilde's *The Picture of Dorian Gray* is superficially
about heterosexual love, it is widely recognized as gay in inspiration and in its none-too-subterranean subtext. As Richard Ellmann
writes, for instance, "More than any other writer of his time in
England, Wilde recognized that homosexuality was the great un-
dercover subject. . . . To express his point of view as directly as he

could, Wilde wrote *The Picture of Dorian Gray*. . . . Wilde was attacked for immorality, but he had cagily left Dorian's sin unspecified, while clearly implying involvements with both sexes" (6). It comes as no great surprise that the most significant changes made in the adaptation of Wilde's novella to the screen involve the foregrounding of heterosexual desire as the motor force of the film. True, the relationship between Dorian and Sibyl (with Sibyl now a singer in a music hall) functions in the film as in the novella to render somewhat ambiguous the simultaneous identification and desire between Dorian and the two principal men in his life. But another female character is added to the film, Gladys, the niece of painter Basil Hallward. Lewin's film begins, as does the novella, with the completion of the portrait of Dorian, but with the difference that a female signature is added to the painting—Gladys is portrayed as a small child who puts the letter "G" under her uncle's signature. After Sibyl's suicide (provoked in the film by Dorian's rejection of her, only now as a result of failing to refuse when Dorian invites her to spend the night with him), the passage of time allows Gladys to mature into a young woman whose childish devotion becomes adult love for Dorian, with somewhat incestuous overtones since Dorian is so closely affiliated with Gladys's uncle. In the film, Dorian asks Gladys to marry him in an attempt to reform and to atone for his guilt over Sibyl's suicide. The same desire for salvation motivates his destruction of the painting, and—as in the novella—he dies while the painting is restored to its original state.

While the character of Gladys lends a more obvious heterosexual component to the film, there is a link between her and the Wilde novella. Two minor female characters in the novella—one actually named Gladys—have some connection with the film character; one is a hostess at a gathering attended by Dorian and Lord Henry, and the other is Hetty, a briefly mentioned "village girl" abandoned by Dorian to protect her from inevitable corruption through his influence. Most important, however, is the familial connection established with Basil Hallward, since the character of Gladys is largely created by dividing the character of Basil in two. Thus Gladys, present at the portrait sitting and cosigner of the portrait, becomes a figure upon whom is displaced any possible sexual attraction between Basil and Dorian.

The addition of Gladys to the film divides the film into two distinct parts, the first dominated by Dorian's relationship with Sibyl, the second by his relationship with Gladys. As objects of Dorian's affections, the two women are not typed according to the virgin/whore dichotomy, but rather according to a dichotomy of class as well as of performance—Sibyl the performer, Gladys a perpetual onlooker. There is a symmetry as well in the representation of the two women, particularly insofar as their male protectors are concerned—Sibyl's brother James, who dies when he attempts to kill Dorian in revenge for his sister's suicide, and Gladys's sometime suitor David, who discovers the secret of Dorian's painting in an effort to obstruct their marriage by whatever possible means.

In what has become known as typical of the classical cinema, then, *The Picture of Dorian Gray* is structured by a series of rhyming oppositions, and the restoration of order in the film occurs when the painting is restored to its original status, and Gladys and David are united in a relationship that is free of the somewhat incestuous overtones of a possible relationship between Dorian and Gladys. The most obvious and foregrounded oppositions in the film center on the representation of the portrait. While Dorian's portrait is described in Wilde's novella, it is not a description that is—to use Roland Barthes's term—"operable"; that is, much of the force of the portrait in the novella is a result of its status as a function of discourse. Not only is the portrait shown in Lewin's film, but its display introduces a striking opposition between black and white and color, for the display of the portrait at three crucial moments in the film occasions the use of glorious technicolor. The use of color gives the painting(s) a certain autonomy, and also makes the difference between the early and late versions of the painting all the more striking.

In one of the most influential essays analyzing film narrative, "Narrative Space," Stephen Heath begins with an analysis of a scene in Hitchcock's *Suspicion*. Two policemen arrive at Lina's (played by Joan Fontaine) home. A play is established in this scene between two paintings, one the realistic portrait of Lina's father which functions as a constant reminder of his law and authority, the other a somewhat abstract "modernist" painting hanging on the wall in the entry hall to the house, and toward which the puzzled attention of one of the policemen is drawn as he enters and again as he leaves. The scene in question demonstrates the construction of narrative space, as a "perfectly symmetrical patterning [that] builds up and pieces together the space in which the action can take place, the space which is itself part of that action in its economy, its intelligibility, its own legality" (20). The tension between the two paintings, one traditional, one modernist, and the function of the modernist painting as "useless" serve "to demonstrate the rectitude of the portrait, the true painting at the centre of the scene, utterly in frame in the film's action" (23). The implication in Heath's analysis is both that the classical cinema constructs a narrative space controlled by the order represented by the father's portrait, and that always at the edges of this construction are the possibilities, so forcefully demonstrated in the Hitchcock scene, of "missing spectacle: problem of point of view, different framing, disturbance of the law and its inspectoring eye, interruption of the homogeneity of the narrative economy, it is somewhere else again, another scene, another story, another space" (24).

A common assumption about textual analysis, and about Heath's contributions to it, is that whatever ruptures, disturbances, or differences emerge are smoothed over and contained by the homogenizing force of classical film narrative. While this is true of some textual analysis, I do not think it is an accurate assessment of Heath's work. This analysis of the scene in *Suspicion* may demonstrate how the articulation of space in classical film narrative marginalizes and relegates to "uselessness" figurations that threaten to upset its order. But the analysis suggests just as forcefully the way in which classical narrative engages in a constant process of negotiation, of flirtation with its own margins. To be sure, no film directed by Hitchcock can be taken as representative of classical Hollywood as a whole—despite claims to the contrary by those who have analyzed the mechanisms of male desire in his films — and the whole painting episode could perhaps be described as a typical "Hitchcock joke," as Heath suggests. But the scene analyzed by Heath finds echoes in other classical Hollywood films. The portrait of Dorian Gray does not occupy the center of *The Picture of Dorian Gray* in the same way as the father's portrait in *Suspicion*; in Hitchcock's film, the portrait is a metaphoric condensation of the authority that dominates Lina and the film, whereas in Lewin's film, the portrait is much more literally the focus of the film. Yet I find echoes of the scene analyzed by Heath in *The Picture of Dorian Gray*, specifically insofar as the articulation of narrative space is concerned.

In the film, a mode of spectatorship is constructed in which there are clear and sharp divisions between innocence and corruption, yet those very divisions are more permeable than they first appear. Spectatorship as it is defined in the film operates on two levels. The first has to do with the portrait itself and the responses to it, with the narcissism of Dorian Gray and the nurturance it finds in Lord Henry, all defined as the excesses which the film must put right — all variations on the common theme of male specular identity, of men as mirrors for other men. The second has to do with how the film constructs a scenography that evokes certain codes and conventions of painting, but in ways more diffuse than merely using literal portraits within the film. Here the objects of such painting-inspired *mise-en-scène* are usually women. Put another way, portraiture in *The Picture of Dorian Gray* occurs on two levels, only one of which has to do with the actual portrait itself; the implications of framing and *mise-en-scène* united the two different levels. Yet the levels are separated by the difference between men and women.

The Picture of Dorian Gray begins with Lord Henry in a carriage on his way to Basil's. While Lord Henry reads, a male narrator speaks in voice-over: "Lord Henry Wotton had set himself early in life to the serious and great aristocratic art of doing absolutely nothing. He lived only for pleasure, but his greatest pleasure was to observe the emotions of his friends while experiencing none of his own. He diverted himself by exercising a subtle influence on the lives of others." The form of spectatorship sketched out here is situated immediately within the realm of an aristocratic aesthete's ideal pleasures. Once he has arrived at Basil's studio, to which he has come out of curiosity about the secrecy of Basil's current painting project, the three men who form the core of Wilde's novella are introduced. Each man performs the activity that will define his spectatorial role throughout the film: Basil creates, Dorian poses and eventually contemplates his own image, and Lord Henry chases and captures a butterfly—presumably yet another metaphoric activity for observing the emotions of others and influencing (not so subtly in this case) their lives. An equivalence is established between these activities as well, since Lord Henry pursues his butterfly at the same time that Basil puts the finishing touches on his portrait and Dorian poses. A dissolve from the live creature, to the dead mounted butterfly, to the portrait makes a clear connection between killing a creature and immortalizing it through art.

While Lord Henry does function in the film, as in the novella, to present a philosophy of pleasure to Dorian, he functions far more obviously in the film as a spectator, to the extent that the portrait is initially as shrouded in secrecy to the viewer as it is to Lord Henry. Rarely if ever do such spectators within the film function unequivocally in the "positions" of address that spectators are assumed to adopt (see Browne). But that a voice-over narrator, never associated with any single character in the film, introduces and contextualizes Lord Henry makes it even more difficult to identify Lord Henry as an authoritative presence in any simple sense. Rather, the central terms of spectatorship in the film are defined by the two polarities which Dorian and Lord Henry represent: for Dorian, mesmerized absorption in his own image; for Lord Henry, somewhat distanced detachment. Basil's role as an artist combines both forms of spectatorship without succumbing to either extreme—he is absorbed and obsessed by his painting, but with the image of another.

While the display of the painting occurs early in the film, in Basil's studio, its appearance is accompanied by enough delay and foregrounding to make the painting the central enigmatic object of the film. Our first sight of the painting coincides with Dorian's first look at the finished product. The portrait is thoroughly realist, an example of classical portraiture. The portrait also is a straightforward representation of what has been seen of Dorian, with two important exceptions—the painting is presented in technicolor, and whereas Dorian has posed for the final moments of his sitting before a painting depicting a group of women bathers, the background to his portrait is blank (figs. 1, 2). The other objects surrounding him—a highbacked chair, a statue of a cat, and a clock—remain in the painting, so that the only erasure is that of the painting. The finished portrait is, of course, entirely in keeping with conventional portraiture, but what remains a matter of some curiosity is the placement of the painting of the women bathers in the first place. This painting is not insignificant in the initial *mise-en-scène* of the studio, since it creates a rhyming structure, against which the still unseen portrait of Dorian is measured.

The next view afforded of the painting occurs within the context of Dorian and Sibyl's relationship. Knowing that Dorian intends to marry Sibyl, Lord Henry has suggested that Dorian test her by

FIGURE 1

FIGURE 2

asking her to spend the night. If she refuses, then she is truly the
superior creature that Dorian believes her to be; if not, then Dorian
will know not to marry her. But when Dorian asks her to spend the
night, she agrees, and Dorian promptly rejects her. The rejection
leads to her suicide, after which the portrait of Dorian is shown
(again in technicolor) with a subtle change: the appearance of what
the narrator, in voice-over, describes as a "cruel look about the
mouth" (fig. 3).

The painting is not seen again until it has been completely
transformed, with Dorian portrayed as a grotesque old man whose
image records the kind of life he leads. The style of the painting has
also changed. It is now in an expressionist mode, with excessive
strokes, bold colors, and a myriad of indistinguishable objects
within the frame (fig. 4). The revelation occurs after Basil has seen
the changes that have occurred in his painting, and Dorian murders him. Whereas Sibyl's death caused the "cruel look about the
mouth" in the earlier painting, Dorian's murder of Basil causes
blood to form on the hands of the deformed and deranged Dorian
represented in the later version. Curiously, there is a change as well
in the sexual quality of the transformed painting. While the

FIGURE 3

evocation of aristocratic wealth in the film allows gay sexuality to be summoned and repressed simultaneously in the name of effete taste and effeminate behavior presumed to be characteristic of the wealthy, there is nonetheless a delicate androgyny in the figure of Dorian represented in the first version of the painting. If the women bathers have disappeared in the portrait, it would be just as easy to see them as having been absorbed into it. But in the final painting, Dorian has become a parody of deranged masculinity.

The most striking changes in the painting, then, are the transformation of a young, somewhat androgynous gentleman into a decrepit old man, and the shift in style from realism to expressionism. The painting changes location, as well. The first part of *The Picture of Dorian Gray*, concerned with the relationship between Dorian and Sibyl, and with the painting as an accurate projection of what we see, contrasts two radically different spaces, the aristocratic home (whether Dorian's or Basil's) and the music hall where Sibyl Vane performs, and where Dorian is treated in awe as a gentleman. The second part of the film, taken up with Dorian's relationship with the grown-up Gladys, contrasts two spaces within the house. When Dorian first notices, the "cruel look about the mouth" in the painting, he decides to hide it away in a room at the

FIGURE 4

top of the stairs. The narrator describes Dorian's decision: "It would be mayhem to allow the thing to remain, even for an hour. Even in a room to which only his friends had access. Henceforth he must always be on his guard. Against everyone. At the top of the house was his old schoolroom, which had not been used for years. No one ever entered it. . . ." The painting thus acquires an aura of secrecy that rhymes with the opening of the film, but transforms secrecy into a threat.

Whereas Dorian negotiated comfortably the spatial opposition between two radically different class environments characteristic of the first part of the film, the tension generated between the two areas of the house initiates conflict heretofore absent, with the added component of temporal opposition as well—the schoolroom is virtually the only reference in the film to Dorian's childhood. While the room is not often shown, it acquires narrative importance. The narrator says, for instance, that "He could not endure to be long out of England or to be separated from the picture. It was such a part of his life." The self-absorption present in the first part of the film is here quite literal. The risk of homosexual implications is managed by drawing an imaginary line across the threshold to the room, a line crossed only by men and never by women, thus identifying bonds between men with the past of childhood.

If the problem generated by the play of the two paintings in *Suspicion* concerns the authority of the father under siege, in this film there is no such equivalence between the classical, realist portraiture of the painting and an authoritative order. Rather, the two versions of the painting are both threats to an implied order, an order which can only be set right by the realignment of reality and representation, and the emergence of that legendary resolution principle for which the classical Hollywood cinema is so famous and so derided — the happy heterosexual couple. For once the death of Dorian brackets the incestuous overtones of his relationship with Gladys, and once the restoration of the portrait to its original state and Dorian's accompanying death erase implicit homosexuality, the male-female couple, Gladys and her patient suitor David, can be united.

What remain a matter of some curiosity in this relationship among male/female, homosexual/heterosexual, and incestuous/ nonincestuous pairs, however, are the different ways painting is evoked in the film to articulate narrative space. For while the portrait of Dorian and its changing status is the obvious center of the film, other devices of *mise-en-scène* partake of the conventions of painting. Particularly striking in this context is an opposition established early in the film between the portraiture of men and the framing of women. Basil's studio is defined as belonging to a community of men, with women framed in a literal and ostensible way. Before Dorian's arrival at the studio at the beginning of the film, Basil and Lord Henry are seated in the garden. In the background we see a woman sewing, framed in a doorway (fig. 5). The pose and the framing are familiar representations of women in Western oil painting, with the woman depicted as if she is observed, unawares, while engaged in a solitary activity, and of which Jean-Honoré Fragonard's "A Young Girl Reading" (1776) is one representative example. Men are defined in terms of how they "look," in both senses of the word, while women are defined in terms of how they look in only one sense of the word. That the only

FIGURE 5

living, breathing female in this scene is the child Gladys emphasizes the rigid sexual hierarchy at work. And Gladys herself enters
the scene of the studio through a doorway, while the construction
of the shot echoes the scene outdoors.

So far, this sounds like the standard "man looks, woman is
looked at" argument—for instance, that painting establishes only
an apparent equivalence between the male and female object of the
look, one betrayed by the status of woman as only the object of the
look (see Mulvey). The matter of curiosity to which I have referred,
however, is that the mostly anonymous women who are framed in
the film are done so in relationship to the position of the spectator,
not in relationship to the three male figures whose spectatorial
activities function so centrally. The composition of the woman in
the doorway engaged in a solitary activity is repeated when the
three men go to the "Two Turtles" to see Sybil Vane perform. We see
Sibyl before them, singing in front of a *trompe-l'oeil* storefront.
Behind the three men, at the opposite end of the theatre, is an
office, where a woman is seen through the open door at work at a
desk (fig. 6). At one point during the performance, we see the stage
at such an angle that images of women, framed identically, are seen

FIGURE 6

on three levels: Sibyl on stage, her mother backstage sewing, and a woman dressing before a mirror (fig. 7). Although these women so obsessively framed within doorways or stages are stereotypical objects of the presumably male gaze, there is a curious contradiction. For the male "spectators" — Dorian, Basil, Lord Henry — seem to be less interested in the spectacle before their eyes, and more interested in each other. And while each of the women is, on her own terms, given a fairly straightforward "frame" of representation, the juxtaposition of the three levels creates an odd, asymmetrical effect. Between the first image of the woman framed in the doorway and the image of the three women, there is a relationship not unlike that between the original and transformed portrait of Dorian, between a conventional composition and a much more excessive one.

It is also curious that while this element of framing has been written about extensively in relationship to gender in film, in this case social class is as much of a determination as gender; at the very least, the device of framing results from the intersection of class and gender determinations. For the woman framed in the doorway at the beginning of the film is a servant, and the women seen at the

FIGURE 7

Two Turtles are defined not just by their sexual status but by their class status as well. While it is much more common for women to be represented as "framed," there are some instances where men— either working-class men at the music hall, or servants—are framed in ways similar to that of the woman sewing. At several moments in the film, servants are portrayed standing stiffly at attention while the wealthy people they serve eat or converse, and the effect is quite similar to that of the woman-in-the-doorway motif.

I am suggesting, then, that the trope of portraiture is a figure of spectatorship to the extent that, in each case, a mode of observation—from narcissistic self-absorption to detached mockery—is foregrounded. There is no single position authorized by each individual instance of portraiture, from Dorian's portrait to the framing of women and servants; rather, spectatorship takes shape as the possible relationships among these different views and their corresponding sites of observation. What seems to me most crucial about this particular example is that it puts into question the automatic equivalence some have assumed between spectatorship in the classical cinema and men possessing women. Not that men don't possess women in this film, but here "possession" is a complex process involving the negotiation and denial of male homoerotic bonds. In addition, the intersection between gender and class in the film does not reduce in any obvious way to a "pure" example of sexual difference, since the notion of property is so excessively defined in class terms as well as gendered ones.

As an instance of that ubiquitous entity, the classical Hollywood cinema, *The Picture of Dorian Gray* is both typical and atypical, as undoubtedly is any Hollywood film. Like many literary adaptations of the 1940s, there is a self-aggrandizing quality about the film, and the numerous references to high art and aristocratic privilege serve simultaneously as windows to a fantasyland and as a self-promoting strategy. Yet unlike other films of the 1940s which deploy opposing definitions of "realist" versus "modern" art in order to elevate the status of the former at the expense of the latter (Waldman), Lewin's film does not condemn any particular version of the aesthetic as inherently corrupt; rather, any and all forms of representation are susceptible to excess. Within the specularity of portraiture in the film is the suggestion that spectatorship involves the simultaneous erection and dissolution of boundaries. Does this therefore mean that *The Picture of Dorian Gray* is "subversive," the exception to the rule of classical cinema? I think not. That a film like *The Picture of Dorian Gray* sits so comforably within the classical cinema, while engaging with an undeniable homoerotic component of spectatorship (at least as far as men are concerned), suggests that textual analysis will perhaps always uncover forms of spectatorship that both conform to and exceed what is assumed to be typical.

Bibliography

Barthes, Roland. *S/Z*. Trans. by Richard Miller. New York: Hill and Wang, 1974.

Bellour, Raymond. "Le blocage symbolique." *Communications* 23 (1975): 235–350. (Special issue on Cinema and Psychoanalysis.)

_____. "The Unattainable Text." *Screen* 16.3 (1975): 19–27.

Bergstrom, Janet and Mary Ann Doane, eds. *Camera Obscura* 21 (1989). (Special issue on The Spectatrix.)

Browne, Nick. "The Spectator-in-the-Text: The Rhetoric of *Stagecoach*." *Film Quarterly* 29.2 (1975–76): 26–38.

Ellmann, Richard. "A Late Victorian Love Affair." In *Oscar Wilde: Two Approaches*. Ed. by Richard Ellmann and John Espey. Los Angeles: University of California Press, 1977.

Haralovich, Mary Beth. "The Proletarian Woman's Film of the 1930s: Contending with Censorship and Entertainment." *Screen* 31.2 (1990): 172–87.

Heath, Stephen. "Film and System: Terms of Analysis." *Screen* 16.1 (1975): 7–77; 16.2 (1975): 91–113.

_____. "Narrative Space." 1976. In *Questions of Cinema*. Bloomington: Indiana University Press, 1981. 19–75.

Jacobs, Lea. "Censorship and the Fallen Woman Cycle." In *Home Is Where the Heart Is: Studies in Melodrama and the Woman's Film*. Ed. by Christine Gledhill. London: British Film Institute, 1987. 100–112.

_____. "The Censorship of *Blonde Venus*: Textual Analysis and Historical Methods." *Cinema Journal* 27.3 (1988): 21–31.

_____. *The Wages of Sin: Censorship and the Fallen Woman Film, 1928–1942*. Madison: University of Wisconsin Press, 1991.

Kuhn, Annette. *Cinema, Censorship and Sexuality, 1909–1925*. London: Routledge, 1988.

Kuntzel, Thierry. "The Film-Work." *Enclitic* 2.1 (1978): 39–62.

Metz, Christian. *Film Language: A Semiotics of the Cinema*. Trans. by Michael Taylor. New York: Oxford University Press, 1975.

Mulvey, Laura. "Visual Pleasure and Narrative Cinema." *Screen* 16.3 (1975): 6–18.

Silverman, Kaja. *The Subject of Semiotics*. New York: Oxford University Press, 1983.

Thomson, David. *A Biographical Dictionary of Film*. 2nd ed. New York: Morrow Quill, 1981.

Waldman, Diane. "The Childish, the Insane and the Ugly: The Representation of Modern Art in Popular Films and Fiction of the Forties." *Wide Angle* 5.2 (1982): 52–65.

Wilde, Oscar. *The Picture of Dorian Gray*. 1891. New York: New American Library, 1962.

6

"How Did You Know He Licked His Lips?": Second Person Knowledge and First Person Power in *The Maltese Falcon*

PETER J. RABINOWITZ

"What Do You Want Us to Think the Facts Are?"
Epistemology and Detective Fiction

Classification is an occupational hazard for any theorist of detective stories—in part because there are so many convenient but competing axes for sorting them out. You can, for instance, differentiate novels according to the location of the guilt they uncover— say, between Hercule Poirot stories (where detective and criminal are kept rigorously separate) and Oedipal stories (where, as in William Faulkner's *Intruder in the Dust* or Raymond Chandler's *The*

A very much shorter version of this essay was delivered at the International Conference on Narrative at Vanderbilt University in April 1992. Thanks are due to members of the audience whose questions helped me sharpen my arguments. Thanks are due, as well, to Brian Richardson for aid in tracking down both second person texts and criticism about them, and to Barbara Andrews, James Phelan, Nancy Rabinowitz, Percy Walton, and Nancy Warren for detailed commentary on earlier drafts, and to Michael S. Rabinowitz for editorial assistance.

Big Sleep, a key discovery is a discovery of the detective's own guilt). Alternatively, you can organize them according to their treatment of time—between backward-facing stories (for instance, Sir Arthur Conan Doyle's *A Study in Scarlet*) where the key events precede the detective's intervention, and stories where the primary events are those provoked by the investigation itself—say, Sara Paretsky's *Bitter Medicine*. It is also popular to distinguish stories stylistically, as between classical British and hard-boiled American.

In this essay I want to work along another axis, looking at detective stories in terms of the way they conceptualize the nature of truth. Mikhail Bakhtin argues that "when the novel becomes the dominant genre, epistemology becomes the dominant discipline" (15), and from this perspective the detective story would seem one of the most novelistic of subgenres. Granted, this is complex terrain that engages a number of intersecting questions, both epistemological *and* metaphysical. Nonetheless, I think we can draw a crucial, if rough, dividing line between two sorts of texts. The first relies on what we might call the Fort Knox notion of truth, a phrase with a double resonance for connoisseurs of early detective fiction, since one of the first attempts to chart out the "rules" for classical detective novels was Ronald Knox's "A Detective Story Decalogue." Fort Knox novels, often embodying positions associated with empiricism, realism, and especially positivism (as Knox puts it, "all supernatural or preternatural agencies are ruled out as a matter of course" [194]), rest on the twin assumptions that the truth exists and that it can be found through rational procedures. That is, their plots are constructed on the belief that the truth value of a particular claim can be determined according to some external and transcendent standard independent of the perspective or context of the individual making the claim, a standard that is available to the skilled detective. Most traditional detectives, from Oedipus and Sherlock Holmes through Mike Hammer and Travis McGee, take the Fort Knox position, assuming, as Michael Holquist puts it, that "the mind, given enough time, can understand everything" (141). Indeed, Ellery Queen built the notion of an independent standard and a single solution into the very format of some of his best novels, offering an explicit challenge to the reader at the point where all the necessary information to reach the one right answer had been provided.

Even many of the traditional novels that appear to trifle with these conventions end up firmly wedded to them. Queen's *Ten Days' Wonder*, for example, reads in part as a subversion of the Fort Knox position, suggesting that more than one solution might fit the available facts. Still, in the end, the novel does not equivocate about what really happened: we may be tricked by false stories, but there is ultimately a difference between true and false accounts, and they can be distinguished in practice, if not always in time to prevent misfortune. Similarly, Anthony Berkeley's *The Poisoned Chocolates Case*, which multiplies the number of possible explanations, ultimately determines one to be the true story.

In contrast, such postmodern detectives as Jacques Revel (in Michel Butor's *L'Emploi du temps* [*Passing Time*]) or Witold (in Witold Gombrowicz's *Cosmos*) resist the siren call of positivism. Philosophically, they're allied with what might be called the barter school of truth, a school often associated with what Katheryn Doran has aptly called the "seductive conflation of epistemological skepticism and metaphysical relativism."[1] Unlike Fort Knox adherents, champions of this position believe that perspective inevitably influences any account (or attempted account) of reality. As a result, what will "count as" truth is always a context-dependent construction.[2]

As I have suggested, there are numerous variations within this broad grouping. In *Les Gommes* (*The Erasers*), for instance, Alain Robbe-Grillet surprisingly combines metaphysical realism with his epistemological skepticism, suggesting that there *is* a true narrative of the events, although it is inaccessible to any of the characters in the world of the novel. *Cosmos* appears to be more thoroughly postmodern, suggesting that no transcendental narrative exists at all, although the novel's (probably coincidental) intertextual references to the life and music of Alban Berg confuse the issue.[3] Still, despite their differences, the novelists in this second camp reject the belief that we can *determine* the truth of particular claims; at most, we *make* truth discursively and rhetorically by telling stories and negotiating among them, bartering truth claims in exchanges that are either taken up or not according to the needs of a particular social context (including its power relations).[4] For these counter-cultural detectives, the search is not for some empirically verifiable "truth" but rather for some coherent story "about" the world, preferably one with enough persuasive power to gain acceptance from whoever needs to be convinced.

For the most part, these novels do not pursue their philosophical quarry all the way to the most radical skepticism (although Paul Auster, in his *New York Trilogy*, comes close). In particular, most do not deny the existence of brute material facts, and do not throw doubt on the possibility of direct observation of the present. But, much like Alain Resnais and Robbe-Grillet's *L'Année dernière à Marienbad* (*Last Year at Marienbad*), they suggest that the past (even the immediate past) exists only in the form of present material objects. "History" (and any detective story necessarily involves its characters in some attempt at historical reconstruction) is consequently a matter of inventing stories about those present objects. Any story that can account for those material objects has equal validity; whether or not it is accepted thus depends not on its fidelity to what is the case, but rather on its barter value for the particular context in which it is presented.

"The Soft Grey Sheen of Lead": Clipping the Wings of the Maltese Falcon

Traditionally, Dashiell Hammett's *The Maltese Falcon* has been read as a straight hard-boiled detective story, with little interest in erudite philosophical issues. This is not to say, of course, that the novel has not been widely read as a serious social critique. Liahna K. Babener, for instance, is typical in claiming that the novel's "target . . . is the duplicity of the Horatio Alger myth" (78). But on the whole, there's been little interest in considering *The Maltese Falcon* as a philosophical novel fundamentally "concerned with stories and storytelling" (Schulman 400).[5]

There is good reason, of course, for the customary readings. The novel first appeared in the context of the early *Black Mask* school, and many of its surface features—its clipped, tough "masculine" dialogue; its complex, fast-moving plot; its cynical antisentimentalism—appear to invite the reader to apply the same reading strategies demanded by other tough novels of the period, rather than, say, the strategies demanded by such then avant-garde contemporaries as Woolf or Pirandello, much less the strategies later demanded by Robbe-Grillet and Auster. Yet different features emerge as significant for readers of different historical periods. And as we grow accustomed to thinking and rereading in postmodern terms, the stability of Hammett's novel increasingly begins to dissolve, as Percy Walton and Kathryn Gail Brock's parodic readings have in their different ways demonstrated.[6] From the arrival of Brigid O'Shaughnessy in Sam Spade's office, it's a novel in which the plot consists not of events, but of continual acts of narrativizing and renarrativizing about events that may or may not have taken place. Even Lieutenant Dundy, the character most committed to meaning what he says (21), finds that he has to invent stories ("Nobody saw it, but that's the way it figures" [22]) and deal with the inventions of others: "What do you want us to think the truth is?" he asks Brigid O'Shaughnessy with a scowl of aggravation (75). The characters are not centered subjects, but assume a dizzying series of self-conscious roles that cast doubt on traditional notions of identity: Brigid O'Shaughnessy's carefully choreographed transformations in particular, from the timid Miss Wonderly clasping her handbag to the teary, love-wracked beseecher of the final confrontation, confirm that this is a world in which the equation between who you are and what your story is is more than a dead metaphor (22). The stability of gender, too, is undermined, not only by the dynamics of the Gutman-Wilmer-Cairo trio or the fight between Cairo and Brigid O'Shaughnessy over the boy in Constantinople (68), but even more by Spade's boyish but femininely seductive secretary Effie Perine. Novelistic clichés—the reliability of women's intuition, the joviality of the fat man—are turned inside out. Messages—even a condolence note to a lover upon her liberation from a husband she detested—are severed from their senders. Clues—for instance, the hole in the newspaper that Spade finds in Cairo's hotel room—are often marked by absence rather than presence, just as Archer's murder in the San Francisco fog is celebrated by the erasure of his name from the door of the detective agency's office.

To the extent that there *is* a story, it is a story of a search without a beginning. Spade's first words to Brigid O'Shaughnessy may be "Suppose you tell me about it, from the beginning" (5), but since he doesn't expect "it" to be believable, he hardly expects that it will have a real origin. More important, the search is a search without an ending, except the promise of endless deferral. It's consistent, then, that in common with much postmodernist thought, the novelistic acid eats away at the distinction between fiction and history. Indeed—and it came as a shock when I called up the OCLC catalog on my computer to check this out—the historical texts that Casper Gutman uses to buttress his story about the falcon turn out to be "actual" historical works, and the stories that he tells fit the facts that we know. Thus, although Ernle Bradford's version of the story puts into question the Knights' power and their undiluted enthusiasm for Malta (which apparently required them, in addition, to garrison Tripoli: "It is indicative of the desperate straits to which the Order had been reduced that they agreed to the Emperor's offer"), his account confirms the basic story of the "annual nominal rent of one falcon" (123).[7] The assessment of Effie Perine's fictional historian-cousin Ted ("the names and dates are all right, and at least none of your authorities or their works are out-and-out fakes" [139]) thus collapses the distinction between the authorial and narrative audiences.[8]

Money—the anchor of capitalism—is deconstructed as well. Gutman may claim that the cash he hands to Spade is "actual money, genuine coin of the realm" that somehow transcends the merely discursive: "With a dollar of this, you can buy more than with ten dollars of talk" (174). But the novel represents a world of counterfeiters, too (119), and even Gutman's apparently legitimate thousand-dollar bills can not only disappear, but even change the very nature of their being: at the end, the one remaining bill has been transformed from a payment into an "exhibit" (215–16).

Then, too, although the novel has sometimes been treated as a Hemingwayesque endorsement of a masculine code of honor and loyalty, the novel's intertextual links with Prosper Mérimée's 1829 short story "Mateo Falcone" serve to undercut that code, too, as well as traditional bourgeois notions of the family. Mérimée's brutal little anecdote concerns a father who executes his own son out of devotion to a higher code of conduct—for the child, bribed with the promise of a silver watch, has turned a fugitive over to the government authorities, becoming "the first of his line to have committed a betrayal" (Mérimée, 65). Hammett twice inverts this scenario: when Gutman, who "feel[s] towards Wilmer just exactly as if he were [his] own son" (178), nonetheless agrees to turn him over to the police in exchange for the falcon, and again when Spade turns over Brigid O'Shaughnessy.

Most striking, of course, is the falcon/phallus itself (what Sam Spade calls a "dingus"): for the transcendental signifier that ostensibly gives meaning and value to the world of the novel displays the "soft grey sheen of lead" (202), as it turns out to be just another counterfeit of a unique original that may or may not exist. No surprise, then, that in this novel, pistols—for instance, the "tools bulging [Wilmer's] clothes" (95)—keep multiplying and changing hands, a thematic ploy that reaches comically Ionesco-like proportions when the guns are all (or nearly all) shut up in the closet during the long negotiation scene. No surprise, either, that the other variant of the phallus—the crucial fall guy—miraculously disappears from a crowded room.

The Maltese Falcon, like most other postmodern detective stories, refrains from challenging the existence of an observable material present, although like them it rhetoricizes history. History becomes a matter of telling stories about present objects, and any story that can account for the material traces of the past—any story, as Spade puts it, that "seems to click with most of the known facts"—will "hold," as long as you have the power to persuade your listeners to go along with it (115). Nor does the novel confront the abyss by endorsing either despair or aesthetic free play. Rather, in common with such other macho preexistentialists as Hemingway,

Hammett seems to be trying to propose a way of controlling one's environment (and preserving "self," in body if not in soul) in a world where truth is relative and where violence (whether in the form of gunshots or of beams falling from construction sites) erupts without warning. Spade's "way of learning is to heave a wild and unpredictable monkey wrench into the machinery" (86), and his refusal to "settle" into a "groove" (64) is, to a large extent, what ensures his survival and success, not to mention his status as a hero.

"Wait Till I'm Through and Then You Can Talk": Power and Narrative Technique

I do not want to overstate the extent of *The Maltese Falcon's* post-modernism. As I pointed out, there are also numerous conventional signals that invite us to read the novel as a traditional hard-boiled text: this is a world of real violence and real corpses, without any of the ghostly ambiguities of perception that haunt Auster's trilogy, and without any of the nagging ambiguities of plot that make the world of Butor's *L'Emploi du temps* (where we never even find out whether or not there was a crime) such an unsettling experience. Still, the presence of these deconstructive counter-forces fundamentally disturbs the equilibrium of the text; and the reader who picks up on the novel's questioning spirit is apt to be taken aback when the novel's postmodern unraveling itself falls apart in the paradoxically tight-knit ending.

The clarity of the conclusion is no doubt partly a result of the pressures of genre: Hammett was apparently not yet ready to give us a detective story without an ending. But there's also a deeper sexual-political cause. If any poststructuralist interpretive doctrine has acquired general currency, it is the belief that texts assert what they're at most pains to deny. And if the clear epistemological and metaphysical structures of traditional realist detective fiction aim to deflect our attention from metaphysical and political aporias, what is being furtively asserted by this text when it so steadfastly refuses to assert anything at all? What I'd like to suggest here is that, through its very rhetorical structure, the novel deconstructs its own postmodern refusal to take a stand—its own rejection of what Casper Gutman calls "plain speaking and clear understanding" (105)—covertly reasserting precisely those traditional values it so ostentatiously undermines, and falling back on an unexamined myth of absence. And the novel does so because it reaches a rhetorical impasse where, in order to follow through on its own barter-school program, Hammett and Spade would be required to accept women as independent subjects.

The novel turns into a self-affirming artifact most clearly through its treatment of embedded narratives, stories within stories. In order to explain how this happens, I'd like to introduce two distinctions: one between two kinds of transmission as a story moves from one level to the next, the other among three types of narration. To begin with transmission: when light waves travel from one medium to another, one of two things can happen. If they hit perpendicular to the surface of the new medium, they continue on in the same direction, in a straight line; but if they hit obliquely, they are refracted, and move off at a different angle. Similarly, when a story moves from one medium to another, one of two things can happen. In straight line transmission, intervening levels of narration do not in any significant way deflect the story being told. In Voltaire's *Candide*, the Old Woman's tale has the same claim to authenticity as the narration that frames it. More elaborately, in Mary Shelley's *Frankenstein*, Safie's letters are presented with four levels of embedding. We know them only from Walton's letters, which include Victor Frankenstein's narrative, which in turn includes the monster's story, which in turn includes the letters—or at least copies that he made of them, copies we're told of, but never shown (108). Nonetheless, as readers, it is as if we have direct access to the letters; the intervening levels don't interfere in any way with *our* rhetorical connection to the originals.

In refractive transmission, by contrast, each intervening level bends the story, so that our attention as readers is necessarily divided between what is narrated and the twists introduced by the act of narration itself. Indeed, such embedded stories are thus both refracted and refractory, in the sense that they resist easy interpretation. Thus, for instance, in Mikhail Lermontov's *Hero of Our Time*, we learn about the characters as much from how they narrate as from what is said about them, and the differences between the accounts given by Pechorin and those given by Maxim Maximich are crucial to our sense of the novel.

Now either type of transmission—straight line or refractive—is in principle consistent with a Fort Knox notion of truth: for while the Fort Knox doctrine hinges on the assumption that the truth is *potentially* available, it does not follow that a particular individual will be capable of (or interested in) actually finding it. Much of Poirot's detection, therefore, consists of sorting out conflicting refracted narratives, some consciously false, some simply mistaken, in order to discover the transcendent truth at their origin. But while the Fort Knox notion does not necessarily entail straight line transmission, straight line transmission *does* entail Knoxism. Straight line transmission inevitably involves both the possibility and the actuality of identity between two versions of a story—not merely a possible partial overlap (as in *As I Lay Dying*, where Cash and Darl may partially confirm each other's narrative of Jewel's past), but an absolute match between the telling and the told, *as well as* a way of determining that that match has occurred. Because of this, we can't have straight line transmission in a world where the very act of perception changes (in some versions, even creates) what is perceived. The barter notion of truth therefore necessarily requires refractive transmission.

My second distinction is among first, second, and third person narration. Although this distinction is commonplace in narrative theory (enough so that as long ago as 1961, Wayne Booth called it "overworked" [150]), its value has been obscured by the grammatical terminology, which encourages us to concentrate on the surface manifestations of the text. But surface does not always match significant structure: Faulkner's *Intruder in the Dust* uses third person grammar, but the narrative has all the characteristics of a retrospective first person novel. I would like to propose, then, that we reconsider the terminology, and think of narrative person not as a grammatical category—nor even what Genette calls a "narrative posture" (*Narrative Discourse* 244)—but rather as a rhetorical situation embracing not only the teller but the audience as well.[9]

To be schematic for a moment: let us assume that narrator A says to audience B that referent C did something. (I'm using the term "referent" here because the terms "subject" and "object" introduce too many ambiguities of meaning.) In the simplest type of what I'm calling third person narrative, the three positions (A, B, and C) are clearly distinct, and the third of them is, moreover, absent from the scene of reception. "A photograph of Mama Chona and her grandson Miguel Angel—Miguel Chico or Mickie to his family—hovers above his head on the study wall beside the glass doors that open out into the garden. When Miguel Chico sits at his desk, he glances up at it occasionally without noticing it, looking through it rather than at it." So begins Arturo Islas's *The Rain God* (3), and we know that Miguel Chico is neither telling nor being told the story. In first and second person narration, however, some of these positions are collapsed. In the simplest type of first person narration, it is the narrator and referent who are collapsed: "Last year, on the evening of March 22, I had a very strange adventure" (Dostoevsky 1). And in second person narration, most often found in spoken discourse (or its novelistic representation), it's the distinction between audience and referent that's collapsed: "You are about to begin reading Italo Calvino's new novel, *If on a winter's night a traveler*. Relax. Concentrate. Dispel every other thought" (Calvino 3).[10]

For the most part, these rhetorical categories overlap with the traditional grammatical categories. Thus most first person narratives in my sense are composed in the grammatical first person. But as I've suggested, *Intruder in the Dust* is rhetorically a first person narrative, since narrator and referent are identical, despite the grammatical construction that describes Chick in the third person throughout. Likewise, we learn at the end of Albert Camus's *La Peste* (*The Plague*) that we've been reading a first person narrative in which the narrator refers to himself in the third person.

PETER J. RABINOWITZ

Despite such famous exceptions as Butor's *La Modification* and Calvino's *If on a winter's night a traveler*, second person is rarely used as the top—that is, the most inclusive—level of narration (I'm calling on this rather informal terminology in large part because the more familiar terms Genette uses in *Narrative Discourse*— extradiegetic, diegetic, metadiegetic—are so cumbersome).[11] Indeed, even some of the rare texts that are second person in grammar are not second person in rhetoric. For instance, Rex Stout's *How Like a God* (1929) is written, except for the brief interchapters, in a grammatical second person. But, as the third person interchapters make clear, it's really a variant of first person narration—an internal monologue that we might call narcissistic narration—in which the narrator is speaking to himself about himself.[12]

This relative scarcity of complete second person texts, coupled with the popularity of Genette's homodiegetic/heterodiegetic distinction (which seems to remove second person narration as a serious option [but see *Narrative Discourse Revisited* 133–34]), has resulted in a widespread tendency to brush second person narration aside. But while second person narration is rare on the top level of narrative organization, it's found widely in smaller narrative units. In particular, as Robyn Warhol has shown, it's found in direct address to the reader, especially in eighteenth- and nineteenth-century fiction; and it is frequent in embedded narration— where it is a dramatized *narratee* rather than the narrative or authorial audience of the text as a whole that's being narrativized. It certainly occurs at a crucial juncture in *The Maltese Falcon*.

What is useful about this reconception of person is that by stressing the relationship not only between narrator and story but also between narrator and audience, we get a handle not only on epistemological issues (the questions about what the narrator knows stressed by so many traditional studies of point of view) but on issues of power as well. In particular, this analysis underscores that second person narration, especially second person refractive transmission, opens up the possibility of feedback—feedback not in its current trendy meaning, as when a Dean tells faculty or students to provide some "feedback" on the latest course evaluation form, but in its more precise acoustic/electronic meaning, the screech that occurs when an infinite loop is created between a microphone and a speaker that is simultaneously serving as both the input and the output of the microphone. That's because in second person narration, the referent of the story, being also the audience, is *present* at the site of reception, and thus always has the potential to insist on retelling his or her story in his or her own way, a further act of narration that can itself become embedded in the story that the original narrator is telling, and so on *ad infinitum*. In contrast, a third person narration, even when refracted, has an absent referent, and hence closes down the possibility for feed-back. When Spade tells Brigid O'Shaughnessy the Flitcraft story, for instance, his transmission is clearly refractive. The curve be-tween Flitcraft's own story and Spade's story about that story shows up in Spade's ironic stance toward the story he tells, in the judgmental element introduced through the act of telling: "I don't think he even knew he had settled back naturally into the same groove he had jumped out of in Tacoma. But that's the part of it I always liked" (64). But the feedback potential in that ironic distance never drowns out the present rhetorical situation, for Flitcraft—if he exists—isn't present, and hence has no opportunity to provide commentary on the tale.

It is more difficult, however, to reduce feedback in second person refracted narrative. There are two primary ways of silencing a referent-audience: conversion and coercion. Conversion has sev-eral variations. One can, for instance, seduce the audience into accepting the narrator's version of the story by offering pleasure. That kind of seduction forms the central intrigue in *Marienbad*, as X tries to persuade A that his stories about what happened to them last year are worth believing. In a very different way, we see the same kind of technique when Spade tries to create a story that will work with the District Attorney: "He's more interested in how his record will look on paper than anything else. . . . To be sure of convicting one man he'll let half a dozen equally guilty accomplices go free. . . . That's the choice we'll give him and he'll gobble it up" (180).[13] Alternatively, one can mediate between conflicting stories until some mutually acceptable version is found: that's what happens, for instance, in the conversation between Violet Stoke and Charles Watkins in Doris Lessing's *Briefing for a Descent into Hell*, or between Spade and Gutman when they negotiate a trade of the fall guy for the falcon.

But whether in the form of seduction or mediation, conversion-generated silencing places the audience in a subject position—a position to make choices. One can avoid that necessity through the second alternative, sheer force—what Spade resorts to when casting Wilmer as the fall guy. When dealing with men, these two alternatives seem adequate—even when dealing with gay men, although Spade (and Philip Marlowe, too) seems to prefer violence as an alternative to offering subjecthood. Violence is especially characteristic of his dealings with Wilmer. He alternately beats up and negotiates with Cairo, but he never extends the option of serious negotiation to Wilmer, who seems to get more deeply under his skin—perhaps because his "hard masculine neatness" (93) casts more doubts on the meaning of Spade's own masculinity than does the effeminacy of Cairo, with his smell of *chypre*. Spade beats up Wilmer before he tells him, "This will put you in solid with your boss" (121), and Spade's brief second person narrative before Wilmer is chosen as the fall guy ("Two to one they're selling you out, son") is similarly accompanied by silence rather than feedback ("The boy did not say anything" [184]).

Something quite different, though, happens in his final scene with Brigid O'Shaughnessy. There's certainly no literal violence at this climax of the plot (perhaps some residue of chivalry makes him squeamish about knocking her out—although it's significant that he's willing to force her to strip in his quest for the palmed thousand-dollar bill). But neither is Spade willing to give her the freedom to negotiate her future. This refusal is all the more strikingly noticeable because of its jarring contiguity with the lengthy give-and-take with Gutman. One cannot, of course, be absolutely sure of Spade's (or Hammett's) reasons for this: Spade may feel (although the prior events in this novel would hardly support this belief) that she is more duplicitous than Gutman. It may be, as I've suggested earlier, that Hammett feels an aesthetic need to close off the infinite possibilities of his text.

Still, it's hard to ignore Spade's uncharacteristically obsessive insistence that he "won't play the sap" for her (212–15). He's told her earlier, half in jest, that "You don't have to trust me, anyhow, as long as you can persuade me to trust you" (65), and there is good reason to believe that, because of her sexual allure—because it's "easy enough to be nuts about" her (214)—her powers of persuasion are more than Spade wants to handle. Certainly her sexual power has been deadly for Thursby, Captain Jacobi, and especially for Miles Archer. Spade, of course, considers himself less "dumb" (208) than Archer ("You've got brains, yes you have" he tells his leering partner sarcastically when he starts to make his move on Brigid O'Shaughnessy [10]), and less of a "sucker for women" than Thursby (207). But there's evidence that Gutman's claim "We mere men should have known better than to suppose ourselves capable of coping with her" (192) applies to Spade more than he would sometimes like to believe. After all, Gutman requires drugs to shut Spade up, but Brigid O'Shaughnessy manages to shut him up by simply putting "her open mouth hard against his mouth" (89).

In the final scene, Spade is intensely aware of this power as he reviews his past with Brigid O'Shaughnessy: "You came into my bed to stop me asking questions" (212). And he's well aware of the way that the continued presence of her body, always an embarrassment in an act of narration, makes the outcome of a life-threatening seduction or negotiation doubly doubtful ("Last night you came here with them and waited outside for me and came in with me. You were in my arms when the trap was sprung" [212]), especially since she is fully aware of both the danger of the situation and the source of her power ("God damn you—you've counted on that" [215]). There is much to be said about the reasons for and implications of Hammett's and Spade's attitudes toward women—it's significant, for instance, that both Brigid O'Shaughnessy and Effie Perine are consistently objectified by the author's (although not the characters') insistence on calling them by full name, first and last.[14] But for my purposes here the effects, not the causes, are of primary concern. For finding himself unwilling to have Spade either batter Brigid O'Shaughnessy or let her negotiate, Hammett silences her with a rhetorical, rather than a physical, coercion, a sleight of pen that reinscribes what Percy Walton has called the "dominant colonizing norm," a "singularizing effort . . . that . . . ignores difference when it accepts its own desires as more important than the desires of the space it seeks to dominate" ("Paretsky's V.I." 203–4).

Specifically, in their famous final confrontation, second person narration is *treated as* a third person narration. That is, although Brigid O'Shaughnessy is literally both audience and referent of the discourse, Spade's account of her story is made definitive, as she is rhetorically objectified as absent and hence silent (her few remaining snippets of dialogue do nothing to challenge the narration). What makes this rhetorical sleight-of-hand possible? She says nothing because she has nothing to say: no feedback loop is started up because—and both Brigid O'Shaughnessy and Spade *know* this—no dissonance is registered between her perception and his. "How did you know he—he licked his lips and looked—?" she asks (209), and in asking this question, she affirms the consonance of their stories, and consequently affirms the straight line of his transmission. On the surface, perhaps, the potential for dialogue continues: "Wait till I'm through and then you can talk," he tells her (214). But because she has already accepted the congruence of the stories, she can do nothing but confirm the correctness of his version of her story; she tries one last barter—with body, rather than text (215)—but it's a futile gesture, and the doorbell rings just as she puts her arms around him.

It's worth distinguishing between Hammett's and Spade's performances here. It's Spade who tells the story, but it's the implied author who creates Brigid O'Shaughnessy's assent. That assent serves to end the story and contain the woman without violence, and its sheer dramatic power makes it easy for the reader to accept without question. But under the surface, the ending comes at tremendous epistemological cost. For in order to guarantee that assent, Hammett has to resort, at this key moment, to a straight-line embedded narrative. And in this apparently purely formal choice, Hammett smuggles in precisely the Fort Knox conception of truth that his novel has been at such pains to resist. It grounds Spade's story as true, but it deconstructs the patient deconstruction of foundationalism that forms the very basis of the novel's epistemological project.

No wonder, then, that Effie Perine seems so depressed at the end—refusing to let Spade touch her—when she has to go along with this epistemological turnaround. As I've suggested, this "lanky sunburned girl" with a "boyish face" (3) has had gender-crossing license throughout the novel—as Spade says, "You're a damned good man, sister" (160). (No doubt her name, with its echoes of "peregrine," gives her some falcon/phallic privileges.) But when she says, "I know—I know you're right" (217), she realizes that there's no longer any opening for the kind of dialogue that has enlivened their relationship up until now. For most of the novel, Spade has given her the choice of siding with Brigid O'Shaughnessy, even against him ("You're sore because she did something on her own hook," she argues; "Why shouldn't she?" [153])—and Effie Perine has belied the clichés about women's rivalry by remaining steadfast in her loyalty to Brigid O'Shaughnessy, even though they're both sexually attracted to the same man. But the ending of the novel proves that female bonding has been a mistake—that there is, in fact, a right and wrong to the situation, and that Effie Perine has simply been wrong.

Spade's situation is no more upbeat than Effie Perine's. Throughout the novel, he has prided himself on his flexibility and unpredictability. But although he enters his office with cheerful lines on his face and clear eyes, the superficially bland final sentences strike a very different note. Effie Perine enters Spade's inner office to announce that Iva Archer, the indefatigable mistress Spade has been trying to elude for the entire novel ("I wish to Christ I'd never seen her" [27]), has arrived once again at the office. " 'Yes,' he said, and shivered. 'Well, send her in' "·(217). The echo of his decision to turn Brigid O'Shaughnessy in to the police ("I'm going to send you over" [211]) underscores the connection between Spade's rhetorical victory over Brigid O'Shaughnessy and his philosophical defeat.

For in the wake of the Knoxian solution has come a chilling kind of return to things as they were—and while sentimental readers may want to see that final shiver as a sign of despairing romantic loss, it's more likely that it comes from a resigned recognition that he has forfeited his philosophical decenteredness and that, like Flitcraft, he has found himself trapped once again in the same groove that he has been trying to jump out of for the entire novel.

Notes

1. Personal communication.

2. This distinction, of course, has close connections to Steven Mailloux's distinction between foundationalist accounts of interpretation and rhetorical hermeneutics in *Rhetorical Power*. There is, as well, a link to the two ways of conceptualizing truth often classed as correspondence theories (where statements are deemed "true" according to their correspondence to some determinable external state of affairs) and coherence theories (where statements are deemed "true" according to internal standards that include such things as consistency, inclusiveness, and logical relations). The distinction, of course, has been important for literary theorists as well, especially for the New Critics. See, for instance, Brooks and Warren (27). I am warned by my philosopher friends, though, that I do not want to wander through the thickets of this distinction. Special thanks to Elizabeth Ring and Katheryn Doran for their invaluable assistance on these issues.

3. For a fuller discusison, see my *Before Reading*, 178–83.

4. In defining the subgenre in this way, I am taking a substantially different route from that of Holquist, in his discussion of "metaphysical" detective stories. He sees postmodern detectives' recognition of chaos ("they dramatize the void" [155]), but does not discuss the novels in terms of the way they *create* a truth.

5. For the most part Schulman, too, views the novel from a social rather than an epistemological perspective, since those stories are motivated by "a market society world that systematically demands improvisation, acting, and the manipulation of appearances, people, and feelings." Still, he is one of the critics who recognizes the philosophical issues as well. See in particular 408–9.

6. My thinking in this direction was begun through conversations with Kathryn Gail Brock nearly a decade ago, and the influence of her "parodic" reading on the following paper is enormous. Walton's argu-

ments, in "You're in My Burg," similarly stress parodic elements in the text; and although she is less interested in determining an authorial reading than I am, the overlap between our essays is considerable.

7. See, for instance, Carutti: "Gli abasciatori di Malta vennero a rendere omaggio al nuovo Re e offerire il falcone, annuo tributo che Carlo V avea imposto all'Ordine dei Cavalieri gerosolimitani in ricognizione della movenza dell'isola dalla corona di Sicilia" [The ambassadors of Malta came to render homage to the new king and to offer the falcon, the annual tribute which Charles V had imposed upon the order of the Knights of Jerusalem in recognition of his granting of the island from the crown of Sicily.] (391). Thanks to Maureen Miller for help with historical research.

8. For fuller discussion of the difference between authorial audience, narrative audience, and narratee, see *Before Reading*, chapter 3.

9. See also Genette's discussion of the problematic nature of grammatical categories, *Narrative Discourse Revisited* 104 ff. See also Bal 121 ff. In refusing to discuss grammatical difference, though, Bal skims over other differences that, as we shall see, really matter.

10. Of course, there are any number of possible variants. For instance, we might want to distinguish between "normal" third person and what I call third person *private,* where the narrator and audience are identical, as when someone writes a note to him- or herself, or a secret diary entry about someone else. And when we introduce the distinctions between implied author and narrator, or between authorial audience and narrative audience, the possible permutations increase radically.

For valuable discussions of second person narration in particular, see also Kacandes, Morrissette, McHale, Richardson, and Bonheim. McHale's "calculus" of "possible communicative situations" (96) provides one useful way of sorting out texts; Richardson's distinction among three different types of second person narration—which he conceptualizes in a way quite different from mine—is likewise illuminating. Bonheim's approach is, in places, similar to my own in its attention to which narrative positions have been collapsed; and his numerous distinctions, too, are often valuable in charting out this hazy area. But especially toward the end of the essay, he puts more stress than I do on grammatical surface. He also minimizes the importance of brief second person interpolations, as well as cases where "the use of the second person is . . . more a matter of rhetoric than of point of view" (71). Although he is here using the term rhetoric in a narrower sense than I am, his essay avoids treating rhetoric in the broader sense too, and hence the issues of power that are central to my argument.

11. For an excellent discussion of Calvino's techniques here, see Phelan, chapter 5. Camus's *La Chute* seems to begin as second person narrative, but it's not really sustained, as much of the novel reverts to first person.

12. See also McHale's discussion of this sort of narration as "self-addressed interior dialogue" (101–4).

13. On the surface, this seems a third person narrative, and at least with respect to its past tense aspects, it is. But there's a double story here, and the main story is intended to narrate to the DA what his role will be: it is hence a future tense second person narrative — or, since the story is never actually told, a hypothetical future tense second person narrative. A Greek term would be useful to describe this kind of narrative situation.

14. Hammett uses a similar technique to create distance in *The Glass Key*, although there is it not tied to gender. For further discussion of Hammett and women, see, for instance, Marling.

Bibliography

Babener, Liahna K. "California Babylon: The World of American Detective Fiction." *Clues* 1.2 (1980): 77–89.

Bakhtin, M.M. *The Dialogic Imagination: Four Essays*. Trans. by Caryl Emerson and Michael Holquist. Ed. by Michael Holquist. Austin: University of Texas Press, 1981.

Bal, Mieke. *Narratology: Introduction to the Theory of Narrative*. Trans. by Christine van Boheemen. Toronto: University of Toronto Press, 1985.

Bonheim, Helmut. "Narration in the Second Person." *Recherches anglaises et américaines* 16 (1983): 69–80.

Booth, Wayne C. *The Rhetoric of Fiction*. Chicago: University of Chicago Press, 1961.

Bradford, Ernle. *The Shield and the Sword: The Knights of St. John*. London: Hodder and Stoughton, 1972.

Brock, Kathryn Gail. "Reason is Convention: Parody in *The Maltese Falcon*." Unpublished manuscript.

Brooks, Cleanth and Robert Penn Warren. *Understanding Fiction*. 2nd ed. New York: Appleton-Century-Crofts, 1959.

Calvino, Italo. *If on a winter's night a traveler*. Trans. by William Weaver. New York: Harcourt, Brace, Jovanovich, 1981.

Carutti, Domenico. *Storia di Vittoria Amedeo II: Il Primo Re Di Casa Savoja*. 3rd ed. Torino: Carlo Clausen, 1897.

Dostoevsky, Fyodor. *The Insulted and the Injured*. Vol. 6 of *The Novels of Fyodor Dostoevsky*. Trans. by Constance Garnett. New York: Macmillan Company, n.d.

Genette, Gérard. *Narrative Discourse: An Essay in Method*. Trans. by Jane E. Lewin. Ithaca: Cornell University Press, 1980.

_____. *Narrative Discourse Revisited*. Trans. by Jane E. Lewin. Ithaca: Cornell University Press, 1988.

Hammett, Dashiell. *The Maltese Falcon*. 1930. New York: Random House/ Vintage, 1989.

Holquist, Michael. "Whodunit and Other Questions: Metaphysical Detective Stories in Post-War Fiction." *New Literary History* 3.1 (Autumn 1971): 135–56.

Islas, Arturo. *The Rain God*. 1984. New York: Avon Books, 1991.

Kacandes, Irene. "Are You in the Text? The 'Literary Performative' in Postmodern Fiction." *Text and Performance* 13 (1993): 139–53.

Knox, Ronald A. "A Detective Story Decalogue." 1929. Rpt. in *The Art of the Mystery Story: A Collection of Critical Essays*. Ed. by Howard Haycraft. New York: Carroll and Graf, 1983. 194–96.

Mailloux, Steven. *Rhetorical Power*. Ithaca: Cornell University Press, 1989.

Marling, William. "The Hammett Succubus." *Clues* 3.2 (1982): 66–75.

McHale, Brian. "'You Used to Know What These Words Mean': Misreading *Gravity's Rainbow*." *Language and Style* 18.1 (Winter 1985): 93–118.

Mérimée, Prosper. "Mateo Falcone." 1829. In *Carmen and Other Stories*. Trans. by Nicholas Jotcham. Oxford: Oxford University Press, 1989. 54–66.

Morrissette, Bruce. *Novel and Film: Essays in Two Genres*. Chicago: University of Chicago Press, 1985.

Phelan, James. *Reading People, Reading Plots: Character, Progression, and the Interpretation of Narrative*. Chicago: University of Chicago Press, 1989.

Rabinowitz, Peter J. *Before Reading: Narrative Conventions and the Politics of Interpretation*. New York: Cornell University Press, 1987.

Richardson, Brian. "The Poetics and Politics of Second Person Narrative." *Genre* 24.3 (1991): 309–30.

Schulman, Robert. "Dashiell Hammett's Social Vision." *Centennial Review* 29.4 (Fall 1985): 400–419.

Shelley, Mary. *Frankenstein*. 1831. New York: Bantam Books, 1981.

Stout, Rex. *How Like a God*. New York: Vanguard Press, 1929.

Walton, Priscilla. "'You're in My Burg': Sam Spade's San Francisco." Paper presented at the meetings of the Popular Culture Association, New Orleans, April 1993.

_____. "Paretsky's V.I. as P.I.: Revising the Script and Recasting the Dick." *Literature/Interpretation/Theory* 4 (1993): 203–13.

Warhol, Robyn R. *Gendered Interventions: Narrative Discourse in the Victorian Novel*. New Brunswick: Rutgers University Press, 1989.

7

Naturalizing *Molloy*

THOMAS G. PAVEL

In contrast with Beckett's own dissident writing, criticism about him is comfortably consensual. Most critics who write on Beckett treat his works as ideal units, assuming that each of them, and perhaps the entire set too, proposes a metaphysical statement about the human condition. Virtually all critics insist on Beckett's antitraditionalist writing and gloomy worldview. Early reviews of *Molloy* exemplify this tendency well. "Beckett settles us in the world of Nothing where some nothings which are men move about for nothing," Maurice Nadeau writes shortly after the publication of the novel.[1] At the end of an enthusiastic article, Georges Bataille strikes a similar chord: "Thus, *literature* gnaws away at existence and the world, reducing to *nothing* (but this *nothing* is horror) these steps by which we go along confidently from one result to another, from one success to another."[2] Later academic criticism belabored these themes at great length. To take only two better known examples: Wolfgang Iser defined Beckett's art as representing subjectivity in the act of canceling itself,[3] that is, as dealing not with events, but with interpretations, and dubious interpretations at that; Leo Bersani proposed an eschatological account, arguing

I wish to thank James Phelan, Peter Rabinowitz, and Donald Brown for their generous criticism of an earlier version of this paper.

that Beckett brings about the end of literature.[4] I would call such views the "apocalyptic" approach.

Taken as an evocation of the Beckettian atmosphere, the apocalyptic view is certainly on target: not only do Beckett's characters make us think of figures in Callot or Goya, but the former's dereliction is somehow deeper than the latter's, in fact deeper than anyone else's since the *Book of Job*. But at the same time, the efforts to describe Beckett's *art* with the help of totalizing concepts such as "the death of the author," "the end of literature," or "the deconstruction of subjectivity" paradoxically go against what Beckett, the prose writer, quite obviously tries to do on every page of his novels: to tell us stunningly concrete stories, which capture the real before and outside its subordination to conventional thought categories. Totalizing concepts like "the end of literature" and "the deconstruction of subjectivity" certainly address questions Beckett's narrations themselves seem to address, especially when examined in isolation from other literary texts. Yet, it is equally true that Beckett's stories are, above all, prose narratives embedded in a long generic tradition, without reference to which their complicated games cannot be fully grasped.

The interpretation of Beckett's narratives thus raises two larger issues: first, the contrast between hermeneutics and poetics; second, the relation between tradition and innovation. The apocalyptic reading of Beckett's narratives assumes that each of these texts incorporates a kernel of wisdom that the critic must recover by attentive contemplation of the text in its unicity. A poetological reading, in contrast, assumes that *placing* the text within its particular family of literary artefacts precedes and helps interpretation.[5] Placing a literary text within, say, a group of generic and thematic relatives highlights not only their common generic features, but also the specificity of the text under consideration. In particular, placing a text helps us get a clearer sense of what is innovative and what is traditional. Since innovation depends as much on following some established codes as it does on breaking some others, a completely revolutionary text is simply unthinkable. It follows that even texts like Beckett's narratives, which have been hailed as radically innovative, might in fact depend on well-established generic and thematic traditions.

Interpretations of Beckett's prose which link it to the European narrative tradition have occasionally been defended. Christine Brooke-Rose and John Fletcher, who hold a moderate historicist view, see Beckett's prose as belonging to a lineage of antinovelists that includes Cervantes, Furetière, Swift, Sterne, and Diderot.[6] For Hugh Kenner, Beckett is a "stoic comedian" belonging to the same lineage as Flaubert and Joyce.[7] Other critics, balancing the apocalyptic and the historicist view of Beckett, relate his work to a pessimistic tradition going from Schopenhauer to Proust.[8] Indeed, Beckett quotes somewhere a revealing passage of Schopenhauer, who defines art as "the contemplation of the world independently of the principle of reason."[9]

The present paper will defend a poetological view of *Molloy*, and attempt to position this text within a set of related literary texts. I will analyze Molloy's monologue, arguing that thematically *Molloy* relies on Beckett's immediate French predecessors, in particular on Sartre's existentialism, while generically it incorporates many elements of quest-romances and ordeal narratives. In contrast with the apocalyptic view, I will conclude that *Molloy* presents a spirited defense of human dignity.

Like most of the "nouveaux romanciers" of his generation, Natalie Sarraute, Michel Butor, Alain Robbe-Grillet, Claude Simon (all discovered and promoted as a group in the early and mid-1950s by Jérôme Lindon at the Editions de Minuit), Beckett writes in a style which challenges both existing narrative conventions and conceptual thought. The peculiar punch of his and his fellows' prose comes from blending two powerful modern traditions: the vitalist and existentialist affirmation of human reality as irreducible to concepts, a favorite theme throughout twentieth-century French philosophy and prose; and the modernist narrative, brought to prominence by Virginia Woolf, James Joyce, and William Faulkner.

In France, the suspicion expressed by philosophy and art toward conceptual thought originates in the wave of vitalist and anti-

intellectualist trends at the turn of the century. Their most successful proponent, Henri Bergson, defended instinct against intel-
ligence and creative energy against rational analysis. Under his
influence, Marcel Proust's *Remembrance of Things Past* painstakingly
showed how conceptual knowledge hinders both artistic and emotional experience. After World War I, following the example of
Søren Kierkegaard, Karl Jaspers, and Martin Heidegger, the French
existentialist thinkers Gabriel Marcel and Jean-Paul Sartre built
sophisticated anticonceptual stands. They certainly did not dis-
pense with concepts entirely, since one cannot advocate anticon-
ceptualism without relying on some concepts. Yet their writings
emphasized the freedom and immediacy of human consciousness,
in direct opposition to the neo-Kantian and Hegelian interest in
abstract concepts. As a novelist, Sartre was fascinated by the same
theme. His early novel *Nausea* narrates the struggle of a young
historian, Antoine Roquentin, to get rid of the inherited conceptual—and, by implication, social—system and grasp existence in
its dazzling concreteness.

Proust and Sartre both wrote first person narratives, narratives
of consciousness. But with all its opposition to conceptual knowledge, Proust's *Remembrance of Things Past* is stylistically rooted in
French classicism as well as in nineteenth-century realism. Likewise, with all its modernist rage against the intellectual and moral
status quo, against conventional thought and bourgeois society,
Sartre's *Nausea* is told in a perfectly conventional, even bourgeois
style: transparent, realist, sensitive, often sentimental. And while
Proust's character turns in the end to art, Sartre's rejection of
abstract ideas in favor of concrete existence does not free his
character, Roquentin, from dependence on abstract categories:
after experiencing a quasi-mystic state, during which he becomes
one with viscous, incomprehensible reality, Sartre's character comes
back to conceptual thought as usual, or almost. To be sure, in his
existentialist despair he casts off his daily routine, stops writing
history, and dives into the unknown. But when, at the end of the
novel, he believes he has found a ray of hope, it consists in a piece of
music written, he tells us, by a "Jew" and sung by a "Negress": no

individual names given, just social concepts. Could it have been otherwise? As long as we use language, can we ever escape abstraction? In a powerful critique of Sartre's philosophy, Brice Parain argued in 1945 that individual consciousness never frees itself from the spell of language and, through it, from the power of universality.[10]

Dependence on language notwithstanding, Beckett's prose represents a further step in the resistance to conceptual thought.[11] Only that instead of *talking* against general categories and abstract concepts, instead of *pleading* for concrete existence, Beckett's prose *enacts* the flight from abstract concepts and the immersion into immediacy. Not that Beckett would eliminate from his prose all reference to socially accepted categories. Full rebellion against concepts can only lead to silence, a silence which Beckett, as a modern disciple of Geulincx, approaches to some degree.[12] Some categories are present in Beckett's prose, but the narrators never use them in a uniform, reliable way. Moreover, resistance to concepts inevitably breeds hostility to social institutions. Beckett's characters not only doubt the stability and universality of language; like Sartre's Roquentin, they also turn their backs to the world of social conventions.

Take as an instance of the meeting point between language and social stability, identification by profession in *Molloy*. Some characters have a clear profession, but no name: thus the various policemen who haunt the first part of the novel. Others have both a name and a profession: Father Ambrose, for instance, in Moran's monologue. Yet others, endowed with a name, are involved in unclear, ambiguous professions: Gaber, we are told, is a messenger, working for Youdi, the head of a mysterious agency. The nature of the agency is never made explicit: Gaber and Youdi could be either private detectives or members of a sect or a secret society. Moran, the narrator of the second part, works as one of Youdi's agents, yet rather than give us any clue about the aims of the agency, he gradually turns away from his professional duties, and ends up as a vagabond.

The same mischievous play with categorical borders occurs elsewhere in the story, and Molloy's relation with his mother is a telling example. Nothing should be easier to define conceptually, it would seem, than the kinship between mother and son. But in Molloy's case, the relation is blurred by several factors. One is the leveling effect of the protagonists' age: "we were like a couple of old cronies, sexless, unrelated, with the same memories, the same rancours, the same expectations" (17). Mixed with the ensuing indifference, there lurks an enduring hostility. Molloy, for one, could not bear to be addressed as "son." His mother, in turn, calls him Dan, which is not his name, but, *perhaps*, his father's. In Molloy's terms, "I took her for my mother, she took me for my father." The relation thus rests on a false symmetry between two people who half-forget who they are, and resent the half they still remember. Appropriately, Molloy calls his mother Mag: Ma for Mother, and the guttural g sound canceling the sweet syllable Ma.

To communicate with his mother, Molloy uses a simple, though not elegant, semiotic system: "I got into communication with her by knocking on her skull. One knock meant yes, two no, three I don't know, four money, five goodbye" (18). Even these minimal conceptual distinctions are too difficult for the two characters to remember: "That she should confuse yes, no, I don't know, and goodbye, was all the same to me, I confused them myself." Only requests for money are important—four knocks, yet the mother "seemed to have lost, if not absolutely all notion of mensuration, at least the faculty of counting beyond two." Since by the time Molloy reaches his third knock, his mother has already forgotten the first two, she interprets a request for money as a two-knock message, which, as Molloy noted earlier, can be indifferently understood as yes, no, I don't know, and goodbye. To be more effective, Molloy replaces "the four knocks of my index-knuckle by one or more (according to my needs) thumps of the fist on her skull." Communication gives way to violence: "That she understood." Notice, in passing, the irony of "according to my needs": these could well be financial, but might also be understood as the need to be violent, to act out one's rage and resentment, a capricious resentment which is sometimes satisfied with one thump and sometimes requires more.

Endowed with an uncertain professional status and muddled family links, Beckett's characters seem to lack, or gradually lose, any features that define them as members of an organized community. Their country and cities have no names, their lives have little or no symbolic consistency. Instead the text highlights physical traits and events: the fragility of the flesh, illness, invalidity. In the mother's episode, we learn that, being deaf, she lacks the ability for symbolic interaction. Her vision is barely functioning: "Not that seeing matters, but it's something to go on with," Molloy comments, emphasizing how little humanity was left in his mother. (The French vesion adds an ironic touch: "Non pas qu'il importe de voir, mais c'est un petit commencement"; a "little beginning," as if at his mother's age one could still care about beginnings.) Among bodily functions, her aged body is best at excreting. She recognizes Molloy by his odor, the least codified, least symbolic of all senses, and feels an animal joy: "She knew it was me, by my smell. Her shrunken hairy old face lit up, she was happy to smell me" (17).

To the same polemic against concepts and conventions we can attribute the contrast between Molloy's obsession with his body and Moran's obsession with duty, profession, manners, and external appearance. Endlessly, happily, Molloy speaks about his legs, his declining knees, his vision, his testicles, his anus. Moran, in contrast, is a compulsive respecter of status, duty, and manners. He judges Father Ambrose severely for flattering himself "with being a man of the world and knowing its ways" (100). By implication, Moran knows these ways better. Strict with his son and servant, Moran has at his disposal a rich moral vocabulary. On the priest's face, Moran notices "how shall I say, a lack of nobility" (102). Later, he advises his son: "There is something . . . more important in life than punctuality, and that is decorum. Repeat." He describes with precision the clothes his son must take for their common journey: the school suit, his toiletry, one shirt, one pair of socks, and seven pairs of drawers. Notice the worry for anal cleanliness, a compulsive feature in Moran and a relaxed one in Molloy.

Moran's obsessiveness is far from making him happy. At home before embarking upon the journey to find Molloy, Moran complains about virtually every detail of his domestic life: "The stew was a great disappointment. Where are the onions? I cried. Gone to nothing, replied Martha. I rushed into the kitchen, to look for the onion I suspected her of having removed from the pot, because she knew how much I liked them. I even rummaged in the bin. Nothing. She watched me mockingly" (102). It is as if a rule-governed life, a life which respects norms, conventions, and social symbols inevitably leads to bickering about their fulfillment. Wherever there is a norm, there also is the probability that it will be infringed. To live by the concept means permanently to witness its neglect. Moreover, what if the rules are themselves mistaken? "Thus to my son I gave precise instructions. But were they the right ones? Would they stand by second thoughts? Would I not be impelled, in a very short time, to cancel them?" (103). In contrast, Molloy's invalidity, by keeping him close to his own body and far from the rule-governed world, makes him a more dignified, even happier character. Neither Molloy nor Moran ever complain about their growing infirmities. The decay of the body (decay of function and structure) is perceived as a liberation.

We certainly are a long way from the subtle vitalism of Bergson and Proust, as well as from the overtly articulated *Angst* of Sartre's Roquentin. Nevertheless, the same suspicion toward concepts that informs Proust's and Sartre's narratives gives *Molloy* its bite. The difference between the latter and the former is that while in Proust and Sartre the message is safely conveyed in the crystal-clear language of representational narrative, Beckett speaks a more recent and disturbing idiom.

Born as a reaction against conventional narrative techniques, the modernist narrative counters the objectivist bias of these techniques and their insensitivity to the spontaneous, meandering stream of the individual consciousness. The creators of modernist prose felt that conventional narratives fail to challenge the sophisticated modern reader; in contrast, texts which use the numerous varieties of modernist techniques make a special effort to puzzle the reader. In opposition to realist and naturalist prose, modernist writing resists naturalizing. Autonomous monologues,[13] for instance, do not bother to depict the outside world too faithfully. Technical details such as lack of paragraph division and punctuation suggest the free flow of thoughts and images and force the reader to pay much more attention to every twist and turn of the text. Hence the reputation for difficulty of many modern texts, *Molloy* included.

Yet just as the most difficult of Faulkner's novels can be analyzed in components involving scenes, dialogue, memories, and impressions, Molloy's monologue doesn't forever resist naturalization. It can, for instance, be divided into three parts, each made up of small narrative episodes, and each involving a journey (successful or not) to the city.[14] The episodes, about fifteen, none shorter than two pages and none longer than ten pages, narrate a long quest, and are permeated by the main theme of the story, resistance to the world of concepts. Once the disorienting effect of typographical innovation (continuous printing) is dispelled, some of the episodes begin to sound surprisingly close to the tone of traditional quest-romances and ordeal narratives.[15]

The beginning, for instance, with its gloomy irony and its allusion to bodily decay, is strikingly modernist. Yet looked at more closely, it appears to follow an age-old framing technique, and achieves an effect comparable to the beginning of, say, Defoe's *Moll Flanders* or Emily Brontë's *Wuthering Heights*. Compare "I am in my mother's room. It's I who live there now" with "My true name is so well known in the records, or registers, at Newgate and in the Old Bailey . . . that it is not to be expected that I should set my name or the account of my family to this work" (*Moll Flanders*), and with "1801.—I have just returned from a visit to my landlord—the solitary neighbour that I shall be troubled with" (*Wuthering Heights*).[16] Beckett's and Brontë's narrators start by naming the place where they are or have just been, Defoe's by warning the reader that she shall hide her true name. The simplest and most matter of fact of all is Molloy. His lines look like a conventional autobiography, narrated by a character who, after a life of adventure and sin, has reached a haven of peace.

The three major sections making up the body of the story are: first, Molloy's adventures before he meets Lousse, a sequence of six short episodes; second, his sojourn at Lousse's house, another six episodes; finally, his wanderings toward the beach and back to the city, wanderings which become more and more arduous as his infirmities worsen dramatically. Each section narrates a part of Molloy's quest, shedding new light on his idiosyncracies and phobias, in particular on his distrust of human communities and their conventions, linguistic or social. And while the monologue certainly cannot be reduced to a mere replay of traditional techniques, we should not neglect the features which emphasize the readability of *Molloy*.

The episodes containing Molloy's initial journey between open country and the city begin with Molloy watching two vague characters, called A and C (modernist innovation? Moll Flanders too was stingy with her names) walking toward each other. Next, Molloy meets one of the two characters, a gentleman with a cigar, sandshoes, and a dog. Molloy expresses his doubts about the world of appearances and the words depicting them: "But was not perhaps in reality the cigar a cutty, and were not the sandshoes boots, hobnailed, dust-whitened, and what prevented the dog from being one of those stray dogs that you pick up and take in your arms . . ." (12). Soon the character disappears, and Molloy, alone, reflects on how his infirmity prevents him from getting closer to the man, checking his cigar, his shoes, finding out whether these objects correspond to Molloy's impressions about them. He then takes off his hat, wisely attached at his buttonhole by a long lace and sighs: "I am still alive then. That may come in useful" (14; in French: "Je vis donc toujours. C'est bon à savoir."),[17] as if his own existence were somehow open to doubt.

A short transition, ironically presented as a pause during a musical performance ("An instant of silence, as when the conductor taps on his stand, raises his arms, before the unanswerable clamour" [15]), leads to Molloy's visit to his mother, a good opportunity for the character to show his contempt for rational planning of action: "I needed, before resolving to go and see that woman, reasons of an urgent nature, and with such reasons, since I did not know what to do, or where to go, it was child's play for me, the play of an only child, to fill my mind until it was rid of all other preoccupation and I seized with a trembling at the mere idea of being hindered from going there, I mean to my mother, there and then" (15). Is this conscious self-deception? Is it a parody of moral reasoning, with the choice being made first, and the deliberation simulated later? As adverse to conventional moral hypocrisy as Proust's narrator and Sartre's Roquentin, Molloy does not trust his own impulses either, albeit he never quite resists them, as we shall see. Such quirky deliberations make the reader doubt the transparence of the story, increasing its resistance to naturalization.

Leaving his mother's place, Molloy gets in trouble with the police and the law (fourth episode). He alludes in vain to his invalidity and learns (or pretends to learn) from the policeman that in the threatening world of social abstractions, there are not two laws, "one for the healthy, another for the sick, but one only, to which all must bow, rich and poor, young and old, happy and sad." The policeman's rhetoric being lost on Molloy ("I pointed out that I was not sad"), the representative of authority turns hostile. "That was a mistake. Your papers, he said" (20). While enjoying the policeman's speech ("He was eloquent"), Molloy is unable to grasp the part that specifically refers to him ("there are not two laws, one for the healthy, another for the sick"), presumably because the second part of the policeman's sentence ("but one only to which all must bow . . .") omits to refer again to health and sickness. Like his mother, Molloy has a limited memory for abstract terms; moreover, he has trouble in seeing himself, the concrete, real Molloy, as the instantiation of a general concept. The request for papers reinforces the gap between social abstraction and Molloy's humble, bodily worries. While by "papers" the policeman refers to something as exalted as *identity* papers, Molloy takes the word in its everyday sense, as meaning *any* piece of paper. And since "the only papers I carry with me are bits of newspapers to wipe myself, you understand, when I have a stool," the idea of papers as symbolic of social identity is in comic contrast with Molloy's interest in the cleanliness of his anus.[18]

More opposition to social symbols occurs in the next episode, during which Molloy is taken to the police station. Scared by authority, Molloy is unable to answer questions: "I am so little used to being asked anything, that when I am asked something, I take some time to know what. And the mistake I make is this, that instead of quietly reflecting on what I have just heard, . . . I hasten to answer blindly, fearing perhaps lest my silence fan their anger to fury" (21–22). His life is so remote from rules, symbols, and concepts that he fails to remember the most routine information, his own family name and his mother's address. His knowledge is bodily, nonverbal: "As to her address, I was in the dark, but knew how to get there, even in the dark" (22). And when society comes to him in the form of well-organized benevolence, Molloy not only rejects it violently, but also warns his reader against society's intrusions into some of the most intimate bodily acts, swooning and vomiting: "Let me tell you this, when social workers offer you, free, gratis and for nothing, something to hinder you from swooning, which with them is an obsession, it is useless to recoil, they will pursue you to the ends of the earth, the vomitory in their hands" (23–24).

Happiness comes back only when, free again, Molloy rides his bicycle to the open country (sixth episode). "Inside me too, someone was laughing" (26). He sucks one of his pebbles to find peace: "A little pebble in your mouth, round and smooth, appeases, soothes, makes you forget your hunger, forget your thirst" (26). Thus Molloy's first attempt to find his mother, and the first section of his monologue, comes to an end: lying in the ditch "at full stretch, with outspread arms," Molloy, appeased, plays with the grass.

But not for long. In the next episode, the character is on the move again. Molloy's second journey opens with a rural prelude: out of his ditch, he sees a shepherd and his dog, hears the sheep bleating, muses about the countryside, confesses his love for the northern climate, counts his farts. In winter, he tells us, under his greatcoat he wraps his body in swathes of newspaper. "The Times Literary Supplement was admirably adapted to this purpose, of a neverfailing toughness and impermeability" (30). The terms "neverfailing toughness and impermeability," which the author undoubtedly intends as an ironic description of the journal's *intellectual* faults, become *physical* advantages in Molloy's world.

Back in the city, Molloy has trouble identifying its name. Yet he is well aware that in his province there is only one town, his native town, "the only one I knew, having never set foot in any other" (31). Although he claims to be clumsy with words, Molloy's aphasia extends to proper names: "I had been living so far from words so long, you understand, that it was enough for me to see my town, to be unable, you understand" (31). He has doubts about all words, to be sure: "even my sense of identity was wrapped in a namelessness often hard to penetrate," because between words and things, the links fade too easily: "there could be no things but nameless things, no names but thingless names." But saying is not inventing either, for "You invent nothing, you think you are inventing, you think you are escaping, and all you do is stammer out your lesson" (32). Although Roquentin's flight from routine is mirrored in Molloy's antisocial nature, the Sartrean hero's self-righteousness would have made no sense to Molloy.

The core of the second part of Molloy's story is his strange, initially incomprehensible, affair with Lousse, a woman whose dog he kills by running over it with his bicycle (eighth episode). Showing no anger, Lousse asks him to help her carry the dog home and bury it. He complies, although his sarcastic tone suggests he is quite aware of the dangers of Lousse's benevolence: "that she found me likeable enough in spite of my hideous appearance and would be happy to hold out to me a helping hand, and so on, I've forgotten the half of it. Ah yes, I too needed her, it seemed" (34). But Molloy, with his customary dignity, makes "no bones about telling her I needed neither her nor anyone." Which, he scrupulously adds, "was perhaps a slight exaggeration, for I must have needed my mother," (34) toward whom, as it becomes clear toward the end of his monologue, he is pushed by an irresistible impulse.

At this point, Molloy inserts one of his affable commentaries about his problematic relation with language: "I always say either too much or too little, which is a terrible thing for a man with a passion for truth like mine." He again sounds like an eighteenth-century narrator, pondering the tact and transparency of his delivery: "And I shall not abandon this subject [notice the decorous tone], . . . without making this curious observation, that it often happened to me, before I gave up speaking for good, to think I had said too little when in fact I had said too much and in fact to have said too little when I thought I had said too much." The tone is classicist in the first half of the sentence, only to turn Molloyan—that is, dry and punctilious—in the second half. The modern themes: inexpressibility, the gap between intention and utterance, between subjectivity and conventions, are couched in a style that mixes conventional elegance with modernist flatness. None of Faulkner's self-indulgent narrators display such irony and self-control

The next few episodes, which take place at Lousse's house, humorously narrate Molloy's captivity. Because of his infirmity, proudly recounted, Molloy cannot help Lousse bury the dog; his uselessness leads him to considerations about his leg and his testicles, "dangling at mid-thigh," and from which "there was nothing to be squeezed" (34). After the dog's funeral, Lousse feeds him good things—a gesture which, like the policeman's eloquence, is lost on Molloy, for the sour visitor doesn't "much care for good things to eat" (37). In the living room the parrot—an ugly mirror of human speech—from time to time utters "Fuck the son of a bitch!" and "Putain de merde," perhaps as an indication about Lousse's habits of speech and the reasons for her attraction to Molloy. (Generously, he thinks that the parrot must have belonged to French and American sailors before being acquired by Lousse.)

Next morning, Molloy wakes up in a bed, naked: "They had carried their impertinence to the point of washing me, to judge by the smell I gave off, no longer gave off" (38). The room is locked. The episode, perhaps intended as a parody of Proust's *La Prison-nière*, reiterates Molloy's revulsion for civilized life. His interminable musings on various topics include an irreverent spoof on the beginning of Goethe's *Faust*: "yes, I once took an interest in astronomy, I don't deny it. Then it was geology that killed a few years for me. The next pain in the balls was anthropology and the other disciplines, such as psychiatry . . . Oh I've tried everything. In the end it was magic that had the honour of my ruins" (39). Needless to say, Molloy inherits Faust's disgust with acquired knowledge but shares none of his enthusiasm for public works.

The clash with Lousse becomes inevitable when Molloy is told, in the next episode, that his clothes have been burned. As he takes revenge by hitting the furniture with his crutches the clothes are brought back, with only his hat's lace and the pebbles missing. Lousse attempts to keep him in the house, but Molloy does not even listen carefully. Convinced that his benefactor is slowly poisoning him, Molloy, after a long meditation on true love, leaves Lousse's house and hides in the city. To be again free, again alone on his crutches, gives Molloy a sense of rapture: "There is rapture, or there should be [ever prudent Molloy!], in the motion crutches give. It is a series of little flights skimming the ground. You take off, you land, through the thronging sound in wind and limb" (64).

Freedom and joy at the end of the second stage of Molloy's quest bring back the zany theme of the pebbles, as if the intimate contact with the mineral realm would protect Molloy from the attempts of humankind to take him prisoner. The long section on sucking stones (69–74) is the happiest of the entire monologue: it represents Molloy's peak of calm, maturity, effectiveness, and humor. Systematic reason, the episode seems to say, is at its best when taken away from human purposes and put in the service of pure futility.

Again, however, solitary happiness (this time in a cave on the seashore outside the city) cannot last: Molloy embarks on his third journey to the city. By now both his legs are paralyzed, though not in a strictly symmetrical way: "For the old pain, do you follow me, I had got used to it, in a way, yes in a kind of way. Whereas the new pain, though of the same family exactly, I had not time yet to get adjusted to it" (77). Molloy's detailed, compulsive description of his paralysis harbors no complaint. Molloy speaks about his body in an affectionate, yet detached way, as if the discomfort of pain were fully atoned for by the pleasure of being alone with one's own organism. Molloy suffers decorously, because his body, suffering included, is his only source of dignity: like Iphigenia on the altar modestly covering her body before death, Molloy wraps his head in his coat "to stifle the obscene noise of choking" (79). Under an impulse that comes from his muse (Molloy *dixit*, 79), he reinterprets his anus as "the true portal of our being," as an exalting image of rebellious autonomy: "Almost everything revolts it that comes from without and what comes from within does not seem to receive a very warm welcome either" (80).

His advance gradually becomes more arduous, with the image of the Calvary in the background: "I was therefore obliged to stop more and more often, I shall never weary of repeating it, and to lie down, in defiance of the rules" (82). A brief encounter with a charcoal-burner who offers Molloy his hut to share turns sour: the ever independent Molloy hits the stranger with a crutch, leaving him for dead. In the two concluding episodes of his last sortie, Molloy crawls through the woods at a rate of barely fifteen paces a day, turning in circles, vainly trying to catch forest murmurs. At times he would prefer to stay in the forest, for "physically nothing could have been easier" (86). But Molloy turns out to be a moral creature: "I was not purely physical, I lacked something, and I would have had the feeling, if I had stayed in the forest, of going against an imperative, at least I had that impression." The "imperatives," only now explicitly mentioned, are the only things Molloy submits to: different from the conventional symbols he despises so much, Molloy's imperatives come from inside, nearly all bearing "on the same question, that of my relations with my mother, and on the importance of bringing as soon as possible some light to bear on these and even on the kind of light that should be brought and the most effective means of doing so" (86).

Thus, once the resistance of the text to naturalization is overcome, Molloy's journeys to the city turn out to be a series of attempts to break out of his loneliness and establish intelligible relations with another human being. Yet strong as the imperatives initially are, their fulfillment always falters: they soon go silent, "leaving me there like a fool who neither knows where he is going, nor why he is going there" (86–87). It is not only the rule-governed world of policemen, social workers, and intrusive altruists that prevents Molloy from achieving his quest: his own inner impulse goes astray. With this realization, his quest comes to an end. At the ridge of the forest, unable to move forward, he detaches himself from all longing: "There seemed to be rain, then sunshine, turn about. Real spring weather. I longed to go back into the forest. Oh no real longing. Molloy could stay, where he happened to be" (91).

The plot of *Molloy* (part I) thus involves the hero's quest for some form of transparent relations with his mother, a quest that ends, as it were, in failure and transfiguration. As a coda to my reading, I would like to add that the story's rigorous spatial structure highlights the hero's predicament. Molloy meanders through two kinds of spaces: the outdoors and the city.[19] Freedom is to be found outdoors, in the open space, for even the woods are too crowded for Molloy. Yet Molloy cannot stay forever in the open, because his "imperatives" force him back to his quest: he must go back to his mother, in the city. But he cannot stay for a long time in the city either: his oppressors (the police) as well as his unbearable benefactors (the social worker, Lousse) subject him to various ordeals, from which he escapes only thanks to his unabashed misanthropy.

The population of characters is neatly divided into homogeneous sets of individuals who behave in similar ways.[20] Only Molloy crosses the boundary between the city and the open spaces. The others are confined either to the city or to the open country. In the city Molloy interacts quite peacefully, if brutally, with his mother, a character who appears to be helpful from the financial point of view, but entirely insensitive otherwise. The representatives of order (the policemen) terrify Molloy, while the intrusive helpers (the social worker, Lousse) merely repel him, encouraging him to behave deviously. The open country is not free of intrusive helpers either (a group of women on the beach, the charcoal-burner), but it at least contains a few characters who pay no attention to Molloy and his troubles: the two travelers (A and C) at the beginning, and the shepherd in the third part.

The above analysis supports John Fletcher's view that *Molloy* displays a remarkable "firmness of structure" (*Novels of Samuel Beckett* 135). The monologue narrates Molloy's three journeys to his mother's house in the midst of a dangerous city and, on the way, the hero's efforts to protect himself from both oppression and intrusive help. It tells us how the hero's infirmities invariably bring him trouble from the police—an openly hostile group—as well as from aggressive well-wishers. Molloy finds peace only far from society, in loneliness and open spaces. This story embodies something of an ordeal novel and of a quest-romance. A traveler between opposite worlds, Molloy goes through severe tests and cyclic adventures. Those who want to harm him miss, and those who want to help can only harm him: Moran's failure to reach Molloy, in the second part, is in a sense the best way to find him.

Molloy's first person narrative patiently recounts the character's opposition to the world of conventions as well as his move away from and back to happiness. It reveals Molloy's variegated inner life, his failed quest, and, foremost, his self-sufficiency. The alliance between the theme of resistance to concepts and the modernist narrative technique gives new life to an old topos: the solitary hero, struggling to maintain his sense of dignity.

Notes

1. Maurice Nadeau (*Combat*, 1951), in Lawrence Graver and Raymond Federman, 53.

2. Georges Bataille (*Critique*, 1951), in Lawrence Graver and Raymond Federman, 63.

3. Wolfgang Iser, "Subjectivity as the Autogenous Cancellation of Its Own Manifestations" in Bloom.

4. Leo Bersani, "Beckett and the End of Literature," in Bloom.

5. I borrow the notion of placement from Jurij Striedter, *Literary Structure*, 166.

6. Christine Brooke-Rose, "Samuel Beckett and the Anti-Novel," 38–46; John Fletcher, "Beckett and the Fictional Tradition," chapter 5 of *Samuel Beckett's Art*.

7. Hugh Kenner, *The Stoic Comedian*.

8. Steven J. Rosen, *Samuel Beckett and the Pessimistic Tradition*.

9. Harold Bloom, "Introduction," in Bloom.

10. Brice Parain, *L'Embarras du choix*.

11. Among the critics who describe the affinity between Sartre and Beckett's struggle with subjectivity and language, see Olga Bernal, *Langage et fiction dans le roman de Beckett*, the section "Les Mots et le Je"; and Edith Kern, *Existential Thought and Fictional Technique*.

12. On the reference to the Cartesian philosopher Arnold Geulincx (1624–69) in Beckett's *Murphy*, see John Fletcher, *The Novels of Samuel Beckett*, 51–53.

13. This category, introduced by Dorrit Cohn in chapter 6 of *Transparent Minds: Narrative Modes*, emphasizes the differences between realist first person narratives and modernist monologues.

14. John Fletcher, *Novels of Samuel Beckett*, rightly argues that "Only a superficial reading leads one to think that *Molloy* is a rambling monologue leading nowhere in particular; only such a reading can have given rise to the unhelpful, but often-proffered opinion that this is a stream-of-consciousness novel." And he adds: "We blunt our terms by thus misusing them: *Molloy* is no more a stream-of-consciousness novel than is Mauriac's *Noeud de vipères*; in both cases we are confronted with a hard, clear, uncompromisingly honest self-description. A book needs more than a first-person narrator talking to and for himself before it can be bracketed with the last episode of *Ulysses*" (135). Presumably for Fletcher a genuine stream-of-consciousness narrative must convey the sense that the speaker's mind is invaded by unsolicited thoughts and images. In contrast with Faulkner's Quentin (in the second section of *The Sound and the Fury*), Molloy seems to control his thoughts quite well. For the expressive potential of the autonomous monologue, see Dorrit Cohn, 232 ff.

15. Accordingly, I disagree with those critics who read Beckett's *Trilogy* as a set of nonchronological texts. Charlotte Renner ("The Self-Multiplying Narrators" in Bloom) argues that "the trilogy is not only, like most multivocal fictions, nonchronological; it is in fact anti-chronological. In other words, it reverses the traditional order of artistic composition. In most fictions, the implied author is understood to be the prerequisite to the invention of narrating characters . . . in Beckett's trilogy, however, the 'author' . . . has no existence prior to inventing its mutable incarnations" (99). But since in first person narratives the existence of the *implied* author is, as the term "implied" indicates, only inferred from the text, it is difficult to determine whether or not it preexists the narrating characters. For a lucid analysis of *Molloy*'s use of first person narration, see Dina Sherzer, 115–22.

16. Bernal, 44–45, compares the beginning of Molloy with that of

several nineteenth- and twentieth-century novels. In a short memoir about his first meeting with Beckett, his publisher remembers the spellbinding effect of *Molloy*'s first sentence: Jérôme Lindon, "Première rencontre."

17. Among the critics who wrote on Beckett's quite intriguing translations, see the perceptive remarks of Brian Fitch, "L'intra-intertextualité de Beckett," 91–112, and the chapter "The Trilogy Translated" in Leslie Hill, *Beckett's Fiction in Different Words*.

18. This interest is more indicative of personal dignity than of hygiene, as Molloy rushes to make clear: "Oh I don't say I wipe myself every time I have a stool, no, but I like to be in a position to do so, if I have to" (20). For a study of Beckett's comic vein, see Ruby Cohn, *Samuel Beckett: The Comic Gamut*.

19. For the remarks on Beckettian space, I am indebted to Michael Sheringham, *Beckett: Molloy*, and to Ludovic Janvier, "Place of Narration/Narration of Place" in Ruby Cohn, *Samuel Beckett: A Collection of Criticism*.

20. In "Narrative Domains," I argue that narratives can be divided into domains of characters who act or react together.

Bibliography

Bataille, Georges. Review of *Molloy* in *Critique*. 1951. Rpt. in *Samuel Beckett: The Critical Heritage*. Ed. by Lawrence Graver and Raymond Federman. London: Routledge, 1979.

Bernal, Olga. *Language et fiction dans le roman de Beckett*. Paris: Gallimard, 1969.

Bloom, Harold, ed. *Samuel Beckett's Molloy, Malone Dies, The Unnamable*. New York: Chelsea House, 1988.

Brooke-Rose, Christine. "Samuel Beckett and the Anti-Novel." *London Magazine*. Dec. 1958: 38–46.

Cohn, Dorrit. *Transparent Minds: Narrative Modes for Presenting Consciousness in Fiction*. Princeton: Princeton University Press, 1978.

Cohn, Ruby. *Samuel Beckett: The Comic Gamut*. New Brunswick: Rutgers University Press, 1962.

———, ed. *Samuel Beckett: A Collection of Criticism*. New York: McGraw-Hill, 1975.

Fitch, Brian. "L'intra-intertextualité de Beckett: La problematique de la traduction de soi." *Texte* 2 (1983): 91–112.

Fletcher, John. *The Novels of Samuel Becket*. London: Chatto & Windus, 1964.

———. *Samuel Beckett's Art*. New York: Barnes & Noble, 1967.

Hill, Leslie. *Beckett's Fiction in Different Words*. Cambridge: Cambridge University Press, 1990.

Kenner, Hugh. *The Stoic Comedian: Flaubert, Joyce, and Beckett*. Boston: Beacon Press, 1962.

Kern, Edith. *Existential Thought and Fictional Technique: Kierkegaard, Sartre, Beckett*. New Haven: Yale University Press, 1970.

Lindon, Jérôme. "Première recontre." In *Cahiers de L'Herne, Samuel Beckett*. Paris, 1976.

Nadeau, Maurice. Review of *Molloy* in *Combat*. 1951. Rpt. in *Samuel Beckett: The Critical Heritage*. Ed. by Lawrence Graver and Raymond Federman. London: Routledge, 1979.

Parain, Brice. *L'Embarras du choix: Essais*. Paris: Gallimard, 1947.

Pavel, Thomas G. "Narrative Domains." *Poetics Today* 1.3 (1980): 105–14.

Rosen, Steven J. *Samuel Beckett and the Pessimistic Tradition*. New Brunswick: Rutgers University Press, 1976.

Sheringham, Michael. *Beckett: Molloy*. London: Grant & Cutler, 1985.

Sherzer, Dina. "Quelque manifestations du Narrateur-Créateur dans *Molloy* de Samuel Beckett." *Language and Style* 5 (1972): 115–22.

Striedter, Jurij. *Literary Structure, Evolution, and Value*. Cambridge, MA: Harvard University Press, 1989.

8

Travel Narrative and
Imperialist Vision

MARY LOUISE PRATT

Hand in hand with the Industrial Revolution, the late eighteenth century brought a newly intensified period of European exploration, commercial penetration, imperial expansion, and colonization all over the planet. In the main, as we all learned in school, the expansion was a search for markets and raw materials, the two fuels needed by European capitalist economies whose productive capacity, and whose ability to produce surpluses, was rapidly increasing. This period of expansion is one in which we still find ourselves, albeit at a much later stage. All corners of the planet are now integrated to some degree into a global capitalist economic system, while that system itself confronts crises undreamt of two hundred years ago. In the beginning, this burst of expansion in the late eighteenth century was mainly British—Captain Cook's first voyage was in 1768, the same year that James Bruce began his search for the source of the Nile—but the French under Napoleon were not far behind. By the end of the nineteenth century, the United States was on board with the Monroe Doctrine, while every major nation in Europe was participating in the notorious scramble for Africa.

A few sections of this essay are revised from my works of 1986 and 1992 cited in the bibliography.

This process of capitalist expansion was (and still is) witnessed in thousands upon thousands of travel books. Travel literature played an extremely important role in the production of consciousness and the making of ideology in connection with the expansionist enterprise. Of particular interest is its role in producing what is now fashionably called alterity, the process by which certain peoples and places get constituted as an Other positioned in varying ways with respect to a normative European self, and made knowable only, or almost only, through those positionings. Quite often these travel books were written by direct emissaries and purveyors of European expansion: explorers, traders, settlers, missionaries, engineers, surveyors, soldiers, diplomats, and so forth. Sometimes they were written by people whose involvement was more marginal or oblique, like naturalists, game hunters, thrill-seekers, or the wives of those explorers, traders, diplomats, and so on. Sometimes they were written by people who were vehement opponents of the expansion, or even fugitives from it. It is thus in a very rich and varied sense that travel literature has been the place where, as Daniel Defert says, "Europe took consciousness of itself, wrote about itself and read about itself more and more as the basis ('principe') of a planetary process and not as a region of the world" (Defert 26).

I propose to document a shift in the discourse of European travel narratives sometime during the first half of the nineteenth century, making accounts from the turn of the century (1790–1830) very different from those written sixty years later. I will be focusing mainly on British accounts of African exploration, but will make some reference to other materials as well. In the case of Africa, the two periods I am talking about correspond to the two major thrusts of British exploration, first the exploration of the Niger River by Bruce, Park, Clapperton, Lander, Oldfield, and others (few of whom survived to write at all). This first thrust, conducted mainly under the auspices of the Africa Association (founded in 1788), was so unsuccessful that exploration was virtually suspended until after 1850, when a whole series of envoys—Livingstone, Burton, Speke, Grant, Baker, Stanley, Du Chaillu, and others—successfully crisscrossed the interior of the continent, and documented its major geographical features. This second period, the "opening up of Africa," is by far the best known.

As with all exploration, the accomplishments of these travelers were constituted dually by the combination of travel and of travel writing. The opening up of Africa necessarily consisted not just of certain Europeans and North Americans journeying to certain geographical locations, but also and crucially of those Europeans and North Americans producing discourse about their journeyings, to be disseminated in Europe and North America. Put another way, the opening up of Africa to Europe was also the opening up of Europe to Africa, the process by which names like Burton, Speke, Grant, Gondokoro, Ujiji, Unyamwezi, and Matabele became household words. With exploration, and a great many other kinds of travel as well, the journey and the writing about it are inseparable projects—they presuppose each other and create each other's significance. If you don't survive to tell the tale, you might as well never have gone, unless of course someone else survives to bring back your diary. Likewise, journey and account mutually determine each other's shape—what you say in the book has everything to do with what you experienced on your trip, but what you experience on your trip has everything to do with the book you are planning to write. For instance, African exploration was typically organized around the quest for specific, definable "prizes" like the source of the Nile. At least in part the project took this form because exploration books could then have the form of classic quests, in which the hero is finding and bringing home a treasure. As a rule, in the classic quest the hero is simply recovering for the community a missing treasure that rightfully belongs to it but was lost—an idea that fit well with European imperial designs. Indeed, the epic model of achievement might be said to have exerted equal influence on the shapes of the explorers' journeys and the shapes of their accounts. This paradigm, already firmly instilled in the consciousness of every European who had ever heard a fairy tale, legitimizes exploration in a culturally and ideological powerful way, and lends it an air of reality that it might not otherwise have.

For of course the European "discoverer" doesn't really bring home anything at all, only the claim to having seen something with European eyes.

The discursive shift in travel narrative that I propose to discuss is easily introduced by a pair of sample passages. Of the two texts quoted below, the first is from a very famous turn of the century travel book, Mungo Park's *Travels in the Interior of Africa*, which appeared in 1802. The second is from David Livingstone's *Narrative of an Expedition to the Zambesi*, which appeared in 1866. Both passages are representative of the discourse of their respective books, and were chosen because they are in no way exceptional. First the Park text (italics mine):

> About a mile from this place, *I heard* a loud and confused noise somewhere *to the right of my course,* and in a short time was happy to find it was the croaking of frogs, which was heavenly music *to my ears. I followed* the sound, and at daybreak arrived at some shallow muddy pools, so full of frogs that it was difficult to *discern* the water. The noise they made frightened my horse, and *I was obliged* to keep them quiet by beating the water with a branch until he had drank. Having quenched *my thirst, I ascended* a tree, and the morning being calm, *I soon perceived* the smoke of the watering place which *I had passed* in the night; and *observed* another pillar of smoke east-south-east, distant twelve or fourteen miles. Towards this *I directed* my route. (163)

Notice in this passage how everything is anchored in the narrator-protagonist, in his immediate sensory experience, his judgment, agency, and desires (examples are italicized). Notice too how the relevance of everything that is said lies in its immediate bearing on the narrator and his journey. Now contrast the Livingstone passage (italics mine):

> Ten or fifteen miles *north* of Morambala *stands* the dome-shaped mountain of Makanda of Chi-kanda; several others, with granitic-looking peaks, *stretch* away to the north, and *form* the eastern boundary of the valley; another range, but of metamorphic rocks, *commencing* opposite Senna *bounds* the valley on the *west.* After steaming

through a portion of this marsh, we came to a broad belt of palm and other trees, crossing the fine plain on the right bank. Marks of large game *were abundant*. Elephants had been feeding on the palm nuts, which *have* a pleasant fruity taste, and *are used* as food *by man*. Two pythons *were observed* coiled together among the branches of a large tree, and *were both shot*. The larger of the two, a female, was ten feet long. They *are harmless*, and said to *be good eating*. (102)

Here everything is described without reference to a situated observer (the italics show some of the ways this was done). The perceptual process by which someone observed some signs and deduced that elephants had been feeding on the palm nuts is not alluded to; neither is the experience by which it was ascertained that palm nuts have a pleasant fruity taste. We will never know who observed the two pythons, who shot them, who measured them and ascertained their sex, who said they were good eating, and who found that out by experience. Syntactically, observations and claims are given as detached facts rather than anchored in a speaker by such devices as verbs of perception or mental process. Things happen without happening to anybody or being brought about by anybody. The pronoun *I* is about as welcome as a case of dropsy. In contrast with Park, only a fraction of the information Livingstone asserts bears immediately upon the participants and their journey. Here the specifics of the journey mainly function as a pretext for introducing information whose origin and relevance apparently lie elsewhere. The actual elephants and pythons encountered, for instance, are used as pegs on which to hang general information about palm nuts and pythons. The landscape is simply there (described mostly in compass terms which are not deictic to the speaker) with no bearing on the travelers. At the risk of oversimplifying, one could sum up the difference by saying that here everything is conveyed as *information*, while in the Park text everything is conveyed as *experience*.

These characteristics hold not only for Park's and Livingstone's writings, but for much of the production of their contemporaries. Throughout Park's text, and those of many of his contemporaries, the specific episodes and adventures of the journey are the main things to be made known to the home audience. Consequently these are often dramatized at great length, producing texts that sound very novelistic to modern readers. In the mid-century texts, there is very little narrative elaboration or dramatization. The vocabulary of the emotions is also virtually dispensed with, as is the convention of elaborating one's emotive responses to important events or sights. The autobiographical is minimized; writers either abandon or, in Livingstone's case, complain about the opening sketch of the author's life which is conventionally found in earlier texts, often at great length. Clearly two different kinds of authority are at work—for Park, subjectivity and perspectivism are the anchors of textual authority; for Livingstone, impersonal knowledge is what counts. At the same time, Livingstone is obviously not trying to speak the language of science. His text is full of judgments, evaluations, and opinions, and it is unquestionably narrative, not descriptive.

I have pointed out that in Livingstone's writing, the relevance of what is said does not lie in its connection with the immediate interests of the traveler himself. As it turns out, what does make all this detached and detachable information relevant is the imperial agenda itself, an agenda that he alludes to constantly in his narrative, and elaborates on at length in his preface:

> This account is written in the earnest hope that it may contribute to that information which will cause the great and fertile continent of Africa to be no longer kept wantonly sealed, but made available as a scene of European enterprise, and will enable its people to take a place among the nations of the earth, thus securing the happiness and prosperity of tribes now sunk in barbarism or debased by slavery, and, above all, I cherish the hope that it may lead to the introduction of the blessings of the Gospel. (2)

Notice that the term *information* appears here as the object of the enterprise, the thing to be acquired and brought home. The information has power: it will *cause* Africa to become the scene of European enterprise. It is an intense orientation toward the future that led the mid-century explorers to value information (rather than experience) in their discourse. They had a sense of participating in the beginning of a long-term planetary (to use Defert's term) process, which was ultimately going to transform every corner of the world. And they were right.

Mungo Park, by contrast, never alludes to the commercial project in his narrative proper. His preface, however, is as explicit about it as is Livingstone's. Perhaps more so, for Park makes no attempt to link commercial expansion with any interests other than the specific financial ambitions of himself and his backers. Here is what he says in his preface about his objectives and aspirations:

> If I should perish in my journey, I was willing that my hopes and expectations should perish with me; and if I should succeed in rendering the geography of Africa more familiar to my countrymen, and in opening to their ambition and industry new sources of wealth, and new channels of commerce, I knew that I was in the hands of men of honour, who would not fail to bestow that remuneration which my successful services should appear to them to merit. (ix)

Again notice how everything is anchored in specific persons and in the immediate interests of the present. The forces at work are not abstractions like "information" or "European enterprise," but rather the ambition and industry of the specific persons ("men of honour") who belong to the Africa Association. The sense of a global transformative project is absent, and probably for this reason there is also no attempt to construe any hypothetical benefits for the Africans. The notion of a benevolent civilizing mission comes into play later, one suspects, when there is a full-fledged imperial mission that needs mystifying. So it was with the Spaniards in America three hundred years before, and so it is today, in White House pronouncements where "democracy" and "freedom" replace "prosperity" and "salvation" as the goods equated with imperial intervention.

And if the Spanish imperial enterprise in the 1500s emerged from the energies and appetites of a newly consolidated Spain, so the nineteenth-century enterprise is the project of the newly consolidated European nation states who are in the process of forming that polity Livingstone refers to as "the nations of the earth." One of the great historical watersheds that separates David Livingstone and Mungo Park is the rise of the modern state. This watershed determines in part that what for Park is an immediate, personal enterprise is for Livingstone a long-term planetary process.

I have underscored Livingstone's use of the term "information" in his preface, as an unwitting metacomment on his own discourse. There is another such term in that excerpt, namely *scene*. While Park talks about *sources* of wealth and *channels* of commerce (rivers form an apt source of terminology for him), Livingstone talks about Africa as the future *scene* of European enterprise (see quotation above). Mid-nineteenth-century travel accounts contain an enormous amount of landscape description, which is likewise shaped by the expansionist project that so impinges on the consciousness of these writers.

Three different modes of landscape description can be distinguished in these writings. The first, which I call the development mode, is illustrated by the first Livingstone text quoted above. The two characteristics that typify the development mode are, first, that it seeks a panoramic, totalizing sweep, and second, that it combines everyday visual vocabulary with specialized—in this case geological—vocabulary that encodes the region's development potential. The language is mildly aesthetic at times—Livingstone speaks of a *fine meadow*, for instance. The criteria for these aesthetic judgments is also the future use potential of the place. There are enormous amounts of this kind of development-oriented landscape description in the travel literature of mid-century, be it about Africa or any other place being "opened up" to European eyes (as Latin America was, for instance, after its independence in 1820). This discourse did not originate with the explorers of mid-century, but it has great prominence in their writings.

The second landscape convention is in the picturesque mode, in which nature is portrayed as a garden replete with flowers and trees of all colors, among which myriads of insects, butterflies, and hummingbirds busily flit. I am being only partly sarcastic here. This conventional garden scene, which recurs innumerable times on the pages of African travel books, invariably includes the flowers, the butterflies, the hummingbirds, and the verb *flit*. Here is an example from a stunningly nondescript account by naturalist J. Leyland called *Adventures in the Far Interior of South Africa* (1866):

> On this route, and in many other parts of the Colony, the scenery was most enchanting and picturesque; the hills and mountains were adorned in wild profusion with flowers of various hues, and often of the most brilliant and gaudy colours, filling the air with their delicious perfume. Most conspicuous were the geraniums, growing three and four feet high. When the flowers were most abundant, the various kinds of Sun-birds [hummingbirds] and Fly-catchers were seen, and thousands of butterflies flitting hither and thither, distinguished by an endless variety of colours. (72)

Sometimes explicitly, though usually not, these garden scenes embody a privatized domestic fantasy of a *locus amoenus* in which to settle one's family. People familiar with children's literature will find a more recent version of such a scene in the first volume of the Babar books, where Babar, recently returned from his civilizing experience in Europe, selects just such a place on which to found the new city of the elephants.

The third landscape convention, in the mode of the sublime, is the panorama seen from a promontory, a convention familiar to us from the prospect poetry of the eighteenth and early nineteenth centuries. This convention is frequently used to textualize arrivals at major geographical discoveries or landmarks, such as Burton's discovery of Lake Tanganyika, or James Grant's arrival at the Victoria Nyanza. I have elsewhere called this the monarch-of-all-I-survey convention ("Conventions"; *Imperial Eyes*), because so often in exploration literature these prospect scenes encode a relation of dominance of the seer over the seen. Often they include a prophetic vision of the future European domination of the region. For instance, in his description of arriving at Lake Victoria Nyanza, Grant literally sketches in such a prophetic vision (italics mine):

> The now famous Victoria Nyanza, when seen for the first time, expanding in all its majesty, excited our wonder and admiration.

Even the listless Wanyamuezi came to have a look at its waters, stretching over ninety degrees of the horizon. The Seedees were in raptures with it, fancying themselves looking upon the ocean which surrounds their island home of Zanzibar, and *I made a sketch, dotting it with imaginary steamers and ships riding at anchor in the bay.* On its shores are beautiful bays, made by wooded tongues of low land . . . (196)

All three types of landscape description have at least one thing in common. All three, the development description, the garden description, and the promontory description, largely eliminate current inhabitants from the environment. There are gardens but no gardener, meadows but no one tilling them, forests but no one hunting in them, resources but no one already using them. Landscapes are described as more or less virgin territory, not as human environments with histories, already inhabited from time immemorial by populations organized into societies, empires, and above all economies. No trace is registered of vast indigenous trade networks, often already linked up with Europe, even in regions that explorers were coming to for the first time. These were the societies, networks, and economies that Europeans were going to dismantle in order to establish their own hegemony, and which they did dismantle, in the end by the most brutal kinds of mass destruction, murder, and coercion. It is no accident that in the thrilling, heady period of exploration, the potential human complications were so often painted out of the future "scene of European enterprise." But in hindsight, one cannot help seeing in these depopulated verbal landscapes of the travel books the ideological preparation for the real depopulation that was to come.

And there is perhaps another sort of depersonalization to be noted here, as Wlad Godzich has pointed out (personal communication). It is surely not a coincidence that the emissaries of the modern state most often position themselves as an invisible and passive eye looking out over a space, a conduit for information rather than a mediating agent. The reader is by their side, looking with them and not at them. These are not subjects who act in the name of the state—the state will act through them.

There are several points of contrast here with earlier travel and exploration writings. In 1790, a travel writer pausing on a promontory was less likely to describe the sight itself than an emotive response to the sight. For example, when James Bruce in the 1780s describes looking down on one of the great cataracts of the Nile, what he ends up talking about is himself:

> It was a most magnificent sight, that ages, added to the greatest length of human life, would not efface or eradicate from my memory; it struck me with a kind of stupor, and a total oblivion of where I was, and of every other sublunary concern. . . . I was awakened from one of the most profound reveries that ever I fell into, by Mahomet and by my friend Drink, who now put to me a thousand impertinent questions. It was after this I measured the fall and believe, within a few feet, it was the height I have mentioned; but I confess I could at no time in my life less promise upon precision; my reflection was suspended, or subdued; and while in sight of the fall, I think I was under a temporary alienation of mind; it seemed to me as if one element had broke loose from, and become superior to, all laws of subordination . . . (162)

The currency in which the sight is given textual value here is not its visual properties (as it would be for later writers), but the response experienced by the seer. Once again, as with Mungo Park, we have a sentimental discourse, stringently anchored in the subjectivity of the speaker-protagonist, a discourse in which experience rather than information is the principal matter to be conveyed. Notice further that the experience Bruce undergoes here is not one of domination or conquest; if anything, the landscape possesses him, rather than the reverse. Nor does he see a prophetic, civilizing vision—on the contrary, the landscape seems to be *out* of control, not under control. Moreover, Bruce represents *himself* as out of control, announcing limitations to his authority (notably his authority to gather information!). This is the kind of thing the mid-century writers almost never do. Their discourse minimizes reference to its speaking subject, and leaves little possibility for expressing limits to the speaker's authority.

In the earlier, experiential narratives, like those of Bruce and Mungo Park, there is little in the way of landscape and nature description of any kind. This is also true of novels of the period, such as those of Chateaubriand. What predominates overwhelmingly is human and diplomatic drama. The "scenes of European enterprise" in these earlier accounts are dramatic scenes in which the traveler is an actor with a role. The narrative proceeds not by passage through a constantly changing ecology, but by passage from one human encounter to the next—meetings with local chiefs, robbers, benefactors, queens, slaves. These experiential, sentimental texts (other examples include Richard Lander and Gaspard Mollien in Africa, and such figures as John Stedman, John Davie, and John Mawe in South America) are adventure stories, tales of a thousand woes, full of captivities, holdups, narrow escapes and, above all, oh so delicate negotiations with local leaders for the permission and protection without which travel would mean certain death for the outsider. They are full of high melodrama and high comedy, the non-European other often seen as outlandish, bizarre, hilarious, or horrifying, the European self as pathetic, silly, or roguish.

As I mentioned earlier, these late eighteenth-century experiential texts strike the literary critic as extremely novelistic. Mungo Park is the picture of the sentimental hero, Richard Lander a pure picaresque rogue. John Stedman in his *Narrative of a Five Years Expedition against the Revolted Negroes of Surinam* (1790) builds his account around a (true) love story between himself and a mulatto slave, told in tear-jerking fashion worthy of Richardson's *Pamela*. As I have argued elsewhere, however ("Conventions"), it is not that these travel writers are imitating or borrowing from the novel. At this juncture, travel literature and the novel must be seen as sharing a common narrative discourse that is dramatic, experiential, and sentimental. Neither genre can legitimately be seen as the originator or proprietor of this discourse.

In the experiential accounts, both European interlopers and local inhabitants get individualized as characters, and what gets elaborated textually are the idiosyncracies and particularities of persons and occasions. Consider for instance Mungo Park's rendition of one of his many encounters with a local king. Notice again the hero's portrayal of himself as vulnerable, inept, limited in power and understanding, innocently at the mercy of things, as Bruce was at the cataract:

> We reached at length the king's tent, where we found a great number of people, men and women, assembled. Ali was sitting upon a black leather cushion, clipping a few hairs from his upper lip; a female attendant holding up a looking-glass before him. He appeared to be an old man, of the Arab cast, with a long white beard; and he had a sullen and indignant aspect. He surveyed me with attention and inquired of the Moors if I could speak Arabic; being answered in the negative he appeared much surprised, and continued silent. The surrounding attendants and especially the ladies, were abundantly more inquisitive; they asked a thousand questions, inspected every part of my apparel, searched my pockets and obliged me to unbutton my waistcoat, and display the whiteness of my skin; they even counted my toes and fingers, as if they doubted whether I was in truth a human being. (234)

This kind of scene is found all through late eighteenth-century travel narrative. Needless to say, such encounters with local leaders and inhabitants are just as frequent and essential to later travelers, but these encounters are seldom dramatized or elaborated in their accounts. Instead, what acquires prominence as a means of representing local inhabitants is the discourse of tribal features, in which the Other is described collectively as an inventory of traits and customs which exist abstracted from particular persons and experiences. In the passage from James Bruce (1790) quoted above, Bruce refers to his native companions by name and represents himself in dialogue with them. In the excerpt from James Grant (1864), on the other hand, Grant refers to his native companions by tribal labels—the Wanyamuezi, the Seedees—and characterizes them in terms of tribal characteristics and responses. Often, as in Richard Burton's classic *Lake Regions of Central Africa* (1861), local inhabitants are removed altogether from the journey narrative and are discussed in separate chapters on the "geography and ethnology" of the region. It is the discourse of "social science," just beginning to consolidate itself in the mid-nineteenth century. Whatever the explanatory power of this discourse, there can be no doubt about its potential for reifying, dehumanizing, and distancing those whom it is used to characterize. You can't talk to a set of tribal features (though you might be able to organize them into a work force). By abstracting traits away from organized social and material life, this discourse verbally dismantles human societies. As with the kinds of nature description I mentioned above, it pulls people out of the landscape.

It would be incorrect to say that this discourse of tribal features is absent from earlier travel accounts. It is not. But it is counterbalanced there by the particularizing, experiential narrative. For instance, when Mungo Park offers some "general observations on the character and disposition of the Mandingoes," his point of departure is the specifics of his own interaction with them. He says, for example, "Perhaps the most prominent defect in their character was the insurmountable propensity which the reader must have observed . . . to steal from me the few effects I was possessed of" (239). This account is anchored differently from, say, Richard Burton's description of the Wanyamuezi, which begins "They are usually of a dark sepia brown, rarely coloured like diluted India ink . . . the effluvium from their skin especially after exercise or excitement, marks their connection with the Negro. The hair curls crisply. . . ." (II: 20).

There is a risk in this discussion of falling into a simple good guys/bad guys story. One does not want to say that the late eighteenth-century sentimental travelers were somehow less imperialist than their successors at mid-century. If I have been constructing what looks like a moral tale, my objective has been not to idealize the earlier accounts, but to use them to make available to us aspects of the later ones. The difference is in the way the imperial enterprise is encoded in the travel narrative. In the mid-century writers, the tendency toward depersonalization and dehumanization, the projection toward a future global transformation, the positioning of the traveler as an invisible, passive observer, are all characteristic of imperialist vision under the modern nation-state. In the sentimental travelers, the expansionist enterprise is encoded largely in what Daniel Defert calls the language of universal diplomacy of pre-nineteenth-century Europe, a pan-continental code in which power relations are understood through courtly ritual and etiquette. As James Clifford has observed (personal communication), part of the appeal of these sentimental accounts today lies in the fact that this dramatic, diplomatic mode allows for dialogue, for power and personhood on both sides, in contrast with the reifying discourses of racism that were to follow. That sense of dialogue in turn lets Europeans think they won fair and square. Though it reads non-European peoples entirely in terms of European social hierarchy and mores, the discourse of diplomatic drama at least concedes their humanity and even allows them a little "class." (One recalls the similar treatment of the Aztec court in the accounts of the conquest of Mexico three hundred years earlier.) Indeed, one of the ways the experiential accounts mystify the imperialist enterprise is by portraying the European travelers as less powerful, less clever, less ruthless than their opponents. Who can keep in mind that such hapless boobies as Mungo Park, always getting robbed, imprisoned, lost in the desert, poked at by ladies, or paralyzed by reveries, are the advancemen of European domination? Yet the appeal of these boobies today lies not just in their innocence, but also in their power of individual action. They do things, they don't just stand there looking or complaining. They are not circumscribed and immobilized in webs of social and ideological control.

Defert says that this courtly, diplomatic code disappeared with the rise of the nation-state in the nineteenth century, and it becomes almost completely superseded in travel narrative by the mid-nineteenth-century conventions I have been discussing. But in the turn of the century texts the courtly code was already under attack, as indeed it was in Europe itself. For the traveler-heroes of the sentimental travel accounts are members not of European courtly aristocracies, but of the rising bourgeoisie who were in the process of replacing the aristocracy as the dominant class. (A surprising number were physicians, interestingly enough.) The ideological struggle between court-based aristocracy and rising bourgeoisie has been examined at some length by Norbert Elias in his belatedly recognized masterpiece, *The History of Manners*. As this struggle developed in the late eighteenth century, it took quite different shapes in different countries (Elias in particular contrasts France and Germany). But in general the European bourgeoisies developed ideologies of their own in opposition to courtly values; these ideologies were in some cases absorbed into courtly life to a degree (as in France, Elias argues) while in others they and their bearers were rigidly excluded (as in Germany). In any case, Elias sees romanticism as an oppositional ideology, expressive of the bourgeoisie's sense that its interests, values, and lifeways were opposed to those of the court. Romanticism's stress on feelings stands in opposition to courtly values of reason over passion; its focus on individual, intrinsic self-worth and personal achievement stand in opposition to courtly emphases on lineage and externals like dress and manners; its chastity, naturalness, and simplicity in opposition to courtly unnaturalness and decadence.

One thing late eighteenth- and early nineteenth-century travel accounts do is dramatize this bourgeois struggle for hegemony on a displaced plane (plain?). In the courts of Arab and African kings and chieftains, the hapless, sincere, and passionate bourgeois emissary confronts the horrors of courtly decadence and immorality. Time and time again, these guileless arrivistes are robbed, imprisoned, left to die, only to be helped in the last instance either by Providence or by the spontaneous generosity of an invariably female slave. Time and time again, the court is satirized, ridiculed, or made an object of utter disgust. Consider, for instance, James Bruce's dehumanizing description of his work as court physician to the harem of one Ethiopian sultan:

> I must confess, however, that calling these the fair sex is not preserving a precision in terms. I was admitted into a large square apartment, very ill-lighted, in which were about fifty women, all perfectly black, without any covering but a very narrow piece of cotton rag about their waists. While I was musing whether or not these all might

be queens, or whether there was any queen among them, one of them
took me by the hand and led me rudely enough into another apartment. . . . I shall not entertain the reader with the multitude of their
complaints; being a lady's physician, discretion and silence are my
first duties. It is sufficient to say, that there was not one part of their
whole bodies, inside and outside, in which some of them had not
ailments. . . . Another night I was obliged to attend them, and gave
the queens, and two or three of the great ladies, vomits. I will spare
my reader the recital of so nauseous a scene. The ipecacuanha had
great effect, and warm water was drunk very copiously. The patients
were numerous, and the floor of the room received all the evacua-
tions. It was most prodigiously hot, and the horrid, black figures,
moaning and groaning with sickness all around me, gave me, I think,
some slight idea of the punishment in the world below. (234–35)

Unquestionably, part of the ideological force of these sentimental
travel books lay in their representation of European class struggle
in a way so dramatic and so congenial to the interests of their
bourgeois readerships. And one can see the ideological force of
representing capitalism's expansionist enterprise in the image of
the class struggle at home, lending it a kind of glory and legitimacy
(and a thrilling pathos), while mystifying its actual power and
direction. By mid-nineteenth century, however, the struggle between courts and bourgeoisies was largely over. Both courtly idiom
and the oppositional bourgeois idiom it conditioned had disappeared. Travelers were by this time entirely caught up in extending
bourgeois hegemony under the aegis of the state and under the
ideology of the civilizing mission, in whose name we have seen
them gathering information and musing into the future from
cliff tops.

But here the risk of another oversimplification must be acknowl-
edged. For these generalized discourses I have been talking about
never came even close to prevailing absolutely. We know that
dominant ideologies only rarely appear in pure form, and that
human subjects are not monolithic. While travel literature is certainly a place where imperialist ideologies get created, it is equally
certainly a place where such ideologies get questioned, especially

from the realm of particularized and concrete sensual experience. In fact, travel literature is a particularly prominent instance of what discourse analysts like to call polyphony, because it is a genre that has never been consigned to professionals or specialists. Even today, it remains a place to which nonspecialist lay voices—an incredible variety of them—have access. You don't have to be a professional writer to write a travel book. Similar to call-in radio, travel literature is ultimately best seen as a genre not in the sense of a set of conventions, but in the sense of a discursive space which, like a street corner, is continually crisscrossed by all manner of people.

To further complicate the picture I have been drawing, I will end with a couple of mid-nineteenth-century travel texts which do not adopt the detached and dehumanized code of the civilizing mission, and which in fact disrupt it. The first is Paul Du Chaillu's *Explorations in Equatorial Africa* (1861), and the second is Henry Morton Stanley's famed *How I Found Livingstone* (1872). Both were extremely popular books in their time, and both were much vilified by authorities and the British explorer elite. It is not a coincidence that both writers were naturalized Americans, though that is not why I picked them.

In Du Chaillu's book, all the characteristics of both historical periods I have mentioned coexist, producing a hugely contradictory, chaotic, and colorful text, a good deal of which, it turns out, was his pure invention. Like the writers of the 1790s, Du Chaillu describes his emotional states and constantly dramatizes encounters with local inhabitants. Yet he does not play the vulnerable sentimental hero, but the Great White Father revered by the natives. Among his favorite scenes to dramatize is not the courtly encounter, but native "atrocities" like ritual killings, witchcraft, trials by poison, and so on. Modern racism is present in his rhetoric. And like mid-century writers, Du Chaillu goes on obsessively about the need and potential for capitalist development, constantly fantasizes about Africa's "civilized" future, and uses all the kinds of landscape description I mentioned earlier. But one often finds Du Chaillu playing conventions against each other, as he does in the passage that follows. This starts out as one of the view-from-the-promontory scenes I mentioned earlier:

> From this elevation about 5000 feet above the ocean level, I enjoyed an unobstructed view as far as the eye could reach. The hills we had surmounted the day before lay quietly at our feet, seeming mere molehills. On all sides stretched the immense virgin forests, with here and there a sheen of a watercourse. And far away on the east loomed the blue tops of the farthest range of the Sierra del Crystal, the goal of my desires. (23)

The relation of dominance over the terrain is clear here—the hills are now lying in quiet ("virginal") submission to the interloper. As with the Grant sketch quoted earlier, Du Chaillu's view now turns into a vision of a utopian future when the imperial mission will have done its work (it's a particularly American vision, too):

> The murmur of the rapids below filled my ears, and as I strained my eyes towards those distant mountains which I hoped to reach, I began to think how this wilderness would look if only the light of Christian civilization could once be fairly introduced among the black children of Africa. I dreamed of forests giving way to plantations of coffee, cotton, spices, of peaceful negroes going to their contented daily tasks; of farming and manufactures, of churches and schools . . . (23)

It is obvious why this vision makes contemporary readers uncomfortable. But apparently it was intended to make Du Chaillu's contemporaries uncomfortable too, for this grand vision gets interrupted by a concrete experience, quite a dramatic one at that:

> and luckily, raising my eyes heavenward at this stage of my thoughts, saw pendent from the branch of a tree beneath which I was sitting an immense serpent, evidently preparing to gobble up this dreaming intruder on his domains. My dreams of future civilization vanished in a moment. Luckily my gun lay at hand. (23)

Obviously this serpent came here directly from the Garden of Eden, and has appeared to tell the reader among other things that the cozy pastoral-plantation fantasy is forbidden fruit which will lead eventually to expulsion from the garden. In the face of this intrusion of immediate experience, Du Chaillu abandons his role as observer and becomes an agent, and what he does is grab the most fundamental real tool of the civilizing mission, his gun. Du Chaillu is unquestionably invoking the conventions of his contemporaries in order to ironize them, and his means are very reminiscent of the earlier dramatic and experiential travel texts. One of the messages implied is, "Let's not always pretend that this pastoral fantasy is really what we are going to produce here" — as an American in 1860 might well know.

A much more direct challenge to the discourse of the civilizing mission came a decade later from the prolific Henry Stanley, author of *In Darkest Africa*. I believe Stanley can be credited with single-handedly breaking up the mid-nineteenth-century British mode of travel writing, and founding quite consciously a new generation both of explorers and of exploration literature. He does this in part by incessantly challenging the mid-century writers on their own grounds. Over and over in his first blockbuster, *How I Found Livingstone* (1872) he indicts his predecessors, Burton, Speke, Grant, and others, for failing to provide him with INFORMATION that was accurate and useful to him. And he challenges them on sentimental grounds, for being detached and cold, for failing to see that negroes experience the same passions white men do. (This, archaically enough, is his criterion for seeing them as fully human.) Stanley describes landscapes, then breaks frame to ask, "Reader, why am I doing this? — Ah, yes, it is because you and I are looking at this place for *opportunities*" (italics mine). In his preface, he explicitly displaces the informational discourse by announcing that he has "used the personal pronoun first person singular, 'I,'" oftener, perhaps than real modesty would admit. But it must be remembered that I am writing a narrative of my own adventures and travels, and that until I meet Livingstone, I presume the greatest interest is attached to myself, my marches, my troubles, my thoughts, and my impressions" (xxii). This is obviously a presumption that Mungo Park and the others shared two generations earlier, with the difference that they did not have to make it explicit. Stanley explicitly ridicules his predecessors' posture of emotional restraint, and repeatedly depicts himself unable or unwilling to adopt it.

But above all, Stanley portrays a whole, unflattering side of European travel experience in Africa which his predecessors unquestionably shared but which they did not write about: its violence. Over and over again, almost obsessively, Stanley portrays himself beating his servants and bearers, horsewhipping them, putting them in chains, all manner of brutalities — often, he admits, with no justification other than his own irritability. He shows himself abusing his European companions, plundering indigenous communities for food, running roughshod over peoples' territory and customs and making up for it in violence, suppressing rebellion after rebellion among his party without the slightest ear for grievances. Stanley, in short, does a journalistic exposé on himself, and by implication on his decorous mentors. Small wonder he — an illegitimate working-class orphan emigrant who never even got his name till he was eighteen — was hated so by the Royal Society Fellows even as the attention of the world was focused on him.

Of particular interest here is the way Stanley, in forging a new discourse, combines elements of the older, sentimental one (he even uses "thou" in his rendering of dialogues with local leaders) with elements of the new muckraking journalism (his first books were, of course, written for the *New York Herald*). It is also important to note that, as with Du Chaillu, Stanley's critique is a "domesticated" one, in the sense that the challenge occurs within the overall imperialist enterprise. In fact one could argue that, while doubtless alienating some sectors of the home public from that enterprise, the effect of Stanley's exposé on others might have been simply a sense of relief and empowerment at finally knowing what has really been going on under all that detachment and decorum. As my colleague James Clifford puts it, if you want to give people a sense of power, you have to make them feel they are seeing behind the scenes. Who would know this better than Stanley the newspaperman?

In any case, that it was a domesticated critique is eerily borne out by Stanley's subsequent career. For of course it was he who, as the agent of King Leopold of Belgium, stood at the forefront of the infamous Scramble for Africa, the orgy of plunder, forced labor, mass imprisonment, and genocide which in the years between 1890 and World War I devastated Central Africa on the same scale that Central and South America were devastated by the Spanish invasion in the sixteenth century. In the Congo alone—Stanley's particular field of endeavor—the loss of life in this period is conservatively estimated at between 10 and 20 million people. Small wonder that at the end of the nineteenth century, the conventional view from the promontory gets replaced by a new trope, the terrifying jungle-at-night scene where Europeans find themselves immobilized and terrorized in a landscape they cannot see. Small wonder that the climax of those terrifying nights is their recognition that the source of the terror and evil is not Africa, but themselves.

Bibliography

Bruce, James. *Travels to Discover the Source of the Nile*. 1790. Ed. and abridged by C.F. Beckingham. Edinburgh: University Press, 1964.

Burton, Richard. *The Lake Regions of Central Africa: A Picture of Exploration*. 1860. 2 vols. New York: Horizon Press, 1961.

Defert, Daniel. "La collecte du monde: Pour une étude des récits de voyage du XVIe au XVIIIe siècle." In *Collection Passion*. Ed. by Jacques Hainard and Roland Kaehr. Neuchâtel: Musée d'ethnographie, 1982.

Du Chaillu, Paul. *Explorations and Adventures in Equatorial Africa*. New York: Harper, 1861.

Elias, Norbert. *The History of Manners*. 1939. Trans. by Edmund Jephcott. 2 vols. New York: Pantheon, 1982.

Grant, James. *A Walk Across Africa*. Edinburgh: Blackwood & Sons, 1864.

Leyland, J. *Adventures in the Far Interior of South Africa*. London: Routledge, 1866.

Livingstone, David, and Charles Livingstone. *Narrative of an Expedition to the Zambesi*. New York: Harper, 1866.

Park, Mungo. *Travels in the Interior of Africa*. 1802. Edinburgh: Adam and Charles Black, 1860.

Pratt, Mary Louise. "Conventions of Representation: Where Discourse and Ideology Meet." In *Contemporary Perceptions of Language: Interdisciplinary Dimensions*. Ed. by Heidi Byrnes. Washington, D.C.: Georgetown University Round Table, 1982.

———. "Scratches on the Face of the Country, or What Mr. Barrow Saw in the Land of the Bushmen." In *Race, Writing and Difference*. Ed. by H.L. Gates. Chicago: University of Chicago Press, 1986.

———. *Imperial Eyes: Travel Writing and Transculturation*. London: Routledge, 1992.

Stanley, Henry Morton. *How I Found Livingstone*. New York: Scribner, Armstrong, and Co., 1872.

Stedman, John. *Narrative of a Five Years Expedition against the Revolted Negroes of Surinam*. 1790. Ed. by R.J. van Lier. 2 vols. Barre, MA: Imprint Society, 1971.

9

Present Tense Narration, Mimesis, the Narrative Norm, and the Positioning of the Reader in *Waiting for the Barbarians*

JAMES PHELAN

The Simultaneous Present in Waiting for the Barbarians

The elderly magistrate-protagonist of J. M. Coetzee's *Waiting for the Barbarians* narrates a painful and remarkable tale, the story of his complicity with torturers as well as his own experience of being tortured; of his attempts to expiate the pain of one tortured woman, attempts that actually perpetuate her pain and oppression; of his humiliation by the forces of his Empire and his continued complicity with the Empire. He is a man who is self-reflective but not fully aware of what he is doing and why, who wants to have his heart in the right place but is very attached to the pleasures of the body. This character and these experiences would lend themselves very well to a retrospective first person narration in the manner of *Great Expectations*. The magistrate could occasionally judge his former self from his perspective at the time of narration, and part of the narrative tension for the reader would be the question of how the experiencing-I evolves into the narrating-I. Of course, Coetzee could still indicate that the narrator-I's understanding of himself and his situation is severely limited. Such a treatment of the narrative perspective would allow Coetzee, first, to use the magistrate's retrospection to highlight some of the thematic import of the narrative, especially concerning complicity, and, second, to involve the reader in seeing beyond the magistrate, building upon or even revising the narrator's conclusions.

Coetzee, however, has the magistrate tell the story not retrospectively but "simultaneously." That is, the magistrate tells the story in the present tense—not the *historical* present after the fact, but the simultaneous present as events are happening. This narrative strategy, the homodiegetic simultaneous present, places the reader in a very different relationship to the magistrate and to the events of his narrative than would any kind of retrospective account. The strategy takes teleology away from the magistrate's narrative acts: since he does not know how events will turn out, he cannot be shaping the narrative according to his knowledge of the end. Consequently, we cannot read with our usual tacit assumptions that the narrator, however unself-conscious, has some direction in mind for his tale. Instead, as we read any one moment of the narrative we must assume that the future is always—and radically—wide open: the narrator's guess about what will happen next is really no better than our own. In fact, our guess is better because we read with the assumption that Coetzee has shaped his novel, has given it some kind of teleology, and we habitually make tentative inferences about that as we read, inferences that remain subject to radical revision as the magistrate's narrative moves in its necessarily unpredictable direction.

What kind of experience is it to read the account of a self-reflective narrator who is unable to use that power of reflection to shape his tale? How does the present tense position and reposition the reader as the magistrate recounts his series of remarkable events, his year of change which brings him to a position very similar to the one from which he started? And why would Coetzee want to position his reader in these ways rather than in the more common positions fostered by retrospective narration? These questions, I believe, are central to understanding the effects of Coetzee's remarkable novel, and they are the questions with which this essay is ultimately concerned. Before I address them directly, however, I want to situate them in the larger context of recent theoretical discussions of simultaneous (as opposed to historical) present tense narration because that placement will contribute to our understanding of the special quality of Coetzee's achievement. As we will see, some theorists have serious doubts about the efficacy of Coetzee's strategy.

Mimesis and the Narrative Norm

Suzanne Fleischman concludes her recent illuminating study *Tense and Narrativity* by building on Gérard Genette's discussion of the inherent instability of present tense narration. Fleischman argues that narrative, by nature, uses the past as the dominant tense. The presence of the present, then, moves a discourse toward the genres in which present tense is dominant—either the lyric or the drama. Fleischman concludes her discussion with her strongest claim: the "metalinguistic function" of the present tense is "to announce a language that cannot be narrative according to the rules of narrative's own game" (310). Fleischman's position is well-argued, provocative, and, I think, inadequate. It is inadequate because it does not take sufficient account of actual narrative practice, the way in which many recent narrative artists have experimented with the homodiegetic simultaneous present. Consider the range of styles, audiences, and interests in just this short list of experimenters: Coetzee, Bobbie Ann Mason in *In Country*, Margaret Atwood in *The Handmaid's Tale*, and Scott Turow in *Presumed Innocent*.[1]

The gap between Fleischman's theoretical account and the practice of many storytellers suggests that we could profit from a closer look at her "rules of narrative's . . . game." From the perspective of these rules, the problem with present tense narration is that it violates a mimetic standard that says one cannot live and narrate at the same time.[2] But the critical and in some cases popular success of recent present tense narratives invites us to reexamine that standard. In the rest of this section, I will explore the relations among standards of mimesis, theoretical explanations of narration, and fictional practice. This discussion will lead to a new account of the relation between mimesis and fictional narration, which will serve as the backdrop for discussing my questions about *Waiting for the Barbarians*.

Among the many important tasks Fleischman takes up, perhaps the most significant for my purposes is her attempt to make the production and comprehension of narrative part of adult linguistic competence. Just as competent speakers internalize rules about what constitutes grammatical and ungrammatical sentences, so too, Fleischman proposes, they internalize "a set of shared conventions and assumptions about what constitutes a well-formed story" (263). Fleischman calls this set of conventions and assumptions "the narrative norm," and this set is what she means by the rules of narrative's game. The norm has four main rules or tenets:

1. "Narratives refer to specific experiences that occurred in some past world (real or imagined) and are accordingly reported in a tense of the PAST" (263). Note here that the norm does not distinguish between fictional and nonfictional narrative. Note, too, that making past tense the norm means that present tense narration will be the marked case.

2. "Narratives contain both sequentially ordered events and non-sequential 'collateral material' [such as description and evaluation] but it is the events that define narration" (263). Note here that this tenet reinforces the formalist-structuralist distinctions *fabula/sjuzhet* and story/discourse and that it privileges *fabula* as the defining element of narrative.

3. "The default order of the *sjuzhet* in narratives is iconic to the chronology of events in the *fabula* they model" (263). Again the assumption is that *fabula* is the core of narrative.

4. "Narratives are informed by a point of view that assigns meaning to their contents in conformity with a governing ideology,

normally that of the narrator" (263). This tenet gives the *sjuzhet* its due, reminding us that *fabula* alone does not determine the meaning and effect of narrative.

Throughout her book, Fleischman emphasizes that although "the tenets of the norm are commonly infringed, the rhetorical or stylistic effects produced by infringements are possible only because the norm is in place" (263). Thus, for example, breaking the default order of the *sjuzhet* does not make a narrative "ill-formed" but it does foreground the *sjuzhet*'s role in creating a narrative's effects. Given this emphasis, we might expect Fleischman to apply the same logic to the use of the present tense and to argue that infringing the norm about the past tense might produce, say, an immediacy effect, rather than a move away from narrative. We need a closer look.

Tenet 1 (narrative refers to a set of experiences in the past) and tenet 4 (a narrative has a speaker from whose point of view the story is told) allow Fleischman to emphasize that the narrative norm implies "two temporal planes, the present of the speaker (and hearer) and the past of the narrated events" (127). Present tense narration is "inherently unstable" for Fleischman because it erases this distinction between the two temporal planes, causing the text to move in one of two directions. Either the narrator will disappear and the events will be presented as if without a filter, thus moving the text toward drama; or the narrator will become supremely important and the events will be merely an occasion for the discourse, thus moving the text toward lyric. Fleischman uses Genette's commentary on the ambiguity of Robbe-Grillet's *La Jalousie* to demonstrate the rule: Genette argues that the novel can be read either as a wholly objective behaviorist account of events or as a completely subjective projection of the narrator's jealous perspective.

On its own terms, this view is persuasive. If we think of narrative as requiring these temporal planes, then it follows that erasing the distinction between them will make narrative unstable. But ultimately the insistence on the distinction between the two planes and this understanding of the interpretive options for present tense texts depend on an assumption about the way mimesis controls the occasion of narration. As noted briefly above, the present tense is such a problem because it violates the mimetic standard that says a speaker cannot tell her story and live it at the same time—"live now, tell later," as Dorrit Cohn puts it. Stipulating that texts which erase the distinction will be either unfiltered or completely subjective allows the mimetic imperative to be preserved. In the first case, we say that the form of the text means that it has no speaker, no narrator in the usual mimetic sense: the concept of a "narrative perspective" drops out and we seem to have the verbal equivalent to "objective" drama. In the second case, we preserve the strict mimesis by seeing everything as revealing a subjective consciousness. But what happens if we question the standard? Let me first give a warrant for this question by a look at some past tense homodiegetic narration that violates a different mimetic standard.

When the two temporal planes are present, narratives that follow the third tenet of the norm (i.e., that the default order is for *sjuzhet* to follow *fabula*) establish a complicated relation between the "retrospective perspective" of the narrative and the "temporal orientation" of the events narrated. As Fleischman points out, the events remain in the past for the speaker, but the temporal orientation of the narrative is "prospective"—it traces the events as they happened. For the reader, this double temporal perspective means that she has a tacit *awareness* that the account is retrospective but an overt *experience* of the events as unfolding prospectively. In homodiegetic narration, the double orientation leads to the separation between the experiencing-I whose acts are being retraced and the narrating-I who is doing the retracing. According to the mimetic standard that says "knowledge alters perception," whenever a narrating-I unself-consciously tells the story of his or her change in consciousness or understanding, the new understanding should inform the retrospective narration.

For example, in Hemingway's "My Old Man" Joe Butler unself-consciously recounts a series of events that suddenly lead him to give up his belief that his father was "one swell guy" and to entertain the idea that his father was actually a "son of a bitch." According to the standard that knowledge alters perception, Joe's unsophisticated retrospective account should be informed by his present suspicions. But it is not. What's more, this apparent violation of the mimetic standard does not undermine but rather makes possible the effectiveness of the narrative for Hemingway's audience, because that effectiveness depends (in part) on the suddenness of Joe's realization. The violation is not a problem because the reader's temporal orientation is always prospective. Since we do not know what Joe ends up learning (or suspecting) as a result of the experience he is narrating, we cannot know *as we read* that Joe's narration does not square with what he learns.[3]

This example has three important implications for our understanding of mimesis and present tense narration. First, it suggests that mimetic standards may be violated without destroying a narrative's effectiveness or altering its generic status. More generally, it reminds us that mimesis is not a product of faithful imitation of the real (whatever that is) but rather a set of conventions for representing what we provisionally and temporarily agree to be the real. In other words, in this larger view Joe's narration violates a *narrow* standard of mimesis, one based only on imitation-of-the-real ("knowledge alters perception"); but it is consistent with a broader standard of mimesis, one that looks both to the real and to conventions for imitating it. Second, the example of "My Old Man" suggests that these conventions are motivated in part by what they make possible: "My Old Man" is a much more powerful story as a result of its violation of the narrow mimetic logic. If Hemingway followed that logic by having Joe's doubts and suspicions inform the narrative, he would have eliminated the shock accompanying the suddenness of Joe's new understanding and the poignancy accompanying its arrival moments after Joe's father's death; he would, in short, have destroyed much of the story's emotional power. If Hemingway had respected strict mimetic logic by telling the story through a heterodiegetic narrator, he would have sacrificed much of the intimacy between Joe and his audience, an intimacy crucial to the narrative's effect.

Third and most important, both the reader's judgments about mimesis and the sense of what is possible depend upon the reader's tacit awareness that she is reading fiction, that the characters and the events are what I have elsewhere called synthetic constructs.[4] Or, perhaps better, this example suggests that we may construct mimetic standards too narrowly because we do not allow for differences between fictional and nonfictional narrative. Despite all that recent experiments with nonfiction narrative by Tom Wolfe, Joan Didion, Hunter Thompson, and others have taught us about the permeability between fiction and nonfiction, some significant differences remain. If "My Old Man" were nonfiction, then one of three things would happen. (1) A real Joe Butler would not tell the story the way the fictional Joe does, but would have his knowledge inform his narration and, thus, give us a different text. (2) Joe's unreliability, which stems from the fact that his narrative is not informed by his knowledge, would undermine his telling—we would come to feel that the narrative stance was insincere and would therefore feel manipulated. (3) Alternatively, we would come to regard the narrative stance as a highly self-conscious performance by Joe, one that was so skillful he could brilliantly feign unself-consciousness. In each of these cases, we would have a very different relation to the story and its narrator than we do in Hemingway's "My Old Man."

Because we read Hemingway's version with the tacit knowledge that it is fiction, two consequences follow: (1) Joe's unreliability functions effectively as part of a dual communication from Hemingway—a communication from Joe to a narrative audience, which is contained within Hemingway's communication to his authorial audience;[5] and (2) the deviation from the narrow mimetic standard does not undermine the story's mimetic power.

Something similar—but not identical—happens, I believe, in fictional homodiegetic present tense narration. The situation is not identical because the deviation is experienced differently. In "My Old Man," the deviation is not registered as we read, and therefore the synthetic remains in the background. In the case of present tense narration, the fictionality of the text is foregrounded, but this foregrounding does not impede our mimetic engagement with the characters.

These considerations lead me to question the adequacy of Fleischman's formulation of the narrative norm on the grounds that it does not address our acquired competence with *fictional* narrative. I would like, therefore, to propose the following revisions of Fleischman's first and fourth tenets:

1. Nonfictional narratives refer to specific real experiences that occurred in the past and are accordingly reported in a tense of the PAST. Fictional narratives refer to imagined experiences presented *as if* they were real, *sometimes through imaginary instances of narration*.

4. Narratives are informed by a point of view that assigns meaning to their contents in conformity with a governing ideology, normally that of the narrator. In fictional narrative, the relation of the narrator's governing ideology to that of the author is always a part of the narrative's meaning.

Such revisions would recognize that the use of an instance of imaginary narration such as the present tense need neither undermine mimesis nor move a discourse away from narrative.

These formulations are subject to the same caveats as Fleischman's. They do not mean to rule out, say, the use of the simultaneous present in nonfictional narrative but rather to emphasize that such a technique will achieve its effect in part by its deviation from the norm—and to suggest that the effect is likely to be different from the effect of the present tense in fictional narrative.[6] These formulations also do not address the question of the *effects* of present tense narration in fiction. To talk of effects, as we shall see, we also need to look more closely than Fleischman does—or, indeed, as I have done so far—at the audience who feels the effects.

On Effects and Audiences

Like many other critics, I have often discussed how technique X produces effect Y in "us." And like others, I typically have two bases for the effects I claim "we" experience: (1) my own set of responses, and (2) the sources in the text I can point to that evoke those responses. Because I privilege the second basis over the first, the search for sources of response can—and often does—lead to a revision of response. Because of that hierarchy among these bases, I go ahead and claim that my sequence of responses, properly grounded in their textual sources, forms the "experience of the authorial audience."

However, as anyone who has followed the reader-response movement even in passing must already recognize, this mode of analysis depends on the repression of one crucial fact: different readers bring different subjectivities to texts and therefore sometimes have different experiences of the same textual phenomena. Once I acknowledge this fact, I have several directions in which to go. I may decide to establish a hierarchy among readers' experiences— some are more valid/true/legitimate than others. But this direction soon leads to a reproduction of the problem: How can I establish the hierarchy without injecting my own subjectivity into the decision and in effect claiming that it is superior to others'? Alternatively, I may decide to celebrate difference and argue for the incommensurability of different accounts of the reading experience: because you and I are different, we will of course read complicated narratives differently, and the best we can do is compare notes. This solution, though it has the advantage of validating different responses, has the significant disadvantage of endorsing a prison-house of subjectivity.

There are of course middle positions that are far more attractive than either of these extremes; Wolfgang Iser's notion that each of us fills in a text's gaps in her own way is the most well-known, and recently Robert Scholes has elegantly argued that effective reading must be both centripetal and centrifugal, that is, grounded in the text and spinning away from its center. But I would like to offer a model that tries less to compromise between the two extremes than to embrace their differing first principles. In embracing both, I realize that I am also necessarily modifying each; but the modification is motivated less by the impulse to correct than by the desire to maintain as much integrity toward each first principle as possible. To be specific, I want to insist on the effort to enter the authorial audience as a worthy-but-unlikely-to-be-achieved goal, even as I recognize and, indeed, celebrate the inevitable subjectivity of my reading self. Rather than trying to find either the objectively best reading or the subjectively most honest, I collapse the distinction between subject and object, intrinsic and extrinsic. The text is in the reader and the reader is in the text like the fish is in the sea and the sea is in the fish. More specifically, I maintain the concepts of authorial audience and authorial reading as a heuristic to allow me to question my subjective experiences; at the same time, I both recognize and value the subjectivity of my readerly experience because it opens up a two-way street between the life experiences that have gone into shaping my subjectivity (including my reading of other texts) and my experiences as a reader of this text. This model invites me as a reader to seek both comprehension and evaluation, sympathetic understanding and, where necessary, strong resistance.

Perhaps the most striking consequence of this model is that it makes reading endlessly recursive. The more I study the text, the more I am able to interrogate and complicate my understanding of how it works on me; the more I have experiences that are in some way related to those in the text, the more my experience of the text will change. Furthermore, because I read within a community, my discussions with other readers can affect both ends of my transaction; other readers may show me things in the workings of the text that I had not fully accounted for, or they may explain their subjective experiences in ways that allow or require me to reexamine mine.[7]

Criticism based on this model of audience and effects might be presented in such a way that it resembles traditional accounts of "the way the text works" because the critic may regard the specific influences of her subjectivity—if indeed she is able to identify them—as things that she need not inflict on her reader. Alternatively, criticism based on this model might move in a "confessional" direction, where the critic calls attention to his subjectivity either to let his reader beware or to invite the reader into a more personal dialogue with himself and the text under consideration. My own subjectivity leads me to develop the rest of this essay in the first, more traditional direction. But I hope that what I have said here will serve as a reminder of the messy, complicated subjective and intersubjective responses compressed within my subsequent shorthand use of the first person plural.

The Present Tense and Audience Experience in
Waiting for the Barbarians

In the light of the preceding discussion, I find it helpful to restate my initial questions. (1) How does the narration affect us if we seek to participate in the authorial audience's role in the dual communication of the narrative? How do we enter that audience and negotiate our relation to the magistrate and to Coetzee as implied author? How, in other words, are we positioned and repositioned as we move through the narrative? (2) What does the imaginary occasion of narration in *Waiting for the Barbarians* make possible—that is, what does it allow Coetzee to accomplish that he could not accomplish with a realistic past tense narration? Let us begin with the opening of the narrative:

> I have never seen anything like it: two little discs of glass suspended in front of his eyes in loops of wire. Is he blind? I could understand it if he wanted to hide blind eyes. But he is not blind. The discs are dark, they look opaque from the outside but he can see through them. He tells me they are a new invention. "They protect one's eyes against the glare of the sun," he says. "You would find them useful out here in the desert. They save one from squinting all the time. One has fewer headaches. Look." He touches the corners of his eyes lightly. "No wrinkles." He replaces the glasses. It is true. He has the skin of a younger man. "At home everyone wears them." (1)

It will be apparent, I think, that there is neither any plausible "occasion of narration" here nor any violation of narrativity.[8] This narrator is doing the impossible—living and telling at the same time. Furthermore, his discourse locates us in the genre of narrative: his subjectivity is obvious, and his account directs its audience's attention toward the other character and the dynamics of their interaction. The subsequent parts of the text strengthen this location, as the preponderance of criticism about it indirectly attests: most commentators ignore the tense and focus on the thematic component of the narrative.

Perhaps the most notable immediate effect of this imaginary instance of narration is that it accentuates the difference between the magistrate's relation to the text and Coetzee's. As noted earlier, because he is telling as he is living, the magistrate is not at all able to design his narration; the narrative situation puts teleology beyond his control. Yet we approach the narrative assuming that it has a teleology, that Coetzee has imposed a design upon this imaginary narration. For example, we read the magistrate's first paragraph as Coetzee's introduction of a thematic issue about vision and blindness and expect that this issue will be prominent throughout the narrative, but we do not conclude that *the magistrate* is deliberately building this motif into his narrative so that he can do more with it later.[9]

As the narrative progresses, Coetzee combines this effect of present tense narration with one of the magistrate's traits as a character-narrator to create a very powerful representation of the magistrate's dilemma—and to complicate the audience's positioning in relation to the magistrate. Coetzee creates the magistrate to be a reflective individual, but he puts the magistrate in a narrative situation that deprives him of the distance from his experience necessary for his reflection to make coherent sense of it. As a result, the magistrate's understanding comes in pieces and is always subject to revision. At the same time, the absence of any retrospective perspective—even the latent one of a Huck Finn—places the authorial audience's prospective experience of the narrative very close to the magistrate's ongoing experience. This positioning has two very significant effects. First, just as the magistrate's understanding comes provisionally and in pieces, so too does ours. Second, although our awareness of Coetzee behind the magistrate means that our understanding can exceed the magistrate's, we frequently must struggle to attain the necessary distance from the magistrate's views and actions. It is this second effect I will explore first.

Our struggle to see beyond the magistrate becomes progressively greater because Coetzee makes the magistrate much more sympathetic than Colonel Joll, Mandel, and the other officials from the Third Bureau, and because Coetzee shows the magistrate being led by his powers of reflection to oppose these representatives of the Empire and to make some progress understanding the situation in which he lives and acts. Indeed, near the end of the narrative the magistrate reaches conclusions that have the appearance of a final truth, a place of understanding where he and the audience can rest. Through the positioning provided by the present tense narration, Coetzee uses the authorial audience's reading experience up to and after this moment as a way to exemplify one of his major thematic points about complicity. This moment in the magistrate's understanding is so important because it is part of the development of the central instability of the narrative, his relation to his own complicity in the Empire's oppression of the barbarians, especially as that complicity is reflected in his treatment of the woman whom he takes into his apartment.

When the magistrate first invites the woman into his rooms he does not understand his motives and frequently describes his puzzlement at what he is doing. "For the time being, perhaps forever, I am simply bewildered. It seems all one whether I lie down beside her and fall asleep or fold her in a sheet and bury her in the snow" (43). But Coetzee asks us to see beyond that puzzlement and recognize that the magistrate's ritual washing of her body has a double significance. Especially in the early stages when the washing is restricted to the woman's broken feet, the ritual is the magistrate's attempt to atone for the woman's torture, and a tacit admission of the way his complicity with the Empire makes him responsible for what happened to her. Like Christ's washing of the feet of his disciples, it is an act of humility and respect, something that arises out of his feeling for her pain and something that acknowledges her equality with him. At the same time, however, the magistrate's actions continue her oppression, an oppression that becomes greater as he washes more of her body: the woman is with him by his command—he is the official of the Empire; she has no choice but to submit—she is the "barbarian." Coetzee gives several signs that the magistrate is too close to his complicity with the Empire to recognize how his confused effort at expiation actually perpetuates her oppression. These signs include the magistrate's shifting without comment from calling her "woman" to calling her "girl" as well as his protesting too much when he briefly thinks that he is trying to "move her" more than Joll did. "I shake my head in a fury of disbelief. *No! No! No!* I cry to myself. . . . I must assert my distance from Colonel Joll! I will not suffer for his crimes!" (44).

Moreover, the very manner in which he carries out the expiation derives from the habits he has developed in his easy life as magistrate during times of peace. That easy life is filled with sensual pleasure; his drive toward that pleasure leads him to move beyond the washing of the woman's feet toward the giving and receiving of erotic pleasure in his washing the rest of her body. She becomes an object for both his attempted expiation and attempted pleasure. In sum, the effort at atonement is corrupted by the magistrate's complicity—and that very complicity prevents him from recognizing what he is doing.

Significantly, however, after the magistrate has himself been tortured by the forces of the Empire, he is forced to move further away from it, and, as a result of this movement, he acquires a new understanding of his actions toward the woman, an understanding that Coetzee highlights by the length and occasional eloquence of its articulation:

> From the first she knew me for a false seducer. She listened to me, then she listened to her heart, and rightly she acted in accord with her heart. If only she had found the words to tell me! "That is not how you do it," she should have said, stopping me in the act. "If you want to learn how to do it, ask your friend with the black eyes." Then she

should have continued so as not to leave me without hope: "But if you want to love me you will have to turn your back on him and learn your lesson elsewhere." If she told me then, if I understood her, if I had been in a position to understand her, if I believed her, if I had been in a position to believe her, I might have saved myself from a year of confused and futile gestures of expiation.

For I was not, as I liked to think, the indulgent pleasure-loving opposite of the cold rigid Colonel. I was the lie that Empire tells itself when times are easy, he the truth that Empire tells when harsh winds blow. Two sides of imperial rule, no more, no less. But I temporized, I looked around this obscure frontier, this little backwater with its dusty summers and its cartloads of apricots and its long siestas and its shiftless garrison and the waterbirds flying in and flying out year after year to and from the dazzling waveless sheet of the lake, and I said to myself, "Be patient, one of these days he will go away, one of these days quiet will return: then our siestas will grow longer and our swords rustier, the watchman will sneak down from his tower to spend the night with his wife, the mortar will crumble till lizards nest between the bricks and owls fly out of the belfry, and the line that marks the frontier on the maps of Empire will grow hazy and obscure till we are blessedly forgotten." Thus I seduced myself, taking one of the many wrong turnings I have taken on a road that looks true but has delivered me into the heart of a labyrinth. (135–36)

This moment of insight is so powerful because in it the magistrate so clearly articulates the view of himself that Coetzee has asked his audience to adopt. Furthermore, in that articulation, the magistrate is fulfilling one aspect of our desire, a desire that develops out of several converging aspects of the reading experience. As noted above, because our prospective reading experience is so close to the magistrate's moment-by-moment lived experience, we frequently must struggle to see beyond his limited vision. At the same time, our fundamental sympathy for the magistrate moves us to want his vision to be as clear and honest as possible. Once the magistrate's struggle to see clearly leads him to a place where his vision matches ours, we take a certain satisfaction in his achievement, even as we recognize that the truth he voices is a chilling one. Indeed, because we are always positioned so closely to the magistrate's developing consciousness, because we struggle to see beyond his vision, his articulation here is likely to advance our understanding of his situation: he expresses better than we could what we have been feeling.

Strikingly, however, Coetzee does not leave his audience with the satisfaction of fulfilled desire very long. And here we can see the consequences of the way the tense positions us to make our understanding, like the magistrate's, provisional and partial. The magistrate's apparent breakthrough in understanding is not followed by significant changes in his behavior. Once he is freed from his exile, once the forces of the Empire flee the town after their unsuccessful campaign against the so-called barbarians, the magistrate steps back into the role he had before the arrival of Colonel Joll. "In all measures for our preservation I have taken the lead. No one has challenged me. My beard is trimmed, I wear clean clothes, I have in effect resumed the legal administration that was interrupted a year ago with the arrival of the Civil Guard" (145).

The precise nature of the magistrate's position relative to the Empire is not entirely clear, because the Empire's relation to the outpost is no longer clear. Mandel says that the forces will return in the spring, but there is also evidence that the Empire may be on its last legs (no merchant will take the coin of the Empire), that, indeed, we have been reading about the desperate actions of an Empire about to fall. The effect of this uncertainty is to shift our attention from the details of the political situation to the interior consciousness of the magistrate. And the manner in which he takes up his former role shows that he has maintained his complicitous consciousness. Once the magistrate reassumes his role, he returns to thinking of the woman as object. Once his sexual desire returns, he tries to "invoke images of the girl who night after night slept here with me. I see her standing barelegged in her shift, one foot in the basin, waiting for me to wash her, her hand pressing down on my shoulder. . . . From the depths of that memory I reach out to touch myself" (149). That he is unable to arouse himself to orgasm does not alter the fact that he is once again objectifying the woman. His turning to Mai for sex is also a resumption of old habits, his reassumption of his attitude of entitlement to sensual pleasure according to his desires.

Coetzee also uses the magistrate's interaction with Mai to underline his failure to follow through on his understanding about the woman. Mai tells him, "Sometimes she would cry and cry and cry. You made her very unhappy. Did you know that?" Before defending himself to her, the magistrate tells us, "She is opening a door through which a wind of utter desolation blows upon me" (152). This glimpse of the woman's pain at his hands gives the magistrate pain—sorrow, emptiness, desolation—but he soon puts it aside and moves on. The force of our negative judgment becomes greater.

But this account of the magistrate's falling back into his complicity is incomplete. It leaves out a significant countervailing force in the reading experience, something that works against our recognition of the meaning of the magistrate's movement. That force is our own sympathy with the magistrate, and our responses to his situation as the prisoner who is tortured and made an outcast among his own people. While he is being tortured, we share his pain; while he is an outcast, we cringe at his humiliation. And the present tense heightens the effect because it contains no promise of any change; as we read, we recognize that the magistrate's subjection to torture could become a permanent condition. When this sympathetic, reflective magistrate conveys his pleasure and satisfaction in resuming his place of consequence ("In all measures . . . I have taken the lead"), we are inclined to share his satisfaction and, therefore, overlook or not fully register the perpetuation of his complicitous consciousness. In other words, we are inclined to be complicit with his complicity. Eventually, however, the evidence of that complicity becomes too great to ignore.

Nevertheless, even as the evidence of complicity mounts, another realization builds within us: in the magistrate's present situation, he cannot act otherwise. He can momentarily feel the woman's pain and his sorrow but he can no longer relate these feelings to his complicity with the Empire and its representative, Joll. To do that would mean that he could not return to his post without some misgivings about his possible relations to the Empire or its successor, and that he could not so automatically resume his pursuit of the easy, sensual life he had before Joll's arrival. He does not experience such misgivings or give up the pursuit of sensual pleasure because his complicity cannot be so easily escaped. Nevertheless, he does register a vague sense of self-division—he feels some things that he cannot fully articulate. The penultimate section of the narrative ends with him telling his audience: "I think: 'There has been something staring at me, and still I do not see it'" (155). And the whole narrative ends with the sentence, "Like much else nowadays I leave it feeling stupid, like a man who lost his way long ago but presses along on a road that may lead nowhere" (156).

These remarks actually serve a double function for the magistrate. While they show some awareness of his failing, some evidence that he cannot completely eradicate the experiences of the last year, they also allow him to maintain his complicity. Like a white professor who admits to his black students that he is racist in ways that he might not always recognize and then does nothing else about his racism, the magistrate admits that a problem exists, but that admission substitutes for any effort to face it or to solve it. Again, however, because the magistrate has been complicit with the Empire for so long, we must recognize that he is in too deep to do otherwise.

The relation of Coetzee's audience to these developments is extremely complicated. As I have indicated, Coetzee asks us to have a two-fold response to the magistrate's behavior: to recognize that the magistrate's inability to escape from his complicitous consciousness is a grim lesson about the power of complicity, something in the magistrate to be resisted rather than forgiven; and simultaneously to recognize that the magistrate, *given who he is and how he has lived his life,* cannot do anything else. Even more important, however, is that Coetzee asks us to turn the experience of our progressive relationship with the magistrate back upon ourselves. And here the present tense plays a crucial role. When the magistrate achieves his insight that he and Joll are two sides of Imperial rule, it is natural for us to believe that the intellectual knowledge of his complicity will translate into action to change that complicity. But the later experience of the narrative asks us to go back and recognize that, however natural, the expectation was also unfounded. Similarly, when the magistrate resumes his position of importance in the town, it is natural for us to share his satisfaction. But the accumulation of evidence of his complicity leads us to recognize our own complicity.

In the first case, the satisfaction of our desire to have the magistrate recognize his similarity to Joll seduces us into believing that once the magistrate articulates his complicity he will be able to escape it. Our seduction depends upon our underestimating the nature and power of complicity and the depth of the magistrate's. The subsequent experience of the narrative emphasizes that complicity works without the conscious awareness of the complicit individual and that the magistrate's whole adult life has been based on his complicity. If his moment of insight offers us the satisfaction of fulfilled desire, the subsequent events present us with the frustration of thwarted desire. But upon reflection, we can recognize that the frustration we feel is partly at our own blindness, the underestimating or perhaps even forgetting that made our seduction possible. In the second case, when we feel some satisfaction in the magistrate's return to prominence, we have a very powerful experience of the insidious working of complicity: in feeling that satisfaction we unwittingly participate in the magistrate's complicity—but we do so from the best of motives, namely our sympathy and fellow feeling.

Our double experience of complicity—in the events and in our activity of processing them—is, I believe, the most important effect that Coetzee's use of the present tense makes possible. It is above all the magistrate's own lack of perspective on his behavior and our immersion in that behavior as it happens that leads to our complicity. A retrospective narration with even a partially more enlightened magistrate would interfere with our experiencing that complicity. Furthermore, given the magistrate's habits of reflection, he would have to become either more enlightened or more clearly deluded: in either case, we would move further away from the experiencing-I and all his halting, faltering steps. Our own halting and faltering would not occur as effectively as it does here.

By the end of the narrative, we reach a complex judgment of the magistrate that combines resistance to his resumed complicity with an understanding of its inescapability. However, because this judgment is only part of our double experience of complicity, we move away from the effort to achieve a final, definitive evaluation of the magistrate's actions and toward the unsettling recognition of the power of complicity. Because complicity is so insidious, and because we see it and experience it in our reading of this narrative, we must be very wary of adopting any stance based on our moral superiority to others whom we might consider complicit in the perpetuation of racism, sexism, or other dehumanizing ideologies. This wariness does not mean that we ought not make distinctions between, say, the Ku Klux Klan and the average white liberal academic; but it does mean that the average white liberal academic, rather than comforting himself with his moral superiority to members of the Klan, ought to examine his life for evidence of his complicity in the perpetuation of oppression and then do something about it. Coetzee's narrative insists—and our experience of it leads us to agree—that we all are complicit in some way or other. The narrative also insists that, despite the inescapability of complicity, we must seek to eradicate it and the oppression it perpetuates. To do anything else is, in effect, to be complicit with complicity.

Given what I have said earlier about the endless recursiveness of reading, I cannot (and do not wish to) claim anything like definitiveness for this account of the present tense and the positioning of the reader. Indeed, as this examination of Coetzee's technique has led me into a discussion of the narrative's and the reader's ethical stances, I want to recognize that this discussion itself implies a particular ethical imperative: This reading of domination, oppression, and complicity in *Waiting for the Barbarians* cannot be presented as the truth that other readers *should* accept. Consequently, I offer it to my readers as my current best effort at articulating the melding of my experiences as a flesh and blood and authorial reader of Coetzee's challenging narrative. I offer it with the knowledge that it is tentative and with the hope that it makes

some useful connections with Coetzee's text and with the experience of other readers.[10]

Notes

1. The "historical present" poses no theoretical problem precisely
because it implicitly (or even explicitly) acknowledges that the narrator
actually has knowledge-after-the-fact even as it employs the present tense
for the effect of immediacy. The heterodiegetic present, as employed, for
example, in Pynchon's *Gravity's Rainbow*, presents related but different
theoretical problems from those of the homodiegetic present. When I
discuss the present tense in this essay, I will be concerned with the
homodiegetic simultaneous present.

2. Fleischman is not alone in her assumption about the unsuitability of
the present tense for narrative. See also Genette, Rimmon-Kenan, and
others. After hearing a much abridged version of this paper as well as one
on present tense narration by Dorrit Cohn at the International Conference
on Narrative in Nice in 1991, Rimmon-Kenan said that she would "take
back" her assertions in *Narrative Fiction*.

3. For a fuller account of the reader's relation to Joe's narrative and of
the workings of that narrative, see my "What Hemingway and a Rhetorical
Theory of Narrative Can Do for Each Other: The Case of 'My Old Man'"
(forthcoming).

4. See *Reading People, Reading Plots*.

5. I use the terms "narrative audience" and "authorial audience" as
defined by Peter J. Rabinowitz in "Truth in Fiction: A Re-examination of
Audiences," and discussed further in his *Before Reading: Narrative Conventions and the Politics of Interpretation*.

6. Of course a heterodiegetic simultaneous present (such as the broad-
cast of a horse race) is much more likely than a homodiegetic one in
nonfictional narrative, but I don't think we should categorically rule out the
use of the homodiegetic simultaneous present for a particular effect. One
of the lessons writers of the so-called New Journalism have taught us is
how effectively many techniques of fictional narration can be employed in
nonfiction narrative.

7. I am drawing here on the concept of "coduction" developed by
Wayne C. Booth in *The Company We Keep*.

8. For a persuasive discussion of the impossibility of locating any
plausible occasion of narration, see Neumann. At the same time, it is worth

noting that occasionally Coetzee moves from the simultaneous present to the historical present, as in this sentence: "Of the screaming which people afterwards claim to have heard from the granary, I hear nothing" (4–5). I take these moves to be deliberate rather than inadvertent, necessary for Coetzee to accomplish certain local tasks in the narrative. The dominant mode of narration, however, is the simultaneous present.

9. For an extended and insightful discussion of vision and blindness in the novel, see Penner.

10. Here I acknowledge the connections and help that other readers have already given me, especially Peter J. Rabinowitz, Jamie Barlowe, Elizabeth Patnoe, Robert Caserio, Nicholas Howe, and Miriam Clark.

Bibliography

Booth, Wayne C. *The Company We Keep: An Ethics of Fiction*. Berkeley: University of California Press, 1988.

Coetzee, J. M. *Waiting for the Barbarians*. New York: Penguin, 1982.

Cohn, Dorrit. "Fictional versus Historical Lives: Borderlines and Borderline Cases." *Journal of Narrative Technique* 19 (Winter 1989): 3–24.

Fleischman, Suzanne. *Tense and Narrativity: From Medieval Performance to Modern Fiction*. Austin: University of Texas Press, 1990.

Genette, Gérard. *Narrative Discourse: An Essay in Method*. Trans. by Jane E. Lewin. Ithaca: Cornell University Press, 1980.

Iser, Wolfgang. *The Act of Reading: A Theory of Aesthetic Response*. Baltimore: Johns Hopkins University Press, 1978.

Neumann, Anne Waldron. "Escaping the 'Time of History': Present Tense and the Occasion of Narration in J. M. Coetzee's *Waiting for the Barbarians*." *Journal of Narrative Technique* 20 (Winter 1990): 65–86.

Penner, Dick. *Countries of the Mind: The Fiction of J. M. Coetzee*. Westport, CT: Greenwood Press, 1989.

Phelan, James. *Reading People, Reading Plots: Character, Progression, and the Interpretation of Narrative*. Chicago: University of Chicago Press, 1989.

———. "What Hemingway and a Rhetorical Theory of Narrative Can Do for Each Other: The Case of 'My Old Man.'" *Hemingway Review*. Forthcoming.

Rabinowitz, Peter J. *Before Reading: Narrative Conventions and the Politics of Interpretation*. Ithaca: Cornell University Press, 1987.

———. "Truth in Fiction: A Re-examination of Audiences." *Critical Inquiry* 4 (1977): 121–41.

Rimmon-Kenan, Shlomith. *Narrative Fiction: Contemporary Poetics*. London. Methuen, 1983.

Scholes, Robert. *Protocols of Reading*. New Haven: Yale University Press, 1989.

10

Dialogue, Discourse, Theft,
and Mimicry:
Charlotte Brontë Rereads
William Makepeace Thackeray

ELIZABETH LANGLAND

In enthusiastic praise of *Vanity Fair*, Charlotte Brontë wrote, "I regard Mr. Thackeray . . . as the legitimate high priest of Truth" (*Correspondence* 243). Perhaps this reverence has confused critics who see in Brontë's subsequent novel *Shirley* an unsuccessful adaptation of Thackeray's techniques. But to revere is not necessarily to imitate slavishly. And to speak, as have critics in the past, of women's texts as adaptations of men's texts corroborates notions of women's texts as belated, derivative, or secondary to the male tradition. Further, it forecloses in advance some of the most important questions those textual revisions generate. I wish to engage here with a range of concepts under the rubric of intertextuality, all of which are related through their focus on language and its operations, and all of which are informed by the conviction that meaning is a process of differentiation and that every text, therefore, borrows from, echoes, imitates, mimics, parodies precursor texts.[1]

I am interested in setting forth a more complete theory of textual relationships than has been implied by the term "influence." Influ-

to ideological consciousness." He adds that "One's own discourse and one's own voice, though born of another or dynamically stimulated by another, will sooner or later begin to liberate themselves from the authority of the other's discourse" (348). The process of liberation receives further impetus from the constant competition of a variety of alien voices within any individual consciousness, any individual text. All language for Bakhtin is dialogized; that is, it bears within itself the history of its use, a "constant interaction of meanings, all of which have the potential of conditioning others" (426). His addendum—"the internal dialogism of double-voiced prose discourse can never be exhausted thematically" (324)—emphasizes the effect of dialogic language in unsettling established meanings.

Julia Kristeva develops a concept of text as mosaic that borrows from Mikhail Bakhtin's formulation of text as "double-voiced discourse," and in the process of drawing from a powerful precursor to authorize her own voice, she enacts the very pattern that I identify in Brontë's response to Thackeray. Kristeva's theory conceives of "intertextuality" as a "mixture of textual signs, citations, and echoes." Writing in the context of Derrida and Lacan, as well as Bakhtin, Kristeva transforms Bakhtin's emphasis on the *word* to a focus on *texts*: "Any text is constructed as a mosaic of quotations; any text is the absorption and transformation of another" (66). Bakhtin's dialogized word and Kristeva's intertext both pinpoint the inevitable incorporation of one work by another and the effects that textual appropriations may have for liberating an individual's own voice. Quite literally, Kristeva has incorporated Bakhtin's voice to liberate her own, a "self-authorizing strategy [that] she uses often" (Friedman 147). Friedman adds, "This 'misreading' . . . does not eliminate the other, but rather borrows his authority from the position of disciple. Intertextuality was paradoxically born under the guise of influence" (147). Just so, in her imitation of Thackeray's narrative omniscience, Brontë discovered a new capacity to speak authoritatively.

Michel Foucault's concept of discourse lies aslant the Bakhtinian/ Kristevan emphasis on the transformative/liberatory effects of dialogism and mosaic. Foucault defines discourse as "the group of statements that belong to a single system of formation" (107). He continues, "thus I shall be able to speak of clinical discourse, economic discourse, the discourse of natural history, psychiatric discourse" (107–8). Foucault is less interested in the way one text revises another—all part of a literary discourse—than in the way different discursive formations operate and cooperate as a technique or "form of power which makes individuals subjects . . . subject to someone else by control and dependence, and tied to his own identity by a conscience or self-knowledge" (212). Thus, although Foucault's "discourse" is not specifically about literary intertextuality, it bespeaks the fundamental intertextuality of different discursive formations. Applying Foucault, we will conceive of intertextual relations between works not as transformative and liberatory, but as conservative, tending to a consolidation of certain powers. Foucault's concepts give us access to the way different discursive formations interrelate to create a certain kind of gendered subject. However, by working to uncover the mechanisms by which we are subjected, an intertextual approach helps to destabilize a traditional humanistic perspective and so frees us from its normalizing tendencies.

Although Roland Barthes conjoins the death of the author with the birth of the text and so postulates a radical intertextuality where every text is potentially an intertext for every other, in practice Barthes's radical theory is constrained by his reading practice in S/Z, where the "interpretive results do not take one further than a highly skilled, subtle formalist might go" (Clayton and Rothstein 23). Barthes's practice, then, helps justify my practice in this essay, which remains focused on only two texts. Yet the theory remains highly suggestive and indicates a way of beginning to conceptualize the revolutionary potential in the woman's signature. That potential is encoded in Barthes' work as theft: "the only possible rejoinder . . . [is] neither confrontation, nor destruction, but only theft: fragment the old text of culture, science, literature, and change its features according to a formula of disguise, as one disguises . . . stolen goods" (10). Barthes's analogy of borrowing to theft emphasizes the transgressive quality of intertextuality when one deliberately appropriates another's goods and disguises them for her own uses. Barthes's meaning remains playful and oblique, as is his style, which thus becomes an exemplification of his meaning. I will exploit his concept by focusing on theft as a technique to disrupt seemingly stable cultural encodings. Such an approach helps explain the way Brontë plays with the trope of tears in the Victorian novel. Tears serve as a primary Victorian encoding of femininity. Tears both define and undermine the woman, signifying both sensitivity and enfeeblement. That old cultural text must be appropriated—that is, stolen—fragmented and disguised, or re-presented. This process works to effect a transformation.

Like Barthes, Luce Irigaray investigates deliberate, even staged, responses to another's prose, for the purpose of disrupting established meanings. Irigaray identifies "mimicry" as an "interim strategy" for "destroying the discursive mechanism" which has oppressed woman. "It means to resubmit herself . . . to 'ideas,' in particular to ideas about herself, that are elaborated in/by a masculine logic, but so as to make 'visible,' by an effect of 'playful repetition,' what was supposed to remain invisible" (76). This formulation addresses explicitly gender issues, as the other theories do not. Parody and mimicry are strategies in which "the woman deliberately assumes the feminine style and posture assigned to her within . . . discourse in order to uncover the mechanisms by which it exploits her" (220). Applying Irigaray's concepts, I argue that Brontë stages, or exaggerates, the stylization of woman as mermaid and the posture of woman as wife.

Although these concepts of dialogue/mosaic, discourse, theft, and mimicry are related, they should not be conflated with each other, as each offers a unique angle of vision on intertextuality, particularly in *Shirley*, where Charlotte Brontë responds to one precursor text, *Vanity Fair*. Emphasizing as I do the liberatory effects of such intertextual relations, I wish to modify Nancy Miller's phrase "political intertextuality," which stresses a process of "overreading" to discern the woman's signature. I adopt instead the phrase "strategic intertextuality" to suggest both the politics of signature and its transformative potential.

The concept of strategic intertextuality opens the way for an enlarged poetics of fiction, one that shows more clearly how *Shirley* cites, absorbs, and transforms Thackeray's *Vanity Fair*. Brontë accomplishes these ends by adopting a third person narrator who echoes key passages of narrative commentary on the ideology of womanhood, by linking domestic and carceral discourses, by revising the Victorian trope of tears, and by parodying feminine paradigms and traditional plots.

Text as Dialogue/Mosaic

Thackeray is astute about the realities of that Victorian icon, "the Angel in the House." He conflates her fate in the home with that of other institutionalized beings like idiots and madmen confined to insane asylums. And he apparently caught Brontë's attention with this profound glimpse into women's lives, this perception of the discipline, the imprisonment, and the punishment. Thackeray writes,

> O you poor women! O you poor secret martyrs and victims, whose life is a torture, who are stretched on racks in your bedrooms, and who lay your heads down on the block daily at the drawing-room table; every man who watches your pains, or peers into those dark places where the torture is administered, must pity you. . . . (552)

Brontë rewrites,

> You held out your hand for an egg, and fate put into it a scorpion. Show no consternation: close your fingers firmly upon the gift; let it sting through your palm. Never mind: in time, after your hand and arm have swelled and quivered long with torture, the squeezed scorpion will die, and you will have learned the great lesson how to endure without a sob. . . . Bitterness is strength—it is tonic. Sweet mild force following acute suffering, you find nowhere: to talk of it is delusion. There may be apathetic exhaustion after the rack. (128)

Despite thematic parallels, formal differences abound. Thackeray represents the feminine from the comfortable distance of an explicitly male narrator and narratee (e.g., "We are Turks with the affections of our women" [169], and "Oh, be humble, my brother, in your prosperity!" [552]). And, although he adopts an ironic stance, that same male narrator ultimately cannot resist reinscribing an ideology of female selflessness that promises to make his own life pleasant when women "consent to remain at home as our slaves" (169).

The imprisonment and secret suffering of idealized women which pass momentarily under Thackeray's sympathetic patriarchal notice become a major agenda in Brontë's novel. Most notably, of course, she represents the feminine experience from a woman's perspective ("let [the scorpion] sting you through your palm," and "after your hand and arms have swelled and quivered long with torture"). The choice of the second person "you" is significant because it alludes both to the reader and, as a colloquial usage, to the writer. We are inside the experience rather than comfortably outside—the narrator and narratee at this moment share the female position, together in the torture chamber of Victorian ideology, which dictates that "[a] lover masculine so disappointed can speak and urge explanation; a lover feminine can say nothing: if she did, the result would be shame and anguish" (128).

A simple illustration of the difference emerges when we compare the following two narrative generalizations, which echo each other. Thackeray's narrator writes: "The best of women (I have heard my grandmother say) are hypocrites" (165). Brontë's narrator responds: "All men taken singly, are more or less selfish" (183). Virginia Woolf called this capacity for generalization about the other sex "one of the good offices that sex can discharge for sex—to describe the spot the size of a shilling at the back of the head" (94), which neither sex can see for itself.

Although Sandra Gilbert and Susan Gubar are right to say that Brontë adopts a third person narrator like Thackeray's, that claim is still too imprecise to tell us anything about *how* the text is actually working (373). In Gérard Genette's more precise terms, both narrators are heterodiegetic (outside the story they narrate). But Brontë's narrator often resembles more closely the homodiegetic (or first person) narrator of *Jane Eyre* than she does the narrator of *Vanity Fair*. There is a difference in focalization. Genette reminds us of the crucial distinction between who *sees* and who *speaks*, that is, between mood and voice. Who *sees* in Brontë's *Shirley* is often an impassioned and angry woman who exhorts "Men of England," "Men of Manchester," "Men of Yorkshire," and "Fathers" to release their daughters from crippling custom. This focalizer/narrator usually stands at a great remove from the narratee she most frequently postulates, a comfortable and complacent patriarch. Consider this exhortation: "Men of England! look at your poor girls, many of them fading around you, dropping off in consumption or decline; or, what is worse, degenerating to sour old maids, — envious backbiting, wretched, because life is a desert to them. . . ." (378). Sometimes parodic, sometimes complacent, sometimes self-righteous—the focalizer shifts and so testifies, as does her tendentious tone, to the uneasiness of the narrator/narratee-as-patriarch relationship.

The focalizer of Thackeray's novel is, in contrast, a comfortable, genial, and kind patriarch, who ultimately comprehends women's lives within the general tale of vanities he unfolds. Thackeray's novel charts a movement toward a normative position—the carnivalesque atmosphere of a London fair that includes both Becky and Amelia—from which all human life, the generic man, is exposed in the folly of his vanity. The concluding vision is produced from a consonance of values between the focalizer/narrator and narratee: "Which of us is happy in the world? Which of us has his desire? Or, having it, is satisfied?" The third person plural bespeaks an amiable companionship that seems to be denied by the tendentious tone of Brontë's narrator.

By shifting from Thackeray's companionable friendship between focalizer and narratee, Brontë also dramatically shifts the effects of her narrative; and it no longer seems adequate to conclude (as Gilbert and Gubar do in an otherwise insightful discussion) that Brontë was trying to create the calm objectivity and magisterial omniscience of a Thackeray and thereby "becomes enmeshed in essentially the same male-dominated structures that imprison her characters" (373). Indeed, the case appears quite otherwise: Brontë wishes to expose "calm objectivity" as a by-product of ideological conservatism. Rather than enmeshing her in male-dominated structures and ideologies, her revision of Thackeray's calm objectivity becomes a wedge for exposing further the ideological gap that his irony has already opened between the idealization and the reality of women's lives. Thackeray's voice, which Brontë echoes, authorizes her own more urgent tones, but her urgency, which cannot assume congruence with another, in turn lends authority to very different narrative ends.

Text as Discourse

Ideological issues focus on that idealized icon of womanhood in Victorian England, the Angel in the House. In nineteenth-century discourse, the home became an institution encoded as feminine. The celebration of home (with its presiding feminine angel) as a refuge from the harsh realities of the commercial world masked its status as a prison for women, enforcing the kind of self-discipline Foucault points to in *Discipline and Punish*. The disciplinary controls exerted by the home (controls which actually work on the mind as would those in Bentham's proposed Panopticon) are imaged by both Thackeray and Brontë as bodily tortures. Thackeray is comfortably explicit: "[Amelia's] life, begun not unprosperously, had come down to this—to a mean prison and a long, ignoble bondage. . . . How many thousands of people are there, women for the most part, who are doomed to endure this long slavery?" (552). Brontë picks up the echo of Thackeray's idea and extends its historical implications by critiquing the institutionalization and discipline of women's lives, the way in which the normative, the ideology of womanhood, becomes a straightjacket or prison.

To demonstrate the breadth of her grasp and depiction, we may refer to *Discipline and Punish* and its discussion of the emergence of new modes of discipline in the late eighteenth and early nineteenth centuries. These new modes include (1) an unseen but all-seeing surveillance, (2) a regime of the norm, and (3) various techniques of the self and its sexuality (summarized in Miller viii). In discussing the locus and operation of discipline, Foucault notes parenthetically that it would be interesting one day to explore "how intrafamilial relations have become 'disciplined'" (215). Brontë, in fact, anticipates this provocative idea in *Shirley*. There she depicts the disciplinary action of the normative in women's lives, in both Victorian house architecture and domestic occupation. The house and its routines become spaces structured for the inculcation of a social ideology that proves particularly destructive for women.

Foucault points out that the nineteenth-century prison depended on two major principles to enact its reform. The first is strict isolation. Without insisting on a rigid homology between the operations of prisons and the ideal upper-class home, we can still be struck by Caroline Helstone's extraordinary isolation in the novel. Mark Girouard, in *Life in the English Country House*, notes that nineteenth-century architecture began to enact rigid segregations: between masters and servants and between men and women. The essential quality of the Victorian home was privacy (285), but another word for privacy is isolation. In the Victorian house, rooms became encoded as masculine or feminine. For example, the dining room was a masculine space decorated in "massive oak or mahogany" to mirror "masculine importance," while the drawing room became a feminine space capturing "feminine delicacy" in "spindly gilt or rosewood, and silk or chintz" (292).

Such historical details confirm the inscription of sexual difference and the disciplinary action of segregation and isolation in the home. They work on Caroline both to sap her energies and to preclude rebellion or dissent. The narrator tells us at one point, "Caroline was limited once more to the grey Rectory; the solitary morning walk by remote byways; the long, lonely afternoon sitting in the quiet parlour which the sun forsook at noon" (375), a routine which the narrator summarizes as the "solitude, the sadness, the nightmare of her life" (381). The preponderance of nouns, adjectives, and verbs suggesting isolation is noteworthy: "solitary," "remote," "lonely," "quiet," "forsook," "solitude." Rose Yorke describes Caroline's life as a "black trance like a toad's, buried in marble," and "a long slow death." The rectory is a "windowed grave," her life "monotony and death" (384, 385). Caroline longs for a profession or a trade "fifty times a day" because labor can "give varieties of pain, and prevent us from breaking our hearts with a single master-torture. Besides," Caroline adds, "successful labour has its recompense; a vacant, weary, lonely, hopeless life has none" (235). But Caroline is already so well disciplined by her lady's life that she can take no effective action.

The second principle that Foucault articulates as necessary to the regulatory action of prisons is work: "Work is defined, with isolation, as an agent of carceral transformation" (240). Ironically, Foucault cites the women's workshop at Clairvaux as "the perfect image of prison labour." He quotes from Foucher's 1838 text *De la reforme des prisons*: "on a throne, above which is a crucifix, a sister is sitting; before her, arranged in two rows, the prisoners are carrying out the task imposed on them, and, as needlework accounts for almost all the work, the strictest silence is constantly maintained. . . . It seems that, in these halls, the very air breathes penitence and expiation" (243). I term this example ironic because anyone who has read *Shirley* will be aware of the prominence of needlework in Brontë's novel—where sewing is a disciplinary activity.

Caroline first appears in the novel subject to just such a regimen as Foucher described. She is under the instruction of her cousin, Hortense, who is teaching her "fine needlework" (103):

> The afternoon was devoted to sewing . . . unnumbered hours [of] fine embroidery, sight-destroying lace-work, marvellous netting and knitting, and, above all, [of] most elaborate stocking-mending. . . . It was another of Caroline's troubles to be condemned to learn this foreign style of darning, which was done stitch by stitch so as exactly to imitate the fabric of the stocking itself; a wearifu' process, but considered by Hortense Gérard . . . as one of the first "duties of woman." . . . No time did [Hortense] lose in seeking up a hopeless pair of hose, of which the heels were entirely gone, and in setting the

ignorant English girl to repair the deficiency: this task had been commenced two years ago, and Caroline had the stockings in her work-bag yet. She did a few rows every day, by way of penance for the expiation of her sins. (107–8)

Brontë writing on domestic life, employing such terms as "condemned," "penance," "expiation," and "sins," echoes Foucher writing on prison discipline. At one point Caroline argues, "If I sew I cannot listen; if I listen, I cannot sew" (115), pointing to the way sewing curbs and regulates activity of the mind.

When Caroline returns to her uncle at the rectory, he approves her day with the words, "Well, that will do—stick to the needle . . . and you'll be a clever woman some day" (122). At home, if she is not sewing for the Jew basket (134), she is making dresses for herself: "Some gloomy hours had she spent in the interval. Most of the time had been passed shut up in her own apartment [sewing]; only issuing from it, indeed, to join her uncle at meals. . . ." (243–44). Again, Caroline's routine echoes Foucault's discipline of work punctuated by meals. Later, Caroline asks the logical question which is focalized through the narrator's satiric eyes: "What do [fathers] expect [daughters] to do at home? If you ask, —they would answer, sew and cook. They expect them to do this, and this only, contentedly, regularly, uncomplainingly all their lives long, as if they had no germs of faculties for anything else: a doctrine as reasonable to hold, as it would be that the fathers have no faculties but for eating what their daughters cook, or for wearing what they sew" (377).

As assiduously as Caroline sews, Shirley avoids the needle. With heavy irony the narrator relates: "[Shirley] takes her sewing occasionally: but, by some fatality, she is doomed never to sit steadily at it for above five minutes" (372). Or we are told, "After tea Shirley reads, and she is just about as tenacious of her book as she is lax of her needle" (373). Playing the transvestite Captain Keeldar—independent, wealthy, and parentless—Shirley can assume many male freedoms and prerogatives and so throws into relief the narrow disciplines of a woman's usual lot.

Of course, Victorian ladies did not spend all their time in isolation or at their needle. Their isolation might otherwise be enviable; one might see it as privacy, a room of one's own. The corollary discipline in their lives Caroline characterizes as "unprofitable visiting"—the routine of morning calls and afternoon teas (377). I mentioned earlier that the drawing room became a feminine space in Victorian England. Mark Girouard adds that the "drawing room acquired two new functions in the Victorian period, as a result of the inane ceremony of morning calls and the more genial celebration of afternoon tea" (293). Morning calls "(which by late nineteenth century took place in the afternoon) . . . involved carriage visits from one local hostess to another, and a quarter of an hour's polite conversation in the drawing room" (293). Such rituals virtually held mistresses hostage in houses, morning and afternoon, giving and receiving these "inane" visits.

These rituals function in ways similar to Bentham's proposed Panopticon, a prison designed so that the inmates would be constantly under an unseen but all-seeing surveillance. Although ladies at home did not live in glass cells, there was the constant possibility that they would be visited at any moment. They had, in effect, to be always ready for the regulatory gaze of society. Morning calls and afternoon teas served as a continual check over their behavior. This control was further enhanced by a normative code of behavior set out in the etiquette books, a widely popular innovation in the Victorian age.

The first view we have of Caroline Helstone at home presents her subject to just such a disciplinary regimen. The narrator relates, "When she had dined, and found herself in the Rectory drawing-room alone, having left her uncle over his temperate glass of port, the difficulty that occurred to and embarrassed her was—How am I to get through this day" (130). The doorbell interrupts her thoughts, and curates join her uncle in the male space, the dining room. Caroline has a new worry "lest they should stay to tea." Her fate is sealed when four ladies are announced to her in the drawing room, and Caroline wishes herself "meantime at Jericho" (131). The social rituals are an agony to Caroline—her visit with the ladies is punctuated, we are told, by silences of five minutes, and the ordeal leaves Caroline with a full sense of her "ignorance and incompetency." The narrator is both savage and funny in the following comment: "Pause third came on. During its continuance, Caroline was feeling at her heart's core what a dreaming fool she was; what an unpractical life she led; how little fitness there was in her for ordinary intercourse with the ordinary world" (133). She can revive "the flagging discourse" only "by asking them if they would all stay to tea" (133).

One form of discipline gives way to another as Caroline feels the pressure of the normative. Tea must be followed "in the natural course of events" by music. Caroline has opened the piano, we are told, "knowing how it would be" (140). For Caroline, the result of this discipline, called entertaining, is a "sort of brain-lethargy" and a "deadened spirit" (141). She escapes briefly to the dining room and "rested herself—rested at least her limbs, her senses, her hearing, her vision—weary with listening to nothing and gazing on vacancy" (142). This is a characteristically grim picture of institutional control, the power of the normative in women's lives. What began with Thackeray's metaphor for Amelia's imprisonment in "woman's lot" expands in Brontë's novel to become an exploration of the connections and links between two seemingly different discursive formations: the domestic and the carceral.

Text as Theft

To turn from Foucault to Barthes is to take up a dramatically different idea, the notion of cultural revision, and thus to think about intertextuality in a very different way. The "old text of culture" undergoes a change of features, as in Brontë's "theft" of the Victorian trope of tears, a powerful signifier of femininity. Brontë appropriates metonymic associations of tears—sobs, sighs, weepings—as attributes of a landscape, of nature, of fate. So personalized through a feminine trope, the destructive powers of nature and fate are read as woman-inspired, as a consequence of rage simmering below the surface of women's acquiescence in domestic arrangements that disempower them.

Tears were the Victorian trope par excellence for femininity, ushered in with Victoria, the girl queen, and Barrett Browning's poetic paean to her:

> God save thee, weeping Queen!
>   Thou shalt be well beloved!
> The tyrant's sceptre cannot move,
>   As those pure tears have moved!
> The nature in thine eyes we see,
>   That tyrants cannot own —
> The love that guardeth liberties!
> Strange blessing on the nation lies
>   Whose Sovereign wept—
>   Yea, wept, to wear its crown!

In her portrait of a weeping monarch, Barrett Browning attempts to bridge the gap in the signifier "tears" between strength of sensibility and weakness of will.

Why do "real" women cry? The multiple answers to this question embed femininity simultaneously within cultural discourses of sensitivity and enfeeblement. Women cry because they feel deeply. Because they sympathize. Because they love. Because they're tender. Because they're true. Because they're happy. Because they're sad. Because they're weak. Because they're dependent.

Thackeray's genial irony reveals his relish for this feminine trope. In the opening pages of *Vanity Fair*, Amelia Sedley drowns in a rhetoric of tears. Everyone, including Amelia herself, cries at her departure from Chiswick Mall: "[S]he had a pair of eyes, which sparkled with the brightest and honestest good-humour, except indeed when they filled with tears, and that was a great deal too often; for the silly thing would cry over a dead canary bird; or over a mouse, that the cat haply had seized upon; or over the end of a novel, were it ever so stupid" (14–15). From introduction to farewell, Amelia's story is awash in tears: "Emmy's head sank down, and for almost the last time in which she shall be called upon to weep in this history, she commenced that work" (658). Women's work.

For Becky Sharp, Amelia's dark side, "Nobody cried," and the implied inversion also holds true: she cried for nobody (16). At her crisis, discovered by her husband with Lord Steyne, her schemes exploded, she sits "in the midst of her miserable ruins with clasped hands and dry eyes" (516–17). The narrative indictment implicit in her "dry eyes" anticipates Becky's textual reentry as the bewitching, yet treacherous "syren." Thackeray's negative interpretation of the opposing signifier "dry eyes" keeps women under the tyranny of the sign "tears."

In contrast, Brontë pursues what was implicit in Thackeray's representation of Amelia, the way a woman's tears inscribe her within a cultural economy of prescribed suffering. Brontë's narrator in *Shirley* enjoins women to short-circuit the signifying current so that dry eyes encode power. As the tears that image her sensibility dry up, so does her susceptibility to disappointment, disease, death: "You expected bread, and you have got a stone, break your teeth on it, and don't shriek because the nerves are martyrized. . . . You held out your hand for an egg, and fate put into it a scorpion. Show no consternation: close your fingers firmly on the gift; let it sting through your palm. . . . the squeezed scorpion will die, and you will have learned the great lesson how to endure without a sob" (128). In Brontë, the answer to the question "Why not cry?" is plain: "[I]f you survive the test—some, it is said, die under it—you will be stronger, wiser, less sensitive" (128).

Into the narrative spaces left blank because there are no tears to fill them pour the woman's questions, effectively silenced in Thackeray's text: "How am I to get through this day?" (130). "What am I to do to fill the interval of time which spreads between me and the grave?" "What was I created for, I wonder?" "Where is my place in the world?" (190).

It remains, then, for Brontë to fragment the old text of culture, tears, to change its features through disguise: "[Caroline] returned from an enchanted region to the real world: for Nunnely wood in June, she saw her narrow chamber; for the songs of birds in alleys, she heard the rain on her casement; for the sigh of the south wind, came the sob of the mournful east" (189). Women may be dry-eyed, but the world weeps. Rain and winds, disguised sobs and sighs, imbue the world with a feminine sensibility that threatens to rend the fabric of existence. The sobs of the future sound an apocalyptic note: "The future sometimes seems to sob a low warning of the events it is bringing us. . . . At other times this Future bursts suddenly, as if a rock had rent, and in it a grave had opened, whence issues the body of one that slept. Ere you are aware, you stand face to face with a shrouded and unthought-of Calamity—a new Lazarus" (399). What rough beast slouches toward Bethlehem to be (re)born? Is it woman?

Text as Mimicry

Brontë's narrator is often angry, only occasionally antic. Yet the playful impulse erupts at key moments. What confuses, perhaps, is the way Brontë's admiration for Thackeray's art coexists with criticism of his perspectives. The letter in which she identifies the author of *Vanity Fair* as "the legitimate high priest of Truth" continues in a reverential vein: "He, I see, keeps the mermaid's tail below water, and only hints at the dead men's bones and noxious slime amidst which it wriggles; but his hint is more vivid than other men's elaborate explanations" (*Correspondence* 224). Brontë echoes *Vanity Fair*'s narrator, who comments, "In describing this syren, singing and smiling, coaxing and cajoling, the author, with modest pride, asks his readers all round, has he once forgotten the laws of politeness, and showed the monster's hideous tail above water? No!" (617). Nonetheless, that narrator relishes a brief glimpse or two below the waterline, where the mermaid's tail is "writhing and twirling, diabolically hideous and slimy, flapping amongst bones, or curling round corpses" (617).

Dorothy Dinnerstein identifies the mermaid's threat with the element in which she lives, "the dark and magic underwater world from which our life comes and in which we cannot live" (5). That threat also lies in the oppositions she embodies: human/animal, charmer/destroyer. For all of his decorum, the narrator's alignment of Becky "shed-no-tears" Sharp with the mermaid reinforces a figurative economy in which woman's superficial charm conceals a deadly purpose: "They look pretty enough when they sit upon a rock, twanging their harps and combing their hair, and sing, and beckon to you to come and hold the looking-glass; but when they sink into their native element, depend on it those mermaids are about no good, and we had best not examine the fiendish marine cannibals, revelling and feasting on their wretched pickled victims" (617). Who are "they"? Who is "you"? Who are "we"? "They (mermaid/women) beckon "you" (men/the masculine narratee), and thus "we" (male narrator and readers—men/women?) must keep our bodies and minds above water. What happens to women caught and deformed in this syntax, as both third person object/Other and first person subject?

Staging the feminine—the stylization and parody of stereotypes and norms which is Irigaray's recommended tactic—becomes Brontë's strategy as she, too, introduces in *Shirley* the figure of the mermaid. First the narrator inexplicably describes her pure, meek heroine, Caroline Helstone, "combing her hair, long as a mermaid's . . . enchanted with the image" in her mirror (123). In light of her own letter of praise, it seems unlikely that Brontë has forgotten Thackeray's description of mermaids "combing their hair." The point seems to be that this enchantress enchants only herself. The man she dreams of winning resolutely resists her charms and proposes to a woman with money.

The mermaid figure returns when Shirley and Caroline plan a tour to the Faroe Isles; Shirley promises "seals in Suderoe, and, doubtless, mermaids in Stromoe" (248). The world Caroline longs to leave, the world of her uncle's rectory (rather than the mermaid's element) is here associated with "remnants of shrouds, and fragments of coffins, and human bones and mould" (248). Shirley spins out a fantasy of their nocturnal encounter with a mermaid: "an image, fair as alabaster" (249). Her features align her explicitly with Caroline: "The long hair . . . a face in the style of yours [Caroline's] . . . whose straight, pure lineaments, paleness does not disfigure" (249). She holds a mirror in her hand, and serves herself as a mirror. Shirley exclaims: "Temptress-terror! monstrous like-ness of ourselves!" (249). Whereas a man would "spring at the [mermaid's] sign, the cold billow would be dared for the sake of the colder enchantress," the two women "Stand safe though not dread-less." The mermaid "cannot charm," because they are like her, but "she will appal," again because they are like her.

The conflict between Thackeray's "they" and "we" has been resolved in Shirley's identification of woman with mermaid. Car-oline demurs; Mrs. Pryor protests: "We are aware that mermaids do not exist. . . . How can you find interest in speaking of a nonen-tity?" (250). Shirley responds, "I don't know" (250), and the scene abruptly ends. It remains an unassimilable bolus, undigested by the narrative.

Such is Brontë's game. She assumes the feminine style and posture to uncover the mechanisms by which it exploits her; introduces, in short, the "patriarch bull . . . huge enough to have been spawned before the Flood" (249). This creature—not in tradi-tional mythology—takes his place alongside the mermaid. Shirley comments to Caroline, "I suppose you fancy the sea-mammoths pasturing about the bases of the 'everlasting hills' . . . I should not like to be capsized by the patriarch bull." Isn't Thackeray just such a "patriarch bull" to Brontë, who defined his mind as "deep-founded and enduring," and who located in the concluding part of *Vanity Fair* "a sort of 'still profound' . . . which the discernment of one generation will not suffice to fathom" (*Correspondence* 224)? Isn't Thackeray just such a literary leviathan enjoying the authority of the patriarchal bull or, rephrased, the bull of patriarchal authority? He might, indeed, capsize Brontë's small craft.

All parodies risk being recuperated: "Parody by itself is not subversive, and there must be a way to understand what makes certain kinds of parodic repetitions effectively disruptive, truly troubling, and which repetitions become domesticated and recir-culated as instruments of cultural hegemony" (Butler 139). Brontë's revisions of the marriage plot signal a parodic repetition not only of

Thackeray's art but of novel conventions in general. Indeed, Thackeray's own parody of marriage as fulfillment no doubt suggested the whole network of constricting codes, values, and beliefs distinctive to the culture that both he and Brontë inhabited; his iconoclasm in the face of those norms must have encouraged her further parody. At the same time, her novel's traditional conclusion, marriage, seems ultimately to recuperate the very values Brontë set out to parody. That is, we close with the romance we were initially advised to reject in favor of something "real, cool, and solid" (39).

But the parodic impulse is still at play. Although Brontë has not altered the plots in which women's lives are to be circumscribed, she has done something equally radical. She has changed the meaning of that plot, has altered the way in which the women's lives are to be understood. If we return once more to Thackeray's *Vanity Fair*, we recall that he opens his novel with the departure of his female protagonists, Amelia Sedley and Becky Sharp, from Chiswick Mall. They will make their way in the world, where the route to success is, essentially, marriage. Becky immediately and typically queries, "If Mr. Joseph Sedley is rich and unmarried, why should I not marry him?" (25). The narrator ironically asks whether "once landed in the marriage country, all were green and pleasant there" (250). But Thackeray embeds this question within the larger vanitas theme informing his novel so that the question of *women's* fulfillment is not directly engaged.

Brontë's *Shirley* expends one-sixth of its length before a major female character is even introduced. Yet the novel clearly focuses on two women: Shirley Keeldar and Caroline Helstone. Why does Brontë so structure her novel? One immediate and frequently given answer is that we are to see the women's lives within the mercantile world of men and masters, both women and workers suffering from "the dehumanizing effect of patriarchal capitalism" (Gilbert and Gubar 387). Such thematic observations are certainly valid, but the structure and events of the first several chapters also have the significant effect of beginning to unseat patriarchal ideologies of womanhood through mimicry, a process that intensifies when the women are actually introduced.

Brontë opens with a male world devoid of women, except as servants. Women are negligible, insignificant, and ignored. The male world of guns and machinery and power is inaccessible to women or to women's influence. Very subtly, the text raises a question: What meaningful role can women have in men's lives and in a patriarchal culture? We are early vouchsafed an answer: the fable of Mary Cave. Mary Cave was the site of a contest and conflict between Yorke and Helstone. Helstone won her, "a girl with the face of a Madonna; a girl of living marble," "beautiful as a monumental angel" (81). This bride is no sooner invested with her offices as Victorian angel in Helstone's house than she begins a decline that ends in her death. Mary's demise is "scarcely noticed" by her husband because "she is of no great importance to him in any shape" (82). The Victorian myth of woman's regenerative moral sensibility is here mimicked and exploded.

This pattern is repeated when we focus on Robert Moore, the mill owner. He generally avoids his home where his sister, Hortense, presides: "its air of modest comfort seemed to possess no particular attraction for its owner" (91). He prefers the snuggery and isolation of his separate quarters in his mill. After he is wounded by the would-be assassin's bullet, he is apparently transformed, a transformation signaled by his confession to his sister, "I am pleased to come home" (555). The narrator dryly comments, "Hortense did not feel the peculiar novelty of this expression coming from her brother, who had never before called the cottage his home; and to whom its narrow limits had always heretofore seemed rather restrictive than protective" (555).

The narrator builds on this kind of observation by associating both Louis and Robert Moore, the prospective husbands of Shirley and Caroline, with rock or stone. Louis is described as "cool as stone" and like "a great sand-buried stone head" (575). Robert asks Caroline, metaphorically, "if that rose should promise to shelter from tempest this hard, grey stone" (595). The reader inevitably recalls the narrator's angry summary of women's lives: "You expected bread, and you have got a stone; break your teeth on it and don't shriek because the nerves are martyrized" (128). Is the narrator suggesting that, in marrying Louis and Robert, the women have ingested stones that their "mental stomach[s]" must digest? That possibility recalls the metaphor of torture with which we began. The gap opened there has widened and exposed the Victorian ideologies of womanhood as dangerous romances, which, in Mrs. Pryor's words, "show you only the green tempting surface of the marsh, and give not one faithful or truthful hint of the slough underneath" (366).

Aggressively, the narrator entitles her final chapter "The Winding-Up," and opens, "Yes, reader, we must settle accounts now" (587). The chapter is full of metalepses, or moments when the narrator transgresses the boundaries of the narrative, speaking directly to her characters. "Are you not aware, Peter," she asks of one, "that a discriminating public has its crotchets: that the unvarnished truth does not answer; that plain facts will not digest?" (587). Plain facts that don't digest recall stones that the women receive in place of bread, another undigestible morsel. A page later the narrator gloats: "There! I think the varnish has been put on very nicely" (588). Is the narrator varnishing the truth for men who don't wish to digest plain facts? The tendentious tone continues—"you cannot know how it happened, reader; your curiosity must be robbed to pay your elegant love of the pretty and pleasing" (588). The narrator, in effect, tells us that the conclusion is varnish, put on to feed her narratee's love of "the pretty and pleasing." And Charlotte Brontë subverts our expectations that marriage can resolve the conflicts and fulfill our own narrative desires. The marriages, too, are a varnish "put on very nicely."

Thus, although the novel concludes with a pair of marriages, that ending should be read parodically. Brontë begins by promising us something called "reality" and concludes, laughingly, with something looking, at first glance, like "romance." But that romance turns into a "manufacturer's daydreams," something that looks very much like garden-variety industrialization. The fairies and ladies disappear.

Thackeray, in contrast, begins with a puppet show—the Becky and Amelia dolls—and he concludes, ostensibly, with the same "game," as we children are admonished to "shut up the box and puppets." But who can forget the closing injunction: "Ah *Vanitas Vanitatum!* Which of us is happy in the world? Which of us has his desire? Or, having it, is satisfied?" (666)? An *ex cathedra* pronouncement; a brilliant and pithy *summa* on the human condition; a magnificent moral gesture. One might want to argue, however, about whether Becky and Amelia have had their desires or have been had. Or, if one is Charlotte Brontë, one might want to try mimicry: "The story is told. I think I now see the judicious reader putting on his spectacles to look for a moral. It would be an insult to his sagacity to offer direction. I only say, God speed him in his quest!" (*Shirley*, finis).

Summa

This essay has employed a variety of critical concepts, from dialogue to discourse to theft to parody, in order to develop a theory of strategic intertextuality. Such a theory emphasizes not only the signature of the woman in the text, but also engages the transformative potential of woman, which it focuses by engaging the liberatory impulse implicit in certain concepts of intertextuality, as opposed to the conservative bent of influence. Even a Foucauldian emphasis on discourse works to uncover and so destabilize the mechanisms by which one is subjected. My analysis has necessarily privileged Brontë's text over Thackeray's, yet I hope it has also engaged both texts in such a way as to make clear their currency within the general signifying practices of their culture. Assuming such currency provides the basis for any intertextual study, and it suggests the scope of Thackeray's own parodic impulse in the novel, which I have only minimally addressed. It also stresses the way influence and intertextuality become mutually entangled, the way one novel's engagement with another is not a simple process of transmission, but a dynamic encounter with the cultural values that saturate any literary object. That contestation of word with word, text with text, has the power to generate a productive friction that destabilizes the ground of meaning and so facilitates change.

Notes

1. In the concept of intertextuality with which I engage, readers will recognize the influence of Jacques Derrida. His memorable formulation — "*Il n'y a pas de hors-texte*" [There is nothing outside the text] (158) — challenges a traditional mimetic understanding of literature as referring both to world and to precursor works, and thus it opens up rich possibilities for our understanding of narrative interrelationships.

Bibliography

Bakhtin, M.M. *The Dialogic Imagination: Four Essays*. Trans. by Caryl Emerson and Michael Holquist. Austin: University of Texas Press, 1976.

Barthes, Roland. "The Death of the Author." In *Image-Music-Text*. Trans. by Stephen Heath. New York: Hill and Wang, 1981. 142–48.

———. *S/Z*. Trans. by Richard Miller. New York: Hill and Wang, 1974.

———. *Sade-Fourier-Loyola*. Trans. by Richard Howard. New York: Hill and Wang, 1976.

Brontë, Charlotte. *Shirley*. 1849. Harmondsworth, England: Penguin, 1974.

The Brontës: Their Lives, Friendships, & Correspondence in Four Volumes. Ed. by T.J. Wise and J.A. Symington. Vol. 2. Oxford: Shakespeare Head Press, 1932.

Browning, Elizabeth Barrett. "Victoria's Tears." In *The Complete Works of Elizabeth Barrett Browning*. Vol. 2. New York: Thomas Y. Crowell and Co., 1900. New York: AMS Press, 1973.

Butler, Judith. *Gender Trouble: Feminism and the Subversion of Identity*. New York: Routledge, 1990.

Clayton, Jay, and Eric Rothstein, eds. *Influence and Intertextuality in Literary History*. Madison: University of Wisconsin Press, 1991.

Derrida, Jacques. *Of Grammatology*. Trans. by Gayatri Chakravorty Spivak. Baltimore: Johns Hopkins University Press, 1976.

Dinnerstein, Dorothy. *The Mermaid and the Minotaur: Sexual Arrangements and Human Malaise*. New York: Harper, 1976.

Foucault, Michel. *Discipline and Punish: The Birth of the Prison*. Trans. by Alan
Sheridan. New York: Vintage, 1979.

———. "The Subject and Power." In *Michel Foucault: Beyond Structuralism
and Hermeneutics*. Ed. by Hubert Dreyfus and Paul Rabinow. 2nd rev.
ed. Chicago: University Chicago Press, 1983. 208–26.

Friedman, Susan Stanford. "Weavings: Intertextuality and the (Re)birth of
the Author." In Clayton and Rothstein, 148–80.

Genette, Gérard. *Narrative Discourse: An Essay in Method*. Trans. by Jane E.
Lewin. Ithaca, NY: Cornell University Press, 1980.

Gilbert, Sandra, and Susan Gubar. *The Madwoman in the Attic: The Woman
Writer and the Nineteenth-Century Literary Imagination*. New Haven: Yale
University Press, 1979.

Girouard, Mark. *Life in the English Country House*. New Haven: Yale University Press, 1978.

Irigaray, Luce. *The Sex Which Is Not One*. Trans. by Catherine Porter. Ithaca,
NY: Cornell University Press, 1985.

Kristeva, Julia. *Desire in Language: A Semiotic Approach to Literature and Art*.
Trans. by Thomas Gora, Alice Jardine, and Leon S. Roudiez. New York:
Columbia University Press, 1980.

Lentricchia, Frank, and Thomas McLaughlin, eds. *Critical Terms for Literary
Study*. Chicago: University of Chicago Press, 1990.

Miller, D.A. *The Novel and the Police*. Berkeley: University of California
Press, 1988.

Miller, Nancy. *Subject to Change: Reading Feminist Writing*. New York:
Columbia University Press, 1988.

Renza, Louis A. "Influence." In Lentricchia and McLaughlin, 186–202.

Thackeray, William Makepeace. *Vanity Fair*. 1848. Boston: Houghton, Mifflin, 1963.

Woolf, Virginia. *A Room of One's Own*. New York: Harcourt, Brace and
World, 1929.

Contributors

Wayne C. Booth is emeritus professor of English at the University of Chicago. His most recent books are *The Company We Keep: An Ethics of Fiction* and *The Art of Growing Older*, an anthology of poetry with extensive commentary that he considers astonishingly wise. He is now struggling to complete approximately five and one-half projects, all of them more important than anything he has yet written.

Ross Chambers teaches French and Comparative Literature at the University of Michigan. Having recently published *Room for Maneuver* and *The Writing of Melancholy*, both at the University of Chicago Press, he is now creeping up in leisurely fashion on *Loiterature*.

Barbara Foley is Associate Professor of English at Rutgers University, Newark Campus. She has written articles on Marxist criticism, African American literature, and literary theory and has authored two books: *Telling the Truth: The Theory and Practice of Documentary Fiction* and *Radical Representations: Politics and Form in U.S. Proletarian Fiction, 1929–1941*.

Elizabeth Langland is Professor of English at the University of Florida. She is the author of *Society in the Novel* and *Ann Brontë: The*

Other One, and coeditor of *A Feminist Perspective in the Academy: The Difference It Makes, The Voyage In: Fictions of Female Development*, and *Out of Bounds: Male Writers and Gender(ed) Criticism*. She has published articles in *PMLA, Critical Inquiry, Studies in the Novel*, and elsewhere and has recently completed a book about domestic ideology and representations of middle-class women in Victorian culture.

Judith Mayne is Professor of French and Women's Studies at Ohio State University. She is the author of several books on film studies, including *Cinema and Spectatorship* (1993) and the forthcoming *Directed by Dorothy Arzner*.

Susan McClary is Professor of Musicology in the Faculty of Music, McGill University. Her most recent books include *Feminine Endings: Music, Gender, and Sexuality* and *Georges Bizet: "Carmen."* In 1993 she delivered the Ernest Bloch Lectures (University of California–Berkeley), which will be published as *Conventional Wisdom: The Content of Musical Form*. A collection of her essays, *De-Tonations: Narrative and Signification in "Absolute" Music*, is forthcoming from Wesleyan University Press.

Thomas G. Pavel teaches Comparative Literature and Romance Languages and Literatures at Princeton University. His books include *The Poetics of Plot: The Case of English Renaissance Drama, Fictional Worlds*, and *The Feud of Language: A History of Structuralist Thought*.

James Phelan teaches English at Ohio State University. He has written *Worlds from Words, Reading People, Reading Plots*, and *Beyond the Tenure Track*. He has also edited *Reading Narrative*, and currently serves as editor of *Narrative*, the journal of the Society for the Study of Narrative Literature. His essay in this volume is part of a book-in-progress on narrative dynamics.

Mary Louise Pratt is Professor of Spanish and Comparative Literature at Stanford University, where she teaches courses on Latin

American literature, criticism and colonialism, and literary and cultural theory. Her books include *Toward a Speech Act Theory of Literary Discourse, Linguistics for Students of Literature, Women, Culture and Politics in Latin America*, and *Imperial Eyes: Travel Writing and Transculturation*.

Peter J. Rabinowitz, author of *Before Reading: Narrative Conventions and the Politics of Interpretation*, divides his time between music and narrative theory. His published articles cover a wide range of subjects, from Dostoevsky to Mrs. E.D.E.N. Southworth, from detective fiction to the ideology of musical structure, from Mahler to Scott Joplin. A professor of comparative literature at Hamilton College, he is also an active music critic and a contributing editor of *Fanfare*.

Index

Fitch, Brian, 197n. 17
Flâneur 29, 39, 40
Flaubert, Gustave, 180
Fleischman, Suzanne, 224–30, 243n. 2
Fletcher, John, 180, 195, 196n. 12, 196n. 14
Foley, Barbara, 8–9, 11, 12, 13, 133n. 7
Ford, Charles, 95n. 30, 95n. 32
Form: and content, 56; and ethics, 121–22; and politics, 43–62; of *The Wings of the Dove*, 99–135. *See also* Structure
Formal analysis, 6, 99–135
Formal critics, 106. *See also* New Criticism
Foucault, Michel, 8, 10, 13, 19, 248, 249–50, 255–60
Francis, Dick, 108
Frankenstein (Mary Shelley), 165
Framing, 151–55
Freadman, Anne, 36
Free indirect discourse, 47, 59
Freud, Sigmund, 73–74, 138
Friedman, Susan Stanford, 247, 249

Gender: and class, 55, 154–55; and the Communist party, 55; in detective fiction, 161, 163–65, 170–74; and discipline, 20, 255–60; and employment, 29–31; and film narrative, 137, 151–55; and genre, 48, 51–61; and heteroglossia, 48; and intertextuality, 246–51; in "loiterature," 28–34; in musical codes, 76, 82, 87; and objectivity, 255; and plot, 60, 265–70; and realism, 55; and spectatorship, 145–55; in the Victorian novel, 246–71
Genette, Gérard, 100–101, 133n. 7, 167, 168, 175n. 9, 224, 226, 243n. 2, 253–54
Genre: and Samuel Beckett, 179–80, 186, 195; definition of, 36; and gender, 48, 51–61; and politics, 43–64; and reading expectations, 103, 105; and violations of narrative norms,

228. *See also* Detective fiction; "Loiterature"; Ordeal narrative; Quest narratives; Sonata; Travel narratives
Geulincx, Arnold, 182
Gilbert, Sandra, and Susan Gubar, 253, 254–55
Girouard, Mark, 256, 259
Godzich, Wlad, 208
Goethe, Johann Wolfgang von, 49
Golden Bowl, The (Henry James), 123
Gombrowicz, Witold, 159
Grafton, Sue, 108
Grant, James, 200, 201, 211, 218
Gravity's Rainbow (Thomas Pynchon), 243n. 1
Great Expectations (Charles Dickens), 222
Gutman, Casper, 162

Hamacher, Werner, 39, 41n. 15
Hammer, Mike, 158
Hammett, Dashiell, 6, 160–77
Handmaid's Tale, The (Margaret Atwood), 224
Haralovich, Mary Beth, 139
Hardin, James, 50
Hatten, Robert, 92n. 8
Heath, Stephen, 47, 137, 143–45
Hegel, G. W. F., 49, 53, 62n. 1
Heidegger, Martin, 181
Hemingway, Ernest, 227–30
Hermeneutics, relation of, to poetics, 10, 179
Herndl, Diane Price, 49, 78
Hero of Our Time (Mikhail Lermontov), 166
Heteroglossia, 48, 49
Hicks, Granville, 45, 61
Hill, Leslie, 197n. 17
History: and cruising, 35; and detective fiction, 160, 163–64; relation of, to fiction, 3–4, 162–64; and travel narratives, 199–221

THE THEORY AND INTERPRETATION
OF NARRATIVE

———————

*James Phelan
and Peter J. Rabinowitz,
Editors*

Because the series editors believe that the most significant work in narrative studies today contributes both to our knowledge of specific narratives
and to our understanding of narrative in general, studies in the series
typically offer interpretations of individual narratives and address significant theoretical issues underlying those interpretations. The series does
not privilege any one critical perspective but is open to work from any
strong theoretical position.